THE
MENZIES
WATERSHED

THE
MENZIES
WATERSHED

Liberalism, Anti-communism, Continuities
1943–1954

Edited by
ZACHARY GORMAN
ROBERT MENZIES INSTITUTE

MELBOURNE
UNIVERSITY
PRESS

MELBOURNE UNIVERSITY PRESS
An imprint of Melbourne University Publishing Limited
Level 1, 715 Swanston Street, Carlton, Victoria 3053, Australia
mup-contact@unimelb.edu.au
www.mup.com.au

𝗳 🐦 ⓘ

First published 2023
Collection © Georgina Downer, Zachary Gorman, 2023
Text © copyright remains with the individual contributors, 2023
Design and typography © Melbourne University Publishing Limited, 2023

Cover design by Philip Campbell Design
Typeset by Cannon Typesetting
Cover image: *Sir Robert Gordon Menzies in a coat and hat in front of a building, New South Wales, 29 August 1951*, Fairfax Corporation, courtesy National Library of Australia.
Printed in Malaysia

A catalogue record for this book is available from the National Library of Australia

9780522880205 (hardback)
9780522880243 (ebook)

FOREWORD

The Hon John Howard

THE ROBERT MENZIES INSTITUTE is to be congratulated on bringing together *The Menzies Watershed*. The contributors cover the early years of the long Menzies hegemony of Australian politics.

Undeniably the most successful political party in Australian history, the Liberal Party of Australia is Menzies's greatest legacy. Without it, the foundations of modern Australia would not have been laid.

As the individual contributions so vividly illustrate, it was Robert Gordon Menzies who masterminded that 23-year unbroken grip on the direction of our country. His extraordinary gifts of oratory, identification with his 'forgotten people', the resolute partnership with the Country Party and a clear-headed alliance with what he never shirked from calling 'our great and powerful friends', matched the national need. Those gifts gave Australians security, prosperity, confidence, and a justifiable sense of optimism about the future.

Menzies's resilience and return from the political wilderness are legendary. He lost the 1951 referendum seeking constitutional power to ban the Communist Party. Yet he took this in his stride, asserting that the fight against communism would go on, but with one hand tied behind his back. A lesser leader would have sunk into despair. Menzies would lead the Coalition to five more electoral victories. There would be a close shave in 1961.

Contrary to the Labor line that Australia's engagement with Asia commenced with the Whitlam years, it was the Commerce Agreement with Japan in 1957, driven by John McEwen, with Menzies's crucial support which turned the page on old animosities. Evidence of the need for Australia to find abiding friendships in our region are clear in the chapters on foreign policy, particularly the treatment of Percy Spender.

David Lee's chapter on economic policy meticulously details the changes which occurred following the defeat of the Chifley government in 1949. Despite these changes it was nonetheless the case that the pillars of economic policy through the 1950s and 1960s, namely high tariffs, centralised wage fixation, a fixed exchange rate and an unreformed progressive taxation system, were largely supported by both the Coalition and the Australian Labor Party.

Political parties should always treasure their achievements. Those of the Liberal Party during the Menzies era were remarkable. We owe a debt of gratitude to the Robert Menzies Institute for *The Menzies Watershed*.

CONTENTS

Foreword   v
The Hon John Howard

Introduction   ix
Zachary Gorman

1   Menzies's miracle? The Foundation of the Liberal Party
    of Australia   1
    Nicolle Flint

2   Menzies and the Movement: Two Pillars of Australian
    Anti-communism   17
    Lucas McLennan

3   Menzies and the Banks   35
    Anne Henderson

4   Liberalism Applied? Policy Shifts in the Transition From
    Chifley to Menzies   45
    Tom Switzer

5   Early Think Tanks and Their Influence on the Menzies
    Government   61
    Andrew Blyth

CONTENTS

6 What Liberty for the Enemies of Liberty?   77
Lorraine Finlay

7 The Art of Power   91
Troy Bramston

8 Menzies, Evatt, and Constitutional Government   103
Charles Richardson

9 The Forgotten People by the Sea? Liberalism and the
Suburbanisation of the Central Coast of New South Wales
During the 1950s   117
Christopher Beer

10 Menzies and Economic Management, 1950–54   133
David Lee

11 A Prudent and Urgent Measure: The Founding of the
Australian Secret Intelligence Service   149
William A Stoltz

12 An Innovative Realist: Percy Spender's Achievements in
the Liberal Tradition of Australian Foreign Policy   165
David Furse-Roberts

13 Overseas Students in Australia: Before and After
the Colombo Plan   183
Lyndon Megarrity

Appendix: Australia's Greatest Prime Minister?   197
The Hon George Brandis KC

Bibliography   207
Notes   223
Index   256

INTRODUCTION

Zachary Gorman

T HE ELEVEN YEARS that passed between the 1943 and the 1954 elections were arguably some of the most pivotal in Australian history. At the political level the transition could not be starker. At the one end was the Labor Party at its electoral zenith. Led by the wildly popular wartime prime minister, John Curtin, in 1943 Labor utterly obliterated the Coalition, which for the first and only time in its now century-long history faced an election led by the Country Party. This farcical circumstance occurred due to the disintegration of the centre-right's supposed major party, the United Australia Party, into a kaleidoscopic array of smaller groupings, making the 'united' moniker a bitter and ironic joke. Yet, by 1954, Robert Menzies led a vigorous and by now experienced Liberal Party—which had put the Country Party once again in their place as a cooperative and productive junior partner—to overcome the last real electoral challenge the Coalition would face until 1961.

Underlying the varied fortunes of these politicians and political groups was a vital debate over policy. The 1943 election seemed to be a vindication, not just of Labor's wartime leadership, but of its plans for an extensive state-driven program of 'post-war reconstruction' that would greatly increase the role that the federal government played in the everyday lives of ordinary Australians. With Curtin's sudden death in July 1945, that program came to be embodied by Prime Minister Ben Chifley, who made extensive attempts to enact constitutional change, set up government monopolies in areas such as banking and air travel, and provide Australian workers with state-owned homes that would ensure that they did not become 'little capitalists'.[1] Yet, by 1954, Australia had rejected all but the social services referendum (which had arguably only passed because Menzies had supported it) and had given a clear endorsement of the continuing role of private enterprise in driving forward the nation's progress. Under Menzies, Australia's 'free' market would still be mollified by the theories of John Maynard Keynes, as were most around the Western world at the time, but the 'little capitalists' were prospering and multiplying in a manner that would only accelerate in the coming years.

This domestic battle played out against a background of international and, more importantly, regional turmoil. The existential threat of Japanese invasion was defeated, but not before it turned the Asia-Pacific on its head by ousting colonial powers, most of which would fail to fully reassert themselves, leaving a volatile political vacuum. Menzies first heralded Australia's shifting focus to its 'near north' during one of his earliest broadcasts as prime minister in April 1939,[2] but there is little doubt that that 'north' felt all the nearer once its most immediate representative was not the familiar face of the Dutch East Indies, but instead a new and difficult to comprehend Indonesian Republic. Add to that the victory of Mao's Communist Party in the Chinese Civil War in 1949 and the outbreak of communist disturbances in numerous places like Malaya, Indochina, and the Philippines, and direct invasions in Korea, which made a 'Cold War' that had begun in Europe all the more local and tangible. The situation convinced the Menzies government that the onset of World War III was imminent, and would produce lasting legacies like the ANZUS Treaty, the Colombo Plan, and the Australian Secret Intelligence Service.

All of this political, policy, and strategic transition would be manifested in the figure of Robert Menzies who, while being ably assisted by the co-founders of the Liberal Party, a handful of outstanding ministers, and the golden age of the public service mandarins, would navigate the Australian ship of state through these troubled waters. The period is therefore a fruitful ground on which to base the second annual academic conference of the Robert Menzies Institute, a prime ministerial library and museum set up at the University of Melbourne to promote research into and discussion of Menzies, the Menzies era, and its enduring legacy. That conference, which was held in November 2022, forms the basis for this book, which is the second of a four-volume series examining the full span of Menzies's life and career.

The conference was conducted on the back of an open call for papers, a premise which accepts that a volume like this cannot cover every issue imaginable from such a rich period of history, which lasted over a decade. But what it can do is bring together a range of scholars, commentators, and public figures to unearth new perspectives and even largely untouched topics, from what is extremely fertile ground for study. We openly acknowledge that this approach will miss certain topics of great interest and relevance: for example, the expanding political role of women and the targeted appeal of Child Endowment, the comprehensive reforms instigated by Menzies's minister for health, Earle Page, and the advent of Commonwealth Scholarships for university education. We accept such shortcomings as inevitable, and believe that they by no means detract from the original contributions our authors make in those areas on which they have chosen to focus. But we have also generally given a degree of flexibility in going beyond the specified date span where necessary for a particular topic, hence some of these gaps will be filled in the two later volumes.

Fertile ground is seldom left completely untilled, and in our first volume, *The Young Menzies: Success, Failure, Resilience 1894–1942*, my introduction went through a fairly comprehensive list of the existing works on Menzies, including ones of particular relevance to this period (1943–54) such as Stuart Macintyre's *Australia's Boldest Experiment: War and Reconstruction in the 1940s*. Much of that historiography was then analysed in David Kemp's thoughtful chapter on 'The Long Assessment'. Given this, it would be repetitive to provide another overview of existing works, particularly as the following chapters generally do a thorough job of identifying a range of literature pertinent to their respective topics.

That is certainly true of the first chapter, which engages with an existing historical debate. *The Young Menzies* concluded with Nick Cater's examination of 'The Forgotten People' radio broadcast of 22 May 1942, which heralded the first beginnings of Menzies's political revival after his resignation as prime minister in August 1941. That broadcast was made while Menzies had the luxury of time and action enjoyed by a backbencher. However, after the disastrous 1943 election result referred to above, Menzies was elected leader of the fragmentary remains of the United Australia Party, on the stipulated condition that he supersede Country Party leader Arthur Fadden as leader of the Opposition.

That being accomplished, Menzies looked towards reforging the Australian centre-right into a new political entity. There has been a great deal of controversy surrounding just how important Menzies was to the subsequent formation of the Liberal Party of Australia, and how much credit he can take for its organisational success. Nicolle Flint's chapter dives headfirst into this debate, providing an overview of the full history of the various parties that have represented the 'non-Labor forces' in federal politics, and the circumstances the movement faced after the 1943 election, to demonstrate how the Liberal Party and its endurance are a political 'miracle' for which, the author argues, Menzies deserves the lion's share of the credit (which he has tended to receive from Liberal politicians, but less so from some historians). As a former politician with an appetite for academic research, Flint is well placed to bridge the gap between the two perspectives.

Dual perspectives are also central to Lucas McLennan's chapter on 'Menzies and the Movement', which looks at how Menzies's objections to both communism and Labor's milder program of state dominance stemmed from his Anglo-Protestant perspective, which valued independence as a necessary moral virtue. McLennan compares and contrasts that critique with the Catholic perspective enunciated by BA Santamaria and his supporters, demonstrating that they reached similar conclusions on several important issues despite coming from different (and often directly conflicting) traditions. This reveals the diversity of Australian intellectual life in the 1940s, and serves to demonstrate how Menzies was able to later garner a significant amount of support from the Catholic community—challenging the sectarian undertones of Australia's political divide. McLennan's chapter makes a compelling case that there was a surprising philosophical affinity between Menzies and those who would become members of the Democratic Labour Party—and may even be used to defend their oft-discussed preference allocations as being based on overlapping principles.

McLennan's chapter cuts against the grain of Australian historiography, which has tended to view political philosophy as something that has not greatly impacted Australian politics. Australia is often portrayed as a Benthamite utilitarian society,[3] which has practised what Albert Métin famously dubbed 'socialisme sans doctrines', i.e. adopting state intervention as and when necessary with little regard for maintaining an overall coherence of approach.[4] However, there have been moments when ideology has played a fundamental role in shaping the course of national events, and perhaps none more so than Chifley's decision to try to nationalise Australia's banking system. Anne Henderson's chapter provides a lively narrative account of and detailed background for this incident, one which arguably altered the political fortunes of Robert Menzies, both by securing his place at the head of the Liberal Party and generating political momentum ahead of the 1949 poll. It was bank nationalisation which gave the 'socialist tiger' real teeth and claws, allowing Menzies to decisively spear it.

If Chifley's big flaw was that he was too ideological, Tom Switzer's chapter indicates that it was not a trait which Menzies shared. Switzer compares the anti-socialist rhetoric which Menzies used to win power in 1949 with the pragmatic approach he took towards the state once in office, asking the question was 'Liberalism Applied?' Menzies arguably found great benefit in keeping in place the public service chiefs he inherited from his predecessor and giving them reasonable scope to pursue their pre-existing objectives, such as full employment. The essay makes clear that while Menzies successfully held the line against socialism, he was not interested in actively shrinking the size of the state like some modern liberal reformers. WK Hancock said in the 1930s that 'Australian democracy has come to look upon the State as a vast public utility',[5] and Menzies was happy to maintain and even expand that utility; he just believed that it worked best when it harnessed the unmatched creative and economic power of private enterprise.

One of the reasons why Menzies was so reliant on his public servants was likely that there were few other sources of public policy advice available to him in the 1950s. There were, however, a small number of Australian think tanks, most notably the Victorian Institute of Public Affairs, founded in 1943 shortly before the Liberal Party. Andrew Blyth's chapter looks in detail at the IPA and other think tank developments, placing them in a larger framework of think tank evolution throughout the Western world. While Blyth makes clear that Menzies was only mildly swayed by the proposals of the IPA, he demonstrates that Menzies was willing to go outside of the public service for advice when necessary, most notably when hiring Sir Keith Murray to conduct an inquiry into Australia's university system.

Because Menzies was not exposed to a centre-right echo chamber of policy advice, he was generally insulated from big overreaches to rival his predecessor's bank nationalisation. Menzies's attempt to ban the Communist Party in 1951, however, was the clearest example of overreach. This he pursued virtually as the government's priority once coming to power, only to be frustrated by first the High Court and then a failed referendum. Current Australian Human Rights Commissioner Lorraine Finlay tackles the moral and philosophical intricacies of this issue in her chapter, 'What Liberty for the Enemies of Liberty?' As Finlay skilfully unpacks, the Communist Party ban is just one moment in an ongoing debate over how liberal democracies should handle vital national security issues while maintaining their liberal and democratic character. This was an issue over which Menzies agonised, and indeed was one on which he frequently changed his view in response to shifts in Australia's strategic circumstances. It was perhaps because Menzies had initially been opposed to conservative calls for a ban, and therefore understood the deep complexities and nuances of the issue, that he didn't appear particularly disheartened by his failure to ban the Communist Party, and was able to rebound from a political setback that would have seen many other leaders forced to resign from office.

This is somewhat surprising, as Menzies during this period was considered vulnerable both electorally and (partly as a natural consequence) within the Liberal Party. Chris Wallace's recent book, *Political Lives*, has related that Menzies as prime minister in the early 1950s struggled to find a press secretary, as most qualified journalists thought he was destined to lose and did not want to have their reputations tarnished by being associated with his demise.[6] That Menzies was able to hold onto his position was partly due to the fact that he had developed a deep understanding of the responsibilities, procedures, and expectations of the prime minister's office, which allowed him to deal with complex issues as they arose. This is something which Troy Bramston examines in his chapter 'The Art of Power'. As an award-winning biographer who has looked in detail at the careers of several Australian prime ministers, Bramston is well placed to see what was unique and successful in the way in which our longest serving leader approached his job. Some of these insights featured in Bramston's *Robert Menzies: The Art of Politics*, but by taking them out of that broader narrative and expanding on them as their own topic, Bramston reveals a new and original appreciation of Menzies's political talents.

Menzies's success was built upon his intimate knowledge of the institutional framework in which he had to operate, and it is a great tragedy that one of the leading historians of that framework, John Nethercote, passed away in 2022. Before his passing Nethercote was slated to present a paper at the Institute's conference, but it is some consolation that Charles Richardson is carrying on Nethercote's legacy in his chapter on 'Menzies, Evatt, and Constitutional Government'. Richardson examines the way in which Menzies both reacted to and helped shape constitutional developments which saw an evolution in the role of the governor-general in Australian political life, including the granting of the 1951 double dissolution. Richardson even suggests that Australia helped to prove that Westminster democracy could function without a hereditary monarch, helping to lay the groundwork for the great expansion of Westminster-style democratic systems in the post-war world.

While international resonances like these are eye-catching, the Menzies era made its most tangible impact at the local level. The 1950s are known as a period of great prosperity, expanding home ownership, and the rapid growth of suburbia; and Christopher Beer's chapter looks at how the Central Coast of New South Wales acted as a microcosm for these developments. Represented in Parliament by the marginal Division of Robertson, and its hard-working but somewhat lacklustre backbencher Roger Dean, the region was simultaneously 'average' and distinct, with sea-changers and holiday homeowners demonstrating how the 'good times' were enjoyed across a broad socio-economic section of Australian society.

Those 'good times' were predicated on how the Menzies government navigated a complex economic landscape, in which Australia was constrained by membership of the sterling bloc and its vital agricultural exports were tremendously vulnerable to outside fluctuations in the market. David Lee's chapter places Menzies's pragmatic and Keynesian approach to economic management in this context, suggesting that his reliance on the levers of state control was not a straight ideological choice made in a vacuum. Rather, it was a complex picture in which philosophical preferences often reluctantly gave way to compromise and informed advice. Moreover, Lee demonstrates that the economic approach of the Menzies era should not be stereotyped from any one snapshot of time. It was an evolving process, heavily impacted by the Korean War wool boom and its fallout, which Lee hints began to liberalise in the period to be covered by the later volumes.

Lee's chapter is the beginning of an 'international' section of four chapters which conclude this volume by covering the Menzies government's engagement with a changing world. This section is also a chance to look at the impact of some of Menzies's leading ministers, most notably Richard Casey and Percy Spender.

The former served initially as Menzies's minister for supply and development (quickly rebranded to national development), but as William Stoltz's chapter demonstrates, he nevertheless played a central role in the founding of the Australian Secret Intelligence Service. This new agency, dedicated to espionage, intelligence gathering and covert action, was formed with the utmost secrecy via an executive order. With its existence and even its budgetary cost hidden from the vast majority of Parliament, the foundation of ASIS once again raises questions about how far Menzies was willing to distort the principles of democracy in order to protect that democracy. Beyond this question, ASIS shows a government keen to take on a wider role in its region, and crucially to be seen as a more equal partner with what Menzies dubbed our 'great and powerful friends',[7] Great Britain and the United States—a role that was able to directly shape their decision making.

One man who was apparently listened to in both Westminster and Washington was Percy Spender, Menzies's short-lived yet prodigious minister for external affairs. Spender's achievements are significant: the Colombo Plan of foreign aid investment and regional development, Australia's agreement to the Japanese Peace Treaty, and decision to join the Korean War, leading to the signing of the enduring ANZUS pact. David-Furse Robert's chapter takes a new approach to analysing Spender, portraying him as an 'innovative realist', who simultaneously upheld a centre-right approach to foreign policy, with an emphasis on caution and bilateralism, while being willing to break free of that mould as necessary.

Finally, the book's chapters conclude with Lyndon Megarrity covering the most famous aspect of the Colombo Plan, the overseas student program. Megarrity demonstrates that it was the culmination of a long tradition of Australia hosting international students, which continues to this day. The chapter shows that the Menzies government was not unique in trying to teach the future leaders of our neighbours in the region, but it was unique in celebrating that fact and overcoming some of the negative sentiment which naturally flowed from the White Australia Policy. That policy did endure, but for nuanced reasons it no longer seemed to dictate how we were perceived in the Asia-Pacific.

The book finishes with a special appendix featuring George Brandis's keynote address delivered to the second annual conference, which contemplates whether Menzies is worthy of being designated 'Australia's greatest prime minister'. The volume thus concludes without touching on the defection of Vladimir Petrov and the narrow result of the 1954 election, which is where we will pick up the story in volume three, setting the scene for 'the Menzies ascendancy'.

CHAPTER ONE

MENZIES'S MIRACLE? THE FOUNDATION OF THE LIBERAL PARTY OF AUSTRALIA

Nicolle Flint[1]

With the benefit of eight decades of historical hindsight, the formation of the Liberal Party in 1944–45 looms as a pivotal moment in Australian political history. Just four years after the formal inception of the party, the Liberals would win office under Robert Menzies, embarking on a path that would see them become the dominant force in Australian federal politics. Since 1949, they have governed in Coalition with the Country (now Nationals) Party for a total of fifty-one years, double the length of time of their rivals the Australian Labor Party. Demonstrating the strength of the original vision, the party today remains largely unchanged in terms of structure and principle.

However, these facts belie the circumstances the creators of the party faced. History shows that in 1944–45, the formation of an enduring and successful centre-right party could not have seemed less likely. Prior to 1944, the group of people who shared the beliefs that would underpin the Liberal Party had been through five separate iterations from Federation, encouraging scholars to refer to these groupings not as a stand-alone, easily identifiable liberal movement, but as the 'non-Labor forces', defined in contrast to their political foes. These non-Labor groupings were led not once, not twice, but three times by prime ministers who were defectors from the Labor Party.[2]

The five years preceding the formation of the Liberal Party of Australia in 1944 could not have been more chaotic, nor the outcome more unlikely that the most potent Australian political force would emerge from the wreckage of the non-Labor forces, then known as the United Australia Party (UAP). In 1939, UAP Prime Minister Joseph Lyons died in office and was replaced by Robert Menzies, despite the fact that Menzies had only recently resigned from the Lyons ministry. Soon thereafter Australia entered World War II, and within a short period of time Menzies lost the support of his colleagues and resigned as prime minister. The UAP, and its coalition with the Country Party, effectively collapsed and Labor took government. Both Menzies's colleagues and the new Labor government were scathing about his character and performance, and many of his wartime policies. Despite this, in 1944, Robert Menzies brought together eighteen separate non-Labor groups from around Australia to form the Liberal Party of Australia, and he is largely credited with drafting key elements of the new political force, including the policy platform and organisational structure.

But was this extraordinary feat really Menzies's miracle alone, or do other, largely forgotten, individuals deserve greater recognition for their role in creating the structure and stability that have seen the federal Liberal Party, in coalition with the Nationals, become *the* party of government in Australia since this time? Was Robert Menzies the sole or primary reason for the formation of the Liberal Party of Australia in 1944 and 1945? Did Menzies alone create the Liberal Party, a party that remains almost unchanged today in 2023 in terms of organisational structure and platform, or, at a minimum, was he the key driving force?

It is necessary to ask these questions, and re-examine the case for Menzies as the founder of the Liberal Party, because scholars such as

Ian Hancock have presented compelling evidence that the reformation of the Liberal Party was not Menzies's miracle alone. Hancock argues that '[e]ven the most cursory examination of chronology and process would cast doubt on the extravagant claims made about Menzies' role in the formation of the Liberal Party',[3] and that Menzies 'was certainly not the founder of the Liberal Party'.[4] Hancock outlines a number of 'minor and forgotten figures' and 'major and forgotten figures' who assisted Menzies in the formation of the party, arguing they were just as important contributors as Menzies to the new Liberal Party of Australia and its unprecedented organisational success.[5] These include Victorians Elizabeth Couchman, president of the Australian Women's National League, William Anderson, founder of the Services and Citizens' Party, Charles Kemp, economic adviser and later director of the Institute of Public Affairs, and from New South Wales, Ernest White, founder of the Liberal Democratic Party, and Thomas Ritchie, businessman.

Other scholars broadly concur with Hancock's thesis. Graeme Starr, for example, states 'it is true that the Liberal Party was not entirely the work of Menzies'.[6] However, Starr credits Menzies with having 'provided the plans and the cement' and the blueprint for the party structure and platform.[7] Gerard Henderson in *Menzies' Child* states '[i]t was not Robert Menzies' work alone. Yet without Menzies it is unlikely that a unified national non-Labor party could have been formed in the mid-1940s if at all'.[8] Anne Henderson admits that, as Hancock argues, it is true that there were many people involved in the formation of the Liberal Party, but Henderson just as importantly notes 'there is little doubt such an achievement would never have resulted without Robert Menzies. Unity among those disparate groups and individuals did not come easily, even after the Party was proclaimed'.[9] Menzies, Henderson states, 'was the spearhead—and organiser—that made ultimate success possible'.[10]

Given the degrees of attribution provided to Menzies as *the* founder of the Liberal Party of Australia, and considering Hancock's forceful arguments that others rather than Menzies deserve the credit, may it still be argued, overall, that the formation of the Liberal Party should be considered 'Menzies's Miracle'? This chapter puts forward the case that the creation of the Liberal Party of Australia should rightly remain credited to Menzies, for ten intertwined reasons that consider the nature and importance of leadership, the history of previous attempts to form a stable national non-Labor political organisation, and Menzies the man: a political force the like of which Australia had not seen before, and has not since.

Everyone else had failed to create a national, lasting 'non-Labor' party

Until Menzies's attempt to create a new, lasting political force while Opposition leader in 1944, the history of the non-Labor movement was defined by organisational failure at the federal level. Prior to Federation, people describing themselves as 'liberals' had dominated colonial parliaments across Australia, but over the four decades that followed 1901, all attempts to form a properly national and united party eventually failed, even when such bodies were proposed or supported by current or former prime ministers. Between 1901 and 1909, the non-Labor forces were represented by Edmund Barton/Alfred Deakin's Liberal Protectionists and George Reid/Joseph Cook's Liberal Free-Traders (later renamed the Anti-Socialists). In 1909, the 'Fusion' of the Protectionists, Anti-Socialists, and a crossbench group of 'anti-socialist protectionists' known as 'the Corner' (which included Menzies's uncle and political mentor Sydney Sampson), saw the creation of the first unified Liberal Party, which held office as the Deakin–Cook Ministry until it was defeated at the 1910 election.[11]

Reid was the initial driver behind the push to unite the Liberal forces through his anti-socialist campaign of 1905–06, during which he argued that differences over the tariff question were largely irrelevant compared with Labor's adoption of the first form of its 'socialist objective'.[12] Deakin was initially hesitant about this proposition, but the three-time prime minister came to understand the need for a new unified non-Labor entity. Working with his daughter Ivy, son-in-law Herbert Brookes, Cook, and others such as Archdale Parkhill, seven years were dedicated to fleshing out the organisation. Liberal Leagues were established in each state, a magazine was founded, meetings were held, and multiple attempts were made to merge with conservative forces, such as the 50,000-member Australian Women's National League, which staunchly refused.[13] The party achieved some success when Joseph Cook won the 1913 election (the first time a single non-Labor party had won an outright majority at a federal election), but a double dissolution saw the party fall from office in the early stages of World War I, and under the immense imperatives of the war the Liberal Party folded into the new Nationalist Party under Labor defector Prime Minister Billy Hughes in 1917. Margaret Fitzherbert records Herbert Brookes's 'weary frustration' at the final Liberal Party meeting as he noted the tireless work he and Ivy had undertaken over years, and their ultimate failure.[14]

The Nationalists existed as an organisation until 1931, but these years were not without significant challenges. Prime Minister Hughes was forced out of the leadership in 1922 by a combination of Liberal forces in South Australia and Victoria, and the newly established Country Party, which refused to form a coalition with him.[15] Stanley Bruce instead became prime minister, only to be undermined by Hughes in 1929 when Hughes crossed the floor with three colleagues and brought down the Nationalist government, which was defeated at the subsequent election.[16] The result was catastrophic in terms of the number of seats lost, including that of Prime Minister Bruce.[17] The next year, Hughes formed a new party, the Australia Party, and managed to establish seventy-five branches with 4000 members, but a disastrous result at the 1930 New South Wales state election ended the fledgling party's hopes.[18]

Around this time, an abundance of activist leagues and pressure groups gained traction across Australia, causing alarm within political parties, because their express aim was to compete with, and in some instances replace, political parties.[19] South Australia's Citizens League had an impressive 20 000 members, and inspired the creation of the Victorian All for Australia League, which rose to 80 000 members and 320 branches in 1931; at the same time the New South Wales All for Australia League had 160 000 members.[20] The threat was real, but ex-Labor MP Joseph Lyons, assisted behind the scenes by Menzies and others, negotiated with and placated key groups. These groups agreed to combine forces under the banner of the United Australia Movement, which would become the United Australia Party in May 1931 with Lyons as leader.[21]

Lyons would govern as prime minister from December 1931 until his death in office in April 1939.[22] Yet despite Lyons's unrivalled success and personal popularity, 'the UAP failed to develop a functional federal political machine'.[23] The original 1909 Liberal Party had established a federal party infrastructure that had been continued by the Nationalists—the Australian National Federation—which had six state branches, a platform, rules, a federal conference, delegates and a secretary.[24] However, Lyons, and those around him, let the former Nationalist federal structure wither and die.[25] Former PM Stanley Bruce, who was re-elected to his seat in 1931, and Richard Casey, who was first elected in 1931, discussed the pressing need to recreate a federal body. Casey even drafted a proposal that was supported by Lyons, and was supposed to be discussed at the Interstate Committee in 1934, but this did not occur.[26]

To complicate matters, while Lyons and his UAP team were busy winning successive elections in 1931, 1934, 1937, and under Menzies in 1940, the state non-Labor forces were busy in-fighting. Most did not embrace the UAP structure and brand, and by August 1943 when the party suffered a crushing federal election defeat, holding just twelve seats in the House of Representatives, the state non-Labor forces were largely fractured. In New South Wales, non-Labor forces were represented by Ernest White's[27] Liberal Democrats, the Commonwealth Party, One Parliament for All Australia, and the UAP.[28] In Victoria, the non-Labor political forces included Elizabeth Couchman,[29] and the Australian Women's National League, United Australia Organisation, Middle Class Party, and William Anderson's[30] Services and Citizens Party.[31]

The federal election result led the New South Wales Institute of Public Affairs and the Victorian Institute of Public Affairs to bring together these different parties for serious merger talks, which concerned Menzies as he felt such talks may prejudice the formation of any national body which would need the support of other states.[32] Menzies's strongly worded urgent letter to the New South Wales leader of the Opposition of 5 November 1943 noted discussions both there and in Victoria, and stated that the South Australians were 'more than a little disturbed' by these talks, that talk of a new federal organisation must involve all states, and that the 'value of a new organisation will depend upon it becoming known to the public in a completed form and not merely in some half-baked condition'.[33] Ultimately, White and the Liberal Democrats derailed New South Wales merger discussions, in October–November 1943; however, they did participate in the formation of the Liberal Party in 1944.[34] Talks in Victoria were more successful,[35] but all parties to merger talks attended the Canberra conference as individual organisations rather than as a new political force. In light of this history, it is a miracle the new Liberal Party of Australia was formed at all, let alone succeeded and prospered.

Menzies issued the invitations to the Canberra and Albury conferences

At the most basic and practical level, Menzies should be credited with the formation of the Liberal Party of Australia, because he wrote to

eighteen separate groups to invite their delegates to attend a conference in Canberra to discuss the formation of a new political party,
and it has not been suggested that any other individual instigated
the conference. Without a personal invitation from the federal leader
of the Opposition, who was also a former prime minister, would so
many, from so far, have been amenable to attending the meeting?

The intention to hold the conference was reported in *The Sydney
Morning Herald* on 30 August 1944,[36] and Menzies personally
wrote to the groups in September.[37] A letter from Menzies to Frank
Davis, president of the Victorian Young Nationalists Organisation,
of 7 September 1944, inviting his organisation to participate in a
conference in Canberra on 13, 14, and 16 October 1944, is representative of the correspondence sent to each organisation.[38] The letter
outlines the key issues to be considered, which included the need
to 'secure unity of action and organisation among those political
groups which stand for a liberal, progressive policy and are opposed
to Socialism', through 'an efficient Commonwealth-wide organisation', that would debate policy and have a close relationship with
its elected Parliamentarians. The letter also suggests an additional
conference may be necessary.

A subsequent letter of 25 September 1944 from Menzies to Davis
lists the following specific items for discussion at the conference:

(a) The desirability or otherwise of an Australian-wide organisation.
(b) Whether such organisation should be based upon unity of name
    and organisation or whether some loose Federal scheme upon
    the basis of existing bodies will suffice.
(c) The question of name.
(d) The ingredients of a proper organisation, including such matters
    as a Federal secretariat, publicity, State officers and agents in
    selected Constituencies.
(e) The means of financing the movement.

(f) A short statement of the political objectives of the movement.

(g) The means of determining policy from time to time.

(h) Ways and means of obtaining candidates.[39]

Written responses from several invited organisations held in Menzies's papers record policy themes and structural proposals that would come to form the conference recommendations, and subsequent inaugural structure and platform of the Liberal Party of Australia. Of particular note are the detailed submissions from the Western Australians[40] and the Liberal Democratic Party of Australia, New South Wales.[41] Less detailed correspondence from the deputy leader of the Opposition in New South Wales[42] and the Queensland Women's Electoral League[43] also outline key issues that would inform the new organisation and provide evidence of a consistency of themes, values and suggested structures apparent in the various submissions. Similar proposals may also be found in a copy of a letter from H Warby to Sir Sydney Snow dated 1 September 1943, enclosing a detailed outline for a new party organisation, that is held in Menzies's papers,[44] which demonstrates detailed proposals as to a new federal organisation were being drafted and considered by a range of individuals and organisations, not just Menzies. Kemp provides details of the proposals developed by Leech[45] and the Institute of Public Affairs.[46] The full list of participants may be found in Menzies's papers, and included representatives from a range of organisations from Queensland, New South Wales, Victoria, Tasmania, South Australia, and Western Australia, as well as state and federal members of Parliament.[47] Given the diversity of individual organisations who attended from across the nation, it is difficult to argue that anyone but Menzies, as a former prime minister, and leader of the Opposition, could have convinced these people to freely contribute their detailed ideas for a new organisation and make the lengthy trip to Canberra to do so.

Menzies had a national network

After all, Menzies was the only conference attendee with Australia-wide political, parliamentary and public contacts due to his time as prime minister and leader of the Opposition, and he had recently had the opportunity to refresh all of these contacts as he toured the nation to fight the 'no' case on the Powers Referendum in 1944.[48] No other participant in attendance at the Canberra and Albury conferences could claim any semblance of Menzies's federal reach, name and reputation. As such it is unlikely any other individual could have convinced such a broad range of organisations to meet to discuss the formation of a new party.

Menzies's ideas were informed by decades of work

Menzies's political position and personal networks do not, in themselves, refute Hancock's claim that his vision for a new political force and supporting ideas 'were not his exclusive intellectual property'.[49] In light of the detailed submissions he received from groups and individuals, it is tempting to conclude that Menzies's skill was drawing together the individuals, groups and their ideas, and then harvesting them. However, suggesting Menzies was merely a skilled cipher ignores his intellectual contribution to public debate over many decades.

None of the ideas expressed in the several years preceding the Canberra conference were new to Menzies. His ideas were formed and tested from the time he was admitted to the Bar and began his career as a barrister, including High Court success in the *Engineers' Case* in 1920 aged just twenty-five.[50] Menzies then researched and honed his policies and platforms from the time he was elected to the Victorian Parliament in 1928.[51] Taking just a few topics that would form the inaugural Liberal Party platform in 1944, there are early statements by Menzies on Australia and the British Empire,[52] freedom,[53] primary producers,[54] and employment, employers, and employees.[55] Menzies further refined his thinking, policies and platform in the regular radio broadcasts he made throughout 1942 to early 1944, well before any serious merger talks by other organisations were underway. Arguably 'The Forgotten People' speech best encapsulates the platform the Liberal Party would adopt, and was broadcast on 22 May 1942, a full twelve to eighteen months before state-based merger meetings commenced. This broadcast was one of many which developed ideas like 'The Function of Opposition in Parliament' (8 May 1942), 'Freedom of Speech, Expression, Worship, and from Want and Fear' (June–July 1942), and the 'Nature, Sickness, Achievements, and Task of Democracy' (October–November 1942). Judith Brett suggests that Menzies was reading Edmund Burke in December 1942 with a specific interest in a 'body of men united by national interest and particular principles'.[56] Other broadcasts of note include 'After the Ball' (27 August 1943), which addressed the election loss, 'Political Campaigning' (3 September 1943), 'Leading the Opposition' (September 1943), and 'A Liberal Revival' (29 October 1943). Throughout this time, Menzies was drafting and circulating his specific ideas as to the form a new federal organisation should take, in a confidential note to colleagues following the 1943 election defeat[57] and in a 16 June 1944 statement.[58]

Menzies had extensive practical experience with party organisations

Menzies's knowledge of political parties and politics was more than just theoretical. He had personal, lived experience of how political parties worked—or did not work—from a very young age. His father was a local councillor between 1909 and 1912, and the Member for Lowan in the Victorian Legislative Assembly from 1911 to 1920.[59] His uncle, Sydney Sampson, the federal Member for Wimmera from 1906 to 1919, had experienced both the formation of the first united

Liberal Party and its demise.[60] His wife Pattie's father had stood as an Anti-Socialist Protectionist trying to oust a sitting Deakinite in 1906,[61] before being elected to the Victorian Parliament in 1913. He moved to the federal Parliament in 1917, losing his seat in 1919,[62] and was a senator for Victoria from 1934 to 1947.[63] So Menzies, and his wife and confidante Pattie, were exposed to the reality of politics and parties in a very practical way from a young age.

Menzies himself was directly involved in the creation of two political entities. During his time in the Victorian Parliament, Menzies helped to form the Young Nationalists—a group dedicated to attracting young people to politics but also injecting robust ideas and interested debate into Australian political discourse. Menzies served as the group's president,[64] and 'his organising talents were such that half of the UAP members returned in the 1932 state election were Young Nationalists—they had almost trebled their Parliamentary representation'.[65] Around the same time, Menzies was part of a group that convinced Minister Joseph Lyons to defect from the Australian Labor Party, precipitating the formation of the UAP.[66] Menzies became president of the United Australia Organisation, speaking at the first annual conference in September 1932, at which he indicated this was his second term as president.[67] In this address Menzies encourages members to establish new branches to expand the organisation, again evidence of his thorough knowledge of how the organisation worked in practical terms. This practical, lived experience of the structure, organisation and functioning of political parties and movements clearly assisted Menzies when he drafted the Liberal Party structure and platform. Once again Menzies's lived political experience cannot be matched by many, if any, other Australians.

Menzies had unrivalled international experience

Menzies had also travelled in wartime and had exposure to the British and Canadian prime ministers, parliaments and parliamentarians, further enhancing his breadth of observation and interaction with parties and the Westminster system.[68] His knowledge of American politics, while not quite as intimate as his experiences within the British Commonwealth, was notable as well.

Menzies's resilience

While Menzies possessed the intellectual skills to underpin the formation of the new Liberal Party, in the years prior it looked unlikely that he possessed the interpersonal skills. Just two years before the creation of the Liberal Party he had resigned as prime minister, humiliated, and branded with the worst possible slurs. Enid Lyons and others had claimed he was responsible for the death of Prime Minister Joe Lyons,[69] Earle Page called him a coward in the House of Representatives for not enlisting in World War I, and Menzies was generally considered aloof, arrogant, insensitive,[70] impatient, condescending, belittling, dominating, overwhelming, contemptuous, and with a vindictive wit.[71] Despite all these flaws, he had rebounded to be elected leader of the Opposition in 1943, perhaps because the centre-right possessed few other talents at this time, but similarly perhaps because he had modified his approach to colleagues.

Menzies chaired the Canberra and Albury conferences

Evidence from the 1944 Powers Referendum, and in the lead up to, and during, the Canberra and Albury conferences suggests Menzies had in fact successfully curbed these excesses of his personality. The Institute of Public Affairs observers reported after the Canberra meeting that: 'No single factor contributed so much to the success of the Conference as Mr Menzies' personality. His good humour, his patience, his skilful handling of the business of the meetings, were at all times outstanding'.[72]

Menzies's role as Chair is further emphasised by Bramston, who describes how Menzies not only chaired the meeting, but hosted drinks, mingled with delegates, and 'worked the sidelines' during the Canberra Conference, and was the 'pre-eminent figure' at Albury.[73] The success—or otherwise—of any meeting depends on a capable Chair, and there is no argument that Menzies was anything other than outstanding in his role at the pivotal conferences. Even Hancock admits Menzies was a brilliant Chair,[74] writing this about the Albury Conference:

> His real achievements were as a speaker—in articulating a new philosophical direction—and as a chairman—in keeping meetings to the point, in reminding the delegates of what they had to do, in pulling ideas together. He was the visible face of the new party, not its sole founder or progenitor, though certainly its most accomplished and skilful proponent.[75]

It is clear that Menzies carefully crafted and targeted his conference speeches to his audience. He pays tribute to the ideas of the individuals and organisations in attendance, summarising their ideas and contributions and repeating them back to them.[76] For example, Menzies thoroughly praised Charles Kemp,[77] of the Victorian Institute of Public Affairs, for his document 'Looking Forward'.

Menzies had prepared this groundwork through the manner in which he wrote to delegates to invite them to attend. His open-ended letters encouraged delegates to share detailed proposals for a new party and platform, that they then heard repeated back to them in Menzies's key speeches, which made them feel that they had suggested key ideas, encouraging them to take ownership of the new party in a way that had never been previously achieved. This was his skill as organiser, orator and persuader.

Leadership is critical to any business, team or party success

Every successful team, business or political party needs a leader. Similarly, every leader needs a team to succeed, and Menzies's team included a range of outstanding individuals. Elizabeth Couchman persuaded the Australian Women's National League to end their decades-long policy of staying separate from the official centre-right party and encouraged their 12 000 members to join the Liberals.[78] William Anderson merged the Services and Citizens Party with the Liberal Party and became the first president of the new Liberal Party of Victoria, serving between 1945 and 1948, then as federal president from 1951 to 1956.[79] Ernest White, formerly of the Liberal Democratic Party, served on the provisional Liberal executive.[80] New South Wales businessman Thomas Ritchie became the provisional Liberal Party Chair in 1944, inaugural president in 1945, raised large sums of money, persuaded the Queensland's People's Party to join the Liberal Party, drafted the plan for the federal organisation, and worked tirelessly to ensure the new party's success, serving as president from 1944 to 1947, then 1949 to 1951, and as a party trustee until 1955.[81] There is no doubt that the creation of the Liberal Party of Australia in 1944–45 could not have been achieved by Menzies alone. To suggest this is as absurd as suggesting that Menzies alone won every election between 1949 and his retirement in 1966. However, it is also unfair to suggest that without Menzies's leadership the party would have been created and achieved lasting success. The formation of the party was Menzies's miracle, and his alone.

Menzies's success as leader and prime minister cemented the survival of the party

Menzies's most outstanding achievement was the enduring success of the Liberal Party of Australia. Under his leadership, Menzies held the party together through the 1946 election defeat (and it is worth noting that *both* the Nationalists and the UAP had been killed off by their first election losses), and his electoral successes between 1949 and his retirement in 1966 cemented the party's existence and prominence. Even the turmoil of five different Coalition prime ministers in the seven years between 1966 and 1972 could not derail the party, nor thirteen years of Hawke–Keating Labor rule between 1983 and 1996. Menzies succeeded where previous prime ministers—Deakin, Reid, Cook, Hughes, Bruce, and Lyons—failed. Not only did Menzies create the Liberal Party, but through his leadership and electoral success he ensured it thrived and prospered. It was, and remains, Menzies's miracle.

CHAPTER TWO

MENZIES AND THE MOVEMENT: TWO PILLARS OF AUSTRALIAN ANTI-COMMUNISM

Lucas McLennan[1]

FROM 1945 TO 1955, the world rapidly split into pro-American and pro-Soviet blocs. In Australia, the political ramifications of the Cold War contributed to Sir Robert Menzies's success in leading a long-term government. Anti-communism was a core feature of the Menzies program in both opposition and government from 1943 to 1954. Menzies's anti-communism stemmed from his deep commitment to the principles of British liberalism. Menzies, like many Protestants, viewed communism as a threat to the British way of life and the English tradition of ordered liberty. For Menzies, the Liberal Party, the Country Party, and several other institutions and organisations (such as the Institute of Public Affairs), deep-seated anti-communism formed one pillar of opposition to communism in Australia. This opposition was based on the belief that communism threatened Australia's British and liberal culture.

During the same period, another 'pillar' of anti-communism gained prominence in Australia. The Catholic Social Studies Movement, known as 'the Movement',[2] aimed to defeat communism in the labour unions and prevent the growth of communist influence in the Australian Labor Party (ALP). The Movement achieved its most significant victories in the same decade that Menzies formed the Liberal Party and came to power. BA Santamaria and his Movement created a significant political subculture that drew on Catholic social teaching and European political thought to oppose communism.[3] From 1942 to 1955, the Movement functioned as an anti-communist force within the ALP and labour movement, while Menzies successfully used anti-communism to win elections and firmly orient Australia as a US ally. However, for various cultural and sectarian reasons, Santamaria and his followers regarded Menzies and his Liberals as enemies during the period under examination.

From the 1955 federal election onwards, Menzies benefited from the fallout of the Labor split. The Coalition received most of the preferences from the breakaway Democratic Labour Party (and, in Queensland, from the distinct Queensland Labor Party, until a national Democratic Labour Party (DLP) was formed for the 1963 election).[4] Usually, the Coalition was able to win in its own right. However, in the elections of 1961 and 1969 (after Menzies had retired), DLP preferences were vital in electing Coalition majorities over the ALP. Those who left the ALP during the split broadly shared the foreign policy outlook of the Menzies government and its policies of supporting the US alliance and containing communism in South-East Asia.[5] In the period under study (1943–54), the Movement remained very much on the labour side of Australian politics.

A review of the Movement's key publication, *News Weekly,* and other documents written or influenced by Santamaria (such as the Australian Catholic bishops' annual *Social Justice Statements* from the 1940s and 1950s) reveal that both pillars shared similar concerns about the direction of post-war Australia. Their shared concerns began with communism, both internationally and domestically. However, both came to have similar concerns about Labor's post-war reconstruction, the state's role, and centralisation. In this chapter, I explore how Menzies and the Movement drew on distinct traditions to inform their shared anti-communism and approaches to other issues. When the similarities of these two pillars are considered, the political connection between them in the next period of Menzies's political career (1955–66) becomes even more comprehensible.[6]

Shared understandings

Menzies and his heritage

Robert Menzies's staunch opposition to communism grew out of nineteenth-century British liberal ideals that formed the cultural milieu in which he was raised and educated. Modern political debates about whether Menzies was a conservative or a liberal try to impose current political categories on the past. Most readings of Menzies's speeches and writings have concluded that he adhered to a distinct form of Australian liberalism, informed by a 'Whig' reading of British history. Menzies was a conservative because he sought to 'conserve' a British liberal tradition he saw as under attack from the forces of socialism and communism.

Stephen Chavura and Greg Melleuish have argued that Menzies's thinking and attitudes can be described as cultural puritanism. Concepts associated with cultural puritanism include 'sturdiness, independence, freedom, self-scrutiny, Godliness, duty, domesticity'.[7] All these concepts are prominent in the speeches and thinking of Menzies (notably his series of 'Forgotten People' broadcasts during World War II).

Chavura and Melleuish define cultural puritanism as 'an out-growth of the powerful connection between Protestantism and political liberty in British culture', as described by Linda Colley. This Protestantism was strongly connected to the political ideals of liberalism, 'especially Gladstonian liberalism'.[8]

Menzies saw the English and Scottish Reformations, the civil wars of the seventeenth century, the Glorious Revolution, and the *Great*

Reform Act of 1832 as providing ordered liberty under the crown, which was the envy of the world. Slow-moving reform in the direction of liberty was understood as a positive feature of Britishness.

Judith Brett has argued that Menzies's Protestant heritage informed his rhetorical commitment to British liberty, which was focused mainly on Protestant self-conceptions of independence and hard work. A cohesive society required men and families to have the means to be independent of the state and to cultivate a commitment to the community. In Menzies's view, the British Protestant and liberal tradition was best symbolised by the free individual who worked hard, owned property, gained an education, and contributed to the community. These values were under threat from state socialism and even more so from revolutionary communism, which sought to crush the individual into a collective. According to Brett, Menzies strongly believed that 'Independence, a central value of individualism, could be seen as the hallmark of a godly man'.[9] Not surprisingly, Menzies, as Opposition leader, led the Liberal Party in strongly opposing three Labor government referendums (1944, 1946, and 1948), which sought to increase the powers of the Commonwealth over whole areas of the economy.

Andrew Carr and Benjamin Jones have sought to frame Menzies as a civic republican. This is a provocative characterisation, given his staunch commitment to constitutional monarchy, empire, and commonwealth. Menzies was defined as a civic republican due to his understanding that the independent man is responsible for developing virtue and committing to contributing to public life in the community. Such a sensibility would have been developed in Menzies through his classical education and his reading of British history. Menzies's writings reveal a person deeply committed to the ideals of British liberalism. He was an admirer of Cromwell and the primacy of Parliament over the crown, suggesting a man at ease with democracy.[10] The description of Menzies as a civic republican rests on his clear commitment to the separation of powers in a state (stemming from a classical understanding of republicanism) and his sense of the importance of institutions, such as schools and universities, as essential for the formation of civilised individuals in a functioning society.

Many scholars have emphasised Menzies's commitment to a British liberal understanding of society. Menzies's hostility to communism and (closer to home) the forms of social democracy advocated by Labor stemmed from his desire to conserve the tradition in which he had been formed. Menzies made clear his sense of the political struggle in the late 1940s in his 1946 election address:

> This is our great year of decision. Are we for the Socialist State, with its subordination of the individual to the universal officialdom of government, or are we for the ancient British faith that governments are the servants of the people, a faith which has given fire and quality and direction to the whole of our history for 600 years?[11]

Based on this, Menzies would oppose communism, Labor's plans for constitutional reform, and much of the post-war reconstruction agenda.

Santamaria and the Movement

Unlike Menzies, Santamaria was an outsider in relation to the British liberal Protestant world. Born to Italian migrants to Australia in 1915, he was even an outsider in the predominantly Irish Catholic milieu of Archbishop Daniel Mannix's Melbourne.[12]

A brilliant student (like Menzies), he received a scholarship to the Christian Brothers' Saint Kevin's College in Toorak. He studied law and arts at the University of Melbourne. He was involved in the Campion Society and studied the ideas of Catholic thinkers, such as Hilaire Belloc, GK Chesterton, and Christopher Dawson.[13] Archbishop Daniel Mannix appointed him to work at the National Secretariat for Catholic Action. In 1936, he was involved in the publication of the *Catholic Worker* as editor (and claimed he was primarily responsible for writing most of the early editions).[14] The *Catholic Worker* was informed by the Catholic social teaching of the popes and (in the English language) writers such as Belloc and Chesterton. Vehemently opposed to atheistic communism, Santamaria (and the *Catholic Worker*) saw capitalism as irreligious and unjust. They saw capitalism as emerging from the Protestant Reformation and liberal revolutions, both of which were anti-Catholic movements in their day.

Santamaria and his allies were sceptical of communism and the Anglo-Protestant establishment in Australia. Informed by Belloc's ideas on the servile state, Santamaria and the *Catholic Worker* (and later *Freedom/News Weekly*) also critiqued the state-centric view of socialism that had become predominant in Australian Labor circles. Belloc's writings on social and economic questions significantly influenced thinkers and activists in these Catholic circles. Since Federation, Australia had developed a state-centric approach to social welfare. Industrial arbitration and policies such as the living wage were examples of progressive social and economic policies in Australia compared with the rest of the Western world.[15] Belloc shared the concern of many for the situation of the working classes in industrial economies. However, he saw the state acting as an ameliorative force to alleviate the poverty and insecurity of the working classes as simply replacing one master (the owners of capital) with another (the state).[16]

In Belloc's seminal work on social and economic questions, *The Servile State*, he laid out a historical framing that, in the ancient pagan worlds, slavery had been common. Slavery had largely disappeared in the European Middle Ages as the influence of the Church saw the widespread distribution of property. Many people enjoyed a form of both independence and security. However, through industrialisation, the peasant with rights to the land or small-scale ownership returned to a state of servility in urban industrial factories. The efforts of the state to fix the problem through the provision of social welfare only enhanced servility. What constitutes a servile state is defined as:

> That arrangement of society in which so considerable a number of the families are constrained by positive law to labour for the advantage of other families and individuals as to stamp the whole community with the mark of such labour we call THE SERVILE STATE.[17]

In his autobiography (*Against the Tide*), Santamaria denied that Belloc significantly influenced his thought development.[18] Nevertheless, in the early days of the *Catholic Worker*, from 1936 to 1938, the influence of Belloc was apparent. In its first years, the *Catholic Worker* argued against the Lyons government's national insurance scheme. The *Catholic Worker* advocated 'a good distribution of property ... legislation in every state which keeps property broken into little pieces and confirms working-class families in the ownership of property in small parcels is the remedy. There is no other'.[19]

Belloc also wrote directly to the paper, commending its actions in campaigning against national insurance.

Between 1942 and 1943, Santamaria had received an episcopal endorsement for a 'movement' that would rely mainly on Catholics in trade unions to organise and counteract communist activities inside trade unions.[20] In *Freedom* (renamed *News Weekly* in 1946), the Catholic connection was not explicitly made. Nevertheless, many accused it of being an alarmist publication.[21] It sought to promote the post-war reconstruction based on Christian social principles. These principles are best described as being expressed in papal documents, such as *Rerum Novarum*, and in the ideals of Belloc. The *Freedom* program included some of the following points:

1. Public control of monopolies
2. Public control of credit
3. Industrial councils
4. Assistance to small owners
5. Part ownership of industry for workers ...
11. Possession of family homes by all

12. A strong program of regionalism

13. A national campaign of family land settlement.[22]

All these points speak to a desire to enable a greater distribution of ownership and decentralisation of the population. While the government was significant in implementing these goals, they differed from what became the ALP's post-war agenda of nationalisation and the provision of greater forms of social welfare.

Here, we can see similarities emerging between Menzies and the Movement in the 1943–54 period. Both were suspicious of the centralising state at home and international communism abroad. Santamaria and the Movement drew on the ideas of Catholic social thought to come to such positions. In contrast, Menzies and his associates drew on their tradition of British liberal thought. The similarities in the 1943–54 period laid the groundwork for the collision of interest between the two pillars that would emerge in the next period of the Menzies era.

The purpose of this chapter is not to narrate or analyse the successes and failures of the Movement in ALP and trade union politics in the 1940s and 1950s. Neither does the chapter describe the career and thinking of Santamaria in the period. Instead, through a study of the public writings in *Freedom/News Weekly*, I have sought to explain the parallels between the two pillars of Australian anti-communism.

The Movement's perspective on Menzies

During the 1940s, the Movement saw the non-labour parties as representative of a corrupt establishment. After the UAP–Country Party defeat at the 1943 election, *Freedom* editorialised that the Coalition only served the 'gods of big business' and was 'no more democratic than the red fascists and communist bosses'.[23] Later, *Freedom* saw the newly named Liberals as a re-badging of the party of 'bankers, industrialists, and monopolists'.[24] In this framing, the establishment that would come to be represented by Menzies fitted the communist critique. Menzies and the Coalition were seen as a sectional party, like Labor, but in the interests of the big end of town. While such statements are hyperbolic, they also speak to the suspicion of Anglo-Protestant capitalism in much Catholic social thought. Belloc, Dawson, and Chesterton viewed the Reformation as unleashing a social and economic revolution promoting individualism and greed. The Anglo-Protestant establishment was another enemy for their disciples in Australia.

The Movement viewed Menzies's creation of the Liberal Party upon the ashes of the UAP as simply an attempt to put 'war-time clothes' on the old party. The new Liberal Party's commitment to freedom would 'mean nothing. Unless it is ready to fight monopoly, to demand realistic measures to destroy monopoly, and measures which will be economically hurtful to monopoly so that the small man can live, protestations about "freedom" serve only to bring that sacred cause into dispute'.[25]

The Movement could not take the claims of the new Liberal Party seriously over representing the interests of small businesses and small farmers because the Movement saw big business and the state as hostile to the interests of workers and families. From the perspective of the Movement, both an enlarged state and the concentration of power in large businesses threatened the freedom and independence of the common people and their families.

A frequent theme of *Freedom/News Weekly* was that Menzies, an enemy of the Labor movement politically, benefited from its divisions over communism. In 1945, Menzies was accused of playing politics over communism in the trade unions. Whereas Chifley had taken pragmatic measures to ensure the ending of a communist-inspired New South Wales strike in December 1945, Menzies advocated harsh measures (including the imprisonment of some strikers), which the *Freedom* writers believed would have inflamed the situation to the benefit of the communists.[26] In the view of *Freedom*, Menzies could not be relied upon to act as a statesman in such matters because he benefited from any turmoil in the union movement and did not see the union movement as essential to the welfare of Australian working people. The Movement believed that Menzies's policies would harm their efforts to defeat communism in the union movement. In the lead-up to the 1946 election, the Liberal policy to allow the government to break strikes by freezing the funds of striking unions was condemned. According to *News Weekly*, such a policy would 'throw the decent unionist over to the side of the communist agitator'.[27]

Menzies was respected in *Freedom/News Weekly* for his perspective on foreign policy. For example, Menzies joined Mannix and others to speak in 1939 at a pro-appeasement rally in the Melbourne Exhibition Building. Later in the war, the publication praised him for his 'statesman-like talk' on the need for Japan and Germany not to be completely destroyed after victory in World War II. Menzies understood the 'lessons of Versailles'. The 'military caste in Germany and Japan' must be removed, but peace (and stopping communism) required that 'economic prosperity' be available to the people of the defeated nations for the good of the world.[28] The publication also fairly presented Menzies's concerns about the Labor referendums of the 1940s.

Overall, *Freedom/News Weekly* received Menzies and the new Liberal Party 1944–49 as too closely tied to the interests of large businesses. In a more sectarian era, Menzies represented the Anglo-Protestant establishment. Not understanding the social questions that needed to be addressed, he was not viewed as someone able to fight successfully against communism.

Opposition to communism

Opposing international and domestic communism was the central focus for Menzies and the Liberals in opposition and the first two terms of government (1949–54). The Movement shared this commitment, but this placed it in tension with figures in labour politics who sought to avoid the emergence of a Cold War between the Western and Soviet blocs. The Movement strenuously opposed recognition of the People's Republic of China (PRC) after 1949, whereas the official position of the ALP was to provide recognition. Chifley argued in Parliament that the old Nationalist government of China (newly based in Taiwan) had been 'completely corrupt' and that there was 'no question whatever that the only government on the mainland today is the so-called People's Government'.[29] Chifley (the Opposition leader in 1950) saw no practical reason why Australia should not recognise the PRC. Chifley did not see communism as the sole reason for the disturbances in East Asia. He agreed with Nehru that the only way to save 'East Asia from radicalism is an improvement in economic conditions'.[30] Consequently, Australia should have focused on technical and other aid to the emerging nations in Asia in the hope that economic prosperity and social justice would keep them from becoming a single-party communist dictatorship. The Movement saw recognition of China as more than simply a practicality, as communism was understood as an evil. *News Weekly* argued 'that there is such a thing as principles'.[31] According to *News Weekly*:

> Communism is the same the world over, directed by the Kremlin, and inherently evil by nature. It has established itself in portions of Europe and the East by violence. We must refuse to recognise it because it is intrinsically evil, and in justice to the millions of people suffering under its yoke.[32]

The methods of communism, the control of global communism from the Soviet Union, and the immorality of the system all necessitated that a practical approach of realpolitik could not be relied upon when dealing with newly communist states. The Movement, therefore, was allied in its advocacy on the PRC with the position of Menzies's Liberals. The Movement's (and later the DLP's) support for this position helped to forestall Australian recognition of the People's Republic of China into the early 1970s.

Menzies's Liberals and the Movement also shared a perspective on banning the Communist Party of Australia (CPA). However, once again, the fierce anti-communism of the 'Movement' placed it at odds with the broader labour movement in which it operated and which it sought to dominate.

A *News Weekly* editorial argued:

> The issue at the referendum—the only issue—is this: Should the power to act against the Communist Party, already possessed by the six states, be transferred to the Commonwealth? As this power is a necessary corollary to the Defence Act, there can be only one answer—'Yes'.[33]

In continuity with the position on recognition of the PRC, the Movement maintained that communism could not be treated simply as a political ideology. As the CPA had a direct relationship with the Soviet Union through the Communist International, it acted as an agent of a foreign power within Australia. Menzies's position in defence of banning the Communist Party was essentially the same. Some liberals viewed the referendum through the lens of liberty (and Menzies had drawn on the liberal tradition to argue against a ban). However, he ultimately came to the Movement-aligned view that the conspiratorial nature of communism made the threat of communism unique. Opposing communism internationally and nationally led to an alignment between Menzies and the Movement in the 1943–54 period, but this issue was not the only one where there was an overlap.

Post-war reconstruction and centralisation

In the post-war period, strong views emerged that the authority of central governments should be strengthened to create a more egalitarian society. In Australia, such an attitude informed the Curtin–Chifley Labor governments in their approach to the task of post-war reconstruction. As a part of this broader trend, the Curtin and Chifley governments attempted to centralise power in Canberra three times in the 1940s. All except one proposal (social services in 1946) failed.

The editors of *News Weekly* were inspired by Catholic social doctrine to develop extensive proposals for decentralisation, land settlement, and population growth through birth-rate increases and migration. Such issues were a constant feature of the publication between 1943 and 1954. The Movement argued against urbanisation and emphasised the need for immigrants to be directed towards rural areas as 'small farmers' or as 'tradesmen' in regional towns. In taking up the cause of rural development, the ideal of independent families and communities (as opposed to the centralising socialist state advocated by many in Labor) was the focal point.

Due to the Movement's place within Labor politics, they supported Labor's centralising tendencies in the three referendums of the 1940s and stopped short of endorsing the Labor government's plans for a national medical system. However, a close reading of the *News Weekly* commentary on the referendums clarifies that support was limited and with severe caveats, demonstrating the ongoing influence of distributist ideals on the Movement. Parallels with Menzies's and the Liberals' critique of post-war reconstruction can easily be made.

The referendums

The first of the referendums took place in 1944. The referendum was entitled 'Postwar reconstruction and democratic rights'.[34] It was known more popularly as the fourteen powers referendum. The proposals would have given the federal government powers for the rehabilitation of former servicemen, national health, provision of family allowances, employment and unemployment, Indigenous Australians, corporations, foreign investments, monopolies, air transport, railways, marketing, manufacturing, national insurance, and national infrastructure. Additionally, the proposals included provisions for freedom of speech and religion.[35]

The position of *Freedom* on the referendum reflected the suspicion of developing too big a state at the federal level (conflicting with the principles of subsidiarity and independence). However, the Movement was located socially and culturally with the Labor side of politics and the publication provided a fair hearing for the proposals and a tempered endorsement. Australian voters had 'always shown a healthy suspicion of moves to centralise control in Canberra'.[36] Australians had maintained that healthy suspicion despite 'a powerful minority' that preached 'unification'.[37] While Labor had often advocated for centralisation in the past, most of the failed referendums seeking to bring power to Canberra had been overseen by the conservative side of politics. Centralisation in Canberra was, therefore, the agenda of big businesses and labour unions that sought a larger state for their interests. *Freedom* instead recognised that the war situation necessitated some further grant of federal powers; however, it argued that the grant of the new powers should 'be fixed' for only a 'limited period of years'.[38] This argument was made in October 1943 (almost twelve months before the referendum proposal was finalised).

Closer to the referendum itself (in August 1944), *Freedom* still supported a Yes vote but came to criticise the campaign in favour of the powers for its association with communists. The publication argued that the CPA envisaged using the powers for its benefit if a communist revolution succeeded in Australia. The CPA wanted 'a yes vote for their own purposes as, if they came to power in Australia, the government powers would already be heavily centralised'.[39] *Freedom* maintained that it supported the government's proposals, as the federal government genuinely needed the powers for legitimate post-war activities. However, some state parties, like those in South Australia and New South Wales, decided to allow communist involvement in the campaign, which doomed it to failure.[40] A core concern was that the High Court and popular democracy would prevent the new powers from being used to implement industrial conscription (this concern was related to the power over 'employment and unemployment').[41]

Freedom also addressed a critique of Menzies and the Opposition's position on the referendum.[42] Menzies supported the actions of the business-backed Australian Constitutional League. The league saw the referendum as representing socialisation in Australia. *Freedom* saw the Menzies Liberal position as a cynical ploy to begin the defeat of the Labor government.[43] The Movement's viewpoint on Menzies, as not particularly principled, stems from an inability to recognise the Liberals as having any coherent philosophy except as a representative of the business class. *Freedom* ultimately used the referendum's defeat to argue that ALP–CPA collaboration on some pro-Yes committees had been a 'grim lesson'.[44] It reinforced the core Movement mission of fighting communism in the unions.

In 1946, the Chifley government proposed three referendum questions on social services, marketing, and industrial employment. Only the social services question received a majority in all six states and on a national popular vote level. The success of the social services question was largely a result of the bipartisan support offered by Menzies as Opposition leader. Later, in 1948, a single question of federal control of rents and prices was heavily defeated.

Concerning the 1948 question, *News Weekly* argued that the scepticism of the public towards Labor's centralisation agenda was to blame for the defeat.[45] *News Weekly* still supported the Yes case for the referendum and claimed to base its position on 'Christian social principles'. The objective of Christians should be to break up the 'concentration of power wherever it is found' and seek to 'break up concentration of wealth'.[46] True to the principle of subsidiarity, the ideal was for price and rent controls to be 'administered by the states'.[47] However, *News Weekly* argued that the conservative opposition to the referendum was purely based on a desire to destroy anti-inflation measures like price controls altogether. Therefore, *News Weekly* recommended again that the people should vote Yes.

The editors of *News Weekly* took a challenging position. The Movement they represented was hostile towards centralisation and increased government power. However, they were engaged with the labour movement that wanted to support the proposals of the Labor government. Opposing the Labor government's agenda and movements would have placed them in a precarious position. While they expressed concerns about elements of these proposals, they otherwise supported them. However, many of their concerns overlapped with the critiques of Robert Menzies.

National health

The shared understandings of Menzies and the Movement were also apparent in their response to Labor's national health plan. On 6 May 1946, Labor added the development of a national free healthcare scheme to its plans for changing the nation.[48] In a speech he made to a conference of state health ministers, the federal Labor health minister, Senator James Fraser, outlined a plan to implement a national medical service throughout Australia. The service would mean that people would receive free medical service at the point of contact with doctors and hospitals.

The healthcare scheme would have put Australia's healthcare policy development in the same direction as that of the United Kingdom. When debating the legislation enabling the 1946 social services referendum (which, as already mentioned, he eventually supported), Menzies expressed concern that the proposals would lay the groundwork for a national medical scheme that could make all doctors and dentists employees of the state. Menzies contended that he objected strongly to the possibility that the medical profession might be 'nationalised'.[49] The medical profession, represented by what was then still called the British Medical Association in

Australia, objected that any such scheme would lead to a 'loss of professional freedom, and the doctor–patient relationship will suffer'.[50] *News Weekly* editorialised frequently against developing a national health scheme, arguing that 'doctors will have to prescribe according to certain rules and that mild complaints would overrun hospitals and doctor's clinics'.[51] Menzies and the Movement found themselves hostile to another aspect of Labor's plan. It is a further example of the Movement and Menzies sharing a stance against a form of socialisation and central government activity based on core principles.

Conclusion

From 1955 to the end of the era of Liberal political hegemony at the federal level in 1972, the Liberals and the DLP enjoyed a symbiotic relationship built around their shared commitment to anti-communism, both internationally and domestically. This chapter has demonstrated that even before the shattering events of 1954–55, Menzies and the Movement had much in common in their reactions to Labor's post-war reconstruction agenda.

The Menzies government's advocacy of banning the CPA (and its broader commitment to anti-communism as a foreign policy goal) and the fight against communism by the Movement in the trade unions entitled both to be described as pillars of anti-communism in Australia. Delineating the shared understandings of these two pillars in the 1940s and 1950s is essential to appreciate the heterogenous nature of anti-communism in countries like Australia. Both pillars drew from distinct political and cultural traditions to form their positions in the 1943–54 period. These distinct traditions, however, led to a suspicion of centralisation, socialisation, and the erosion of property, and to extolling the virtues of independence. Studying their earlier similarities is vital, given the significance of the relationship between these two pillars in Australian political history.

CHAPTER THREE

MENZIES AND THE BANKS

Anne Henderson[1]

IT WAS A pleasant late winter Saturday afternoon in Melbourne—
date, 16 August 1947. Record snowfalls across the Victorian Alps
meant a crisp chill for a dry but cloudy day. Robert Menzies, federal
Liberal Party Opposition leader, was attending a friend's lawn
tennis party and heard over the radio the very brief words of Prime
Minister Ben Chifley, announcing his government would nationalise Australia's trading banks. The announcement was as brief as it
was sudden.

Menzies's first reaction was to think the move would not be
unpopular.[2] He recalled the anger felt towards banks for their
refusal of credit in the Depression, then a not-so-distant memory.
Ben Chifley, likewise, remembered this but with a longstanding
resentment at the banks, seeing them as a major reason for the failure
of the Scullin government, 1929–31.

Chifley was confident in his move that Saturday, as the manner
of his announcement seemed to indicate. His erstwhile legal expert,
Labor's minister for external affairs, Dr Bert Evatt, had assured him
the legislation would survive any challenges.[3]

The announcement was made in just one sentence to the press, a mere forty-two words after a hastily convened Cabinet meeting in Canberra. Alas, for the Labor prime minister, it would prove to be a sadly misjudged step. In time, it would become his nemesis. Chifley had handed his rival Robert Menzies a platform to campaign on, all the way to the December 1949 election, which would be a landslide for the Liberal and Country parties in coalition.

A showdown between labour and capital had been coming for some three decades. How this would play out in Australia through the late 1940s and 1950s was not to be imagined. Nationalisation of Australia's banks and the notion that private banking lay at the heart of capitalism had existed from the earliest labour days in the 1890s.[4]

After the debacle of the Scullin government, and its failure to manage the credit and financial crisis, not least from its own schism, in 1932 the ALP State Executive in New South Wales produced a report that exonerated Scullin's Labor government and claimed that the solution in the future was the nationalisation of all Australian banking business.[5] Chifley himself, as a member of the Lyons United Australia Party government's 1935–7 Royal Commission into Monetary and Banking Systems, had submitted a minority report that advocated the nationalisation of all private banking.[6]

The war years had seen Australia's private banks having to operate under strict national security regulations. Much of their investments were forcibly secured with the Commonwealth Bank—then regarded as Australia's central bank. At the cessation of hostilities in Europe in May 1945, the banks had looked forward to an easing of the war regulations only to discover the Labor government intended the regulations to continue. Disruption of business from industrial action had increased and this added to inflation. The economic times were challenging and the Chifley government saw the solution in government having greater control of the financial sector.

Under the *Banking Act* of 1945, local authorities and state governments were banned from dealing with private banks. This meant the private banks now found themselves on a battle footing competing with the Commonwealth Bank, as if with one hand tied. With this threat to the independence of Australia's trading banks it was only Leslie J McConnan, chief executive of the National Bank of Australasia (NBA), who attempted any push-back by trying to unite the banks in protest.[7] The other banks, too worried about government reprisals, hung back. McConnan's moment would come, however, after August 1947. He was the man historian Geoffrey Blainey has described as being 'interested least in banking and most in public affairs'.[8]

In such an atmosphere, Menzies did not successfully capitalise on the banking issue during the 1946 election campaign. Subsequently, in May 1947, feeling comfortable in his success at the election, his first as Labor leader, Chifley attempted to widen the orders of the 1945 Act to apply to additional authorities such as local councils. This led to a challenge in the High Court by the wealthy Melbourne City Council, which wanted the right to choose its own bank.

On Wednesday, 13 August 1947, the High Court found against the federal government, a move which angered Chifley. Menzies has written that it was the only time he ever noted Chifley to have lost his temper.[9] The government now faced the prospect of the private banks challenging the entire Act. It was just three days later that Chifley would announce his government's decision to nationalise Australia's banking system.

As Opposition leader and leader of the Liberal Party in 1947, Robert Menzies and his close supporters were fending off a quiet rebellion within the party against Menzies's leadership. The results of the 1946 federal election had not convinced many that this high-minded legal professional had the right style to win back government. In March, a meeting of the Victorian Council of the Liberal Party had heard critics speak of Menzies's 'conceit' and others allege he had a head 'too up in the clouds' before a motion for a change of leadership was voted down.[10] Chifley's move to nationalise the trading banks handed Menzies a cause not just to solidify his leadership but one that was in time to bring down the Chifley government.

Reaction to Chifley's simple statement that he would seek to nationalise the banks was immediate. By the following Monday, newspapers were leading with front page headlines announcing the move as creating national shockwaves. *The Argus* in Melbourne threw the switch to extreme with the heading '"Totalitarianism!" says Banks' Spokesman' with the subheading 'Menzies declares: "To Russia for a parallel"'. *The Sydney Morning Herald* headlined with 'Bank Decision Staggers Community', reporting 'Leading industrialists and others said yesterday that the proposed banking monopoly would endanger the nation's economy and threaten private enterprise and individual liberty'.[11] This was just the beginning of a national outcry fleshing out the negative implications of the move against Australia's private banks.

From the vantage point of some seven decades later, it is hard to conceive that Chifley and Labor might have thought such a move could be sustained in a market economy like Australia's. It smacked of unguarded socialism at the very least. Menzies bolted from the blocks on day one.

In spite of growing disruptions to industry by radical union actions, many influenced by the Communist Party of Australia, it would not be until faced with legislation to nationalise Australia's trading banks that voters were able to connect warnings of communist inspired activity to their actual lives. Jobs had been easy to find in the post-war economy—peacetime, after war, had its own rewards.

As prime minister, Ben Chifley had successfully handled the ongoing repayment of massive war debts—in particular by getting Labor to eventually accept Australia's ratification of the Bretton Woods Agreement, which installed the International Monetary Fund. Ongoing industry disruptions had not, up to 1947, had a real impact on daily life.

But then came the banking protest over nationalisation and—like a referendum campaign—ordinary citizens suddenly were awash with information overdrive as to how socialisation and government control of the market would impact a free economy. Communism as a growing menace in post-war Europe and in domestic union disruption now had resonance in the nationalisation of the banks.

Commentary and accusations filled daily newspapers. There were accusations of government secrecy and plotting to ambush the banks and that the government had become dictatorial, suggestions that nationalisation would soon be extended to the insurance industry, notions that UK banks trading in Australia would close, reports that the government would compulsorily acquire shares in banks at a low price and predictions that there would be large job losses as the trading banks closed. Not only were bank employees on the march, bank customers and other ordinary Australians joined them. Menzies now spoke directly to the middle-class voters he had invoked in his radio talks in 1942–4 and they were massed and angry.

Before the end of August 1947, Menzies was addressing vast rallies of protesting bank employees and other interested individuals such as workers employed in the insurance industry. Photos in newspapers showed crowds spilling out from function centres into the streets, wide expanses of heads and hats, men and women.

The work behind the scenes of Leslie McConnan and his NBA was nothing short of a well-oiled political machine. A good account of it is to be found in Geoffrey Blainey's *Gold and Paper*.[12] And, for a full account of the anti-nationalisation campaign itself, dig out a copy of AL May's *The Battle for the Banks*.[13] *The Sydney Morning Herald* reported on its front page on Thursday, 25 September, that members of Parliament had received some 500 000 signatures on petitions opposing bank nationalisation. By the end of the year, the print industry (in a country of around 8 million) was celebrating rising income from millions of booklets and pamphlets against nationalisation, largely funded by the banks—especially the NBA.[14]

Chifley was not for turning. On Tuesday, 17 September, caucus having approved bank nationalisation the day before, Australians woke to read of the realities of the move. Chifley had announced that the private banks would be 'taken over by the Commonwealth Bank, either by agreement or by compulsory acquisition'. The terms would be 'just' and compensation for property compulsorily acquired would be 'by agreement or, failing agreement, by a Federal Court of Claims'. He added that the changeover might take years.[15] In the Parliament, the prime minister said confidently, even smugly, that there was nothing in the Constitution to prevent the government taking over banking if it was thought appropriate and thus there would be no referendum.[16] This was class war as Australia had never seen it.

In the House of Representatives, on 18 September, Menzies moved a censure motion where he accused Chifley of seeking to avoid the will of electors by refusing a referendum, and not having proposed bank nationalisation at the 1946 election. Menzies further argued that Chifley was resorting to dictatorial government that undermined the financial lives of ordinary Australians; as he put it:

> ... the 'vested interest' of 1,500,000 people who do business with the trading banks. Of that number at least 1,400,000 are, in the very nature of things, people of modest means. Have they no 'vested interest'? Have they no right in this life to control their own finances, or to go from one bank to another for needed accommodation? ... a politically controlled government banking monopoly, the only one to be created in any English-speaking country or any democratic country in the world, will be an instrument of despotism and oppression.[17]

After a day or so, the government gagged debate on the censure motion. The status quo prevailed. Chifley was secure in knowing two years must pass before another election and he had a comfortable majority. Meanwhile, in spite of his energised and resolute campaign,

Menzies was cautious when a sudden, unexpected, Victorian state election was announced and the Liberal Opposition fought it on the banking issue.[18] Menzies had been defeated too often to realise at this point he was on a winner. But the Victorian election held on Saturday, 8 November 1947, in which Menzies campaigned heavily on the banking issue, saw the defeat of John Cain's Labor government by the Liberal/Country Party. At that moment it would have flickered in Menzies's mind that there was now hope that those who said, 'You'll never win with Menzies', were mistaken.

As the Chifley Banking Bill made its way through Parliament in late October and early November 1947, out on the hustings Menzies and his supporters had sensed a return of the mood of late 1931 when the groupings around the newly formed United Australia Party, led by Joe Lyons and of which Menzies was a key figure, stormed into office.

Campaigning during the Victorian state election in 1947, at a large rally in Albert Park, Menzies in 'top form' referred to those 'old-style' rallies or what the reporters referred to as just 'like old times'.[19] Speaking in the House of Representatives and leading the debate on the Banking Bill on the evening of 23 October, Menzies was watched by record filled galleries after hundreds had been turned away.[20]

It was an eloquent flourish by the Opposition leader as there was no chance the bill would fail to pass with the size of Labor's majorities in both houses. But Menzies was making a heady start on an election campaign still two years away. In his speech, Menzies went to the core of Coalition objections to the legislation, saying:

> [The Bill] will create in the hands of the ruling party a financial monopoly, with unchecked power to grant or withhold banking facilities or bank accommodation in the case of every citizen … It will have an operation and effect far beyond the business of money changing. This bill will be a tremendous step towards the servile State … That is the antithesis of democracy.[21]

In return, Labor's minister for information, Arthur Calwell, attacked Menzies for his opposition to the legislation. Calwell was shrill in his condemnation, saying: 'Imagine plunging Australia into a civil war over a few lousy pence … No matter how many millions the banks spend in this campaign, they cannot withstand the tide of progress. They are finished'.[22] Calwell was speaking old-style Labor dreaming. And, sadly for Labor who could not foresee its folly, this decades-long ideological prejudice, strongly supported by the Australian Communist Party, was about to meet its match in Australia's highest courts at the time.

Chifley's banking legislation made it through the Senate at the end of November and within twenty-four hours was challenged in the High Court by the states of Victoria and South Australia. The High Court challenge became the longest in its history, lasting from 8 February 1948 until 15 April—a total of thirty-nine days. Bert Evatt, appearing for the government, spoke for eighteen days. He did not help his case with an aggressive manner and, at the outset, calling for the disqualification of two of the judges, which was overruled by Chief Justice J Latham.

A majority decision against the government in the key finding of the court (Latham and McTiernan dissenting) was handed down on 11 August 1948. It found that the prohibition of business by private banks breached the freedom of interstate trade and commerce protected by section 92 of the Constitution.[23] An appeal to the Privy Council followed.

Beginning in mid-March 1949, Bert Evatt appearing again for the government, the UK's Privy Council hearing lasted thirty-seven days, during which Evatt spoke for twenty-two days. Two judges died before it finished. For all that, the government's appeal was once again lost—the Privy Council handing down its decision on 26 July. Chifley's banking legislation lay in tatters. The federal election was just months away.

For all that, Menzies now worried that the Opposition would not be able to sustain the banking campaign against Labor with the legislation finally rejected. Menzies also had doubts the banks could deliver. It was clear that if the banking issue could be kept alive, the Coalition would defeat Labor. The banks continued to argue they were not safe while Chifley and Labor retained government.

Crucially for Menzies, the NBA's McConnan made a deal. If the Opposition could keep up the momentum of positive hope for change, the bank officers' campaign would be re-energised to defeat Chifley on the banking issue.[24] And it was. Historian David Day has written of the 1949 federal election result that, in view of the anti-bank nationalisation campaign waged by Menzies and the Opposition, 'the adverse vote was … a rejection of further socialisation and a poll on Chifley's plans for bank nationalisation'.[25]

During the Menzies era to follow, reform of Australia's banking system continued. Labor's rejection of sections of the Coalition's legislation to reform the invalid *Banking Act* of 1947 was used to call a double dissolution election in April 1951. The result delivered a healthy majority in both houses for Menzies, after which the 1947 Act was repealed. In 1953, the Commonwealth Trading Bank was established and a further *Banking Act* limited some of the controls that had been imposed on the trading banks. In 1957, the Menzies government began legislation to set up the Reserve Bank of Australia and the Commonwealth Banking Corporation. The legislation was finally passed in January 1960.

Further arrangements in the early 1960s saw the trading banks and the Reserve Bank develop special 'term loan' funds provided by the trading banks to meet Australia's growing development. In 1964, the Australian Bankers Export Re-finance Corporation came into being. In this way, the Menzies years quietly changed Australia's banking system for all time.[26]

In conclusion, I should let Robert Menzies have the final word.

Writing of Ben Chifley and the bank nationalisation saga, decades later, in *Afternoon Light*, Menzies concluded with respect to Chifley as follows:

> By upholding the principles of his party, he paradoxically helped destroy his party. ... if one's ideas are so rigid that they will not bend, the chances are that they will break ... socialisation led Chifley to defeat.[27]

CHAPTER FOUR

LIBERALISM APPLIED? POLICY SHIFTS IN THE TRANSITION FROM CHIFLEY TO MENZIES

Tom Switzer[1]

Introduction

AT THE 1949 federal election, Robert Menzies campaigned on a policy platform which supported free enterprise and freedom of choice, and which conversely opposed socialism and state ownership. This rhetorical framing helped Menzies and his Liberal Party distinguish themselves from the Labor government, which had been in power since 1941 and had frequently been found advocating for an increased role for the state. However, despite the lines of philosophical cleavage being quite clear during the election, after 1949 the incoming prime minister arguably left unchanged many of the achievements of Ben Chifley's interventionist government.

Though Chifley's government was relatively short-lived—from 1945 to 1949—its socio-economic achievements were stupendous: an emboldened welfare state, a development ethos, a larger immigration intake, the imposition of Keynesian demand management at the Treasury, and full employment, were all placed at the heart of government policy.[2]

This proved an enduring settlement. Even though his election defeat in 1949 opened the way to a long period of Coalition governance, none of the prime ministers who succeeded Chifley—Menzies, Harold Holt, John McEwen, John Gorton, William McMahon, Gough Whitlam, Malcolm Fraser—challenged the core elements of this post-war system.

Menzies gave voice to the classical liberal philosophy of limited government based on competition and the widest freedom of individual choice. But he never set out to destroy the post-war economic policy consensus of high tariffs, centralised wage fixing and financial regulation. Some of his critics at the time lamented a fundamental mismatch between his rhetoric and the record.

But Menzies was a creature of his culture, and as Gregory Melleuish has observed, 'cultures are created by people who put into place institutions that mould and shape the pathways of the next generation'.[3] The Federation Settlement of 1901 created a protectionist culture that shaped generations of Australians. It's not surprising, then, that Menzies's early years in power were marked by certainty and predictability, qualities much appreciated after the Depression and World War II.

Still, Menzies scored a great triumph for liberalism in 1949: the defeat of Chifley's plans to introduce socialism in the form of bank nationalisation. (See Anne Henderson's chapter.) Indeed, it is widely agreed among historians that Labor's proposal presented an opportunity for Menzies to revive his floundering political career—as had their earlier attempts to greatly increase the power of the federal government via referendum.

At the time, the media's conventional wisdom had written Menzies's political obituary: after upsetting his colleagues, he had lost power in humiliating fashion during the war in 1941. 'It was the most humiliating personal collapse in the history of federal politics in Australia,' remarked biographer Allan Martin in 2001.[4]

Then Menzies led the newly created Liberal Party to a massive defeat at the 1946 election, and the popular slogan 'You can't win with Menzies' came to haunt the former prime minister. Menzies told his mentor Owen Dixon that he had profound doubts about his political future. According to Martin, Menzies 'knew he was the subject of dislike and hostility throughout the community and thought perhaps his party could not win under his leadership'.[5] But Labor's bank nationalisation changed the political circumstances, and Menzies exploited the opportunity.

In the lead-up to the December 1949 poll, Menzies launched a free enterprise campaign against Labor's bank nationalisation law. 'Australians are now called to a great battle to defend their freedoms against dictatorship at home,'[6] he declared. 'A vote for Labor is a vote for socialism.' Private banks were not safe if Labor were re-elected, because nationalisation was a direct link to the people's private property rights.

Menzies warned of Labor's goal of 'socialism in our time'—that is, the establishment of the 'master state' where,

> as in the monstrous totalitarian states which have disfigured the history of the 20th century, all free choice will have gone ... In brief, socialism is in Australia an alien and deadly growth. We must destroy its political power and its mental and spiritual infection while there is still time ... You cannot socialise the means of production without socialising men and women ...
>
> A resolute reduction in the burdens of government, and with it, in the rates of tax, will mean reduced costs of production.
>
> Socialism, by placing its emphasis on State control, state management, the growth of departments, the notion that security is independent of individual effort, actually discourages production.[7]

Menzies was hardly alone in making the case against socialism. Between 1905 and 1906, George Reid had led a famous campaign warning Australians about the dangers of Labor's 'socialist tiger',[8] while in 1949 Country Party leader Artie Fadden cautioned the electorate: 'If you choose the Labor Party, then your ballot paper will truly be your last will and testament, disposing in your own lifetime of your liberties and your property and condemning your children and your children's children to the living death of socialist regimentation'.[9]

Menzies's 'forgotten people' theme, which he started championing in radio broadcasts from 1942, was a successful attempt to undermine Labor's class-based politics and to broaden the centre-right's image beyond that of representing private enterprise. Menzies's message was directed at small-business people, professionals and migrants, appealing to the 'ordinary' people of the Australian suburbs whose aspiration focused on the family and home—or what Judith Brett has called the 'moral middle class'.[10]

Indeed, many Australians saw a potential threat to their own life implicit in the creation of a government-owned and controlled bank monopoly. As David Kemp has argued, in 1949 Menzies presented the Australian people with a clear choice between liberalism and individuality on the one hand and a monopolistic socialism, with its directed conformity on the other. As a result, he marked a direct link between capitalism and liberty, a link that Chifley and the Labor Party grossly underestimated.[11]

The result on 10 December 1949 was a Liberal–Country Party Coalition victory by 51 per cent to 49 per cent after preferences. Labor retained control of the Senate, but with a 74–47 majority the Coalition held a commanding margin of power in the House of Representatives.[12] To be sure, bank nationalisation was not the overriding issue at the election, but it contributed significantly to the defeat of the Chifley government.

Thanks to its subsequent consolidation, the 1949 election became the watershed poll in Australian history; the most important election in the history of non-Labor politics and in the history of the Liberal Party. According to Paul Kelly, the nationalisation matter represented three key lessons: that Labor best governed by focusing on middle-of-the-road brands of government intervention; that the public valued the economic and moral benefits of free enterprise; and that the nationalisation issue was exploited by Menzies not to repudiate government intervention and state power but to position himself as its most successful champion.[13]

In other words, the 'moderate' Ben Chifley, as Labor partisans had dubbed him, had overreached, whereas the pro-free enterprise Robert Menzies was a 'cautious reformer',[14] as prominent journalist Alan Reid called him, who Kelly credits with taking 'to its zenith the old Labor ideal of civilising capitalism'. As a result, it was Menzies, not Chifley, who consolidated and gave expression to the enduring post-war legacy—an Australia of low unemployment, consistent growth, social stability, high immigration, and the more distinctly Menzian achievement of high home ownership. The World War II generation, represented by the ex-servicemen, had gone Liberal not Labor. The great Australian middle class emerged from the battering it had received in the Great Depression and through wartime taxation, to greatly expand throughout the 1950s. And the economy suffered few external shocks, such as the Korean War wool boom.

The upshot for Labor was that it failed to mobilise the politics of the peace in its favour. Which helps to explain Paul Keating's later lament: 'We built the post-war structures and gave it to the Liberal Party, to Menzies'.[15] The truth is that, as John Howard observed, the Menzies years were 'characterised by an unspoken bipartisanship on issues such as high tariffs, centralised wage fixing and financial regulation'.[16]

Menzies, 1949–54

Menzies had pledged a new era of private enterprise and the repudiation of socialism, but what actually resulted was a period of 'high-risk consolidation.'[17] Menzies was willing to confront an obstructionist

Labor Senate over a new Bank Bill to replace Chifley's totemic legisla-tion, risking just the second double dissolution in Australian history after the first had spectacularly backfired on Prime Minister Joseph Cook. However, once that battle was won and the government faced the inflation boom precipitated by the Korean War, steady economic management took precedent over any real economic reform.

Having a won a great victory to hold the line against socialism, Menzies showed little inclination to actually conquer the enemy's territory. He concluded that deregulation, privatisation, competition policy, tariff cuts etc. were just not on the public-policy agenda in the 1950s, and as a result, Menzies went to great lengths to retain not just the same group of public servants and economists who advised Curtin and Chifley, but also much of their policy agenda.

From the perspective of the public service of the day, though, the return of Menzies (who had been prime minister once before, 1939–41) and all the talk of dismantling controls and celebrating the virtues of private enterprise, initially seemed to indicate that the era of interventionism was about to ebb.[18] After all, Friedrich Hayek had written his 1944 book, *The Road to Serfdom*, which had made him famous among the political and economic elites across the Western world—and Menzies himself had intensively read a copy.[19] There were also powerful figures in the incoming government who viewed with extreme caution the expanded bureaucracy of the war and post-war years. They saw the whole idea of post-war reconstruc-tion as a tool of the socialists. They were deeply suspicious of those who had served the previous Labor administration, and they wanted Menzies to 'cleanse' the public service by jettisoning those who had served in the Department of Postwar Reconstruction.[20]

Chief among the prominent public servants was Dr HC 'Nugget' Coombs, a key Chifley adviser, who had carried out innovative work during the war. As he later made clear, the public servants of the 1940s were generally enthusiastic converts to the ideas of John Maynard Keynes in his *The General Theory of Employment, Interest, and Money*

(1936).[21] Though there were differences in degree, they broadly subscribed to the theory that influenced Labor's plans for full employment, for demobilisation and training schemes for ex-servicemen, and for commissions of inquiry to study aspects of the post-war scene, such as agricultural policy, housing and social security.[22]

Despite the great care he took always to separate Liberal Party policies from those of Chifley and Labor, Menzies disagreed with his colleagues, especially his coalition Country Party ministers, and resisted pressure to replace some of the senior servants he inherited from the Chifley government. Under the British Westminster system of government, Menzies believed, a permanent impartial public service should serve every government, whatever its political orientation: that bureaucrats, whatever their own personal prejudices, would and should serve successive governments equally. John Bunting, later Menzies's permanent head, called him a 'traditionalist' in taking this attitude.[23]

Menzies had great respect for Coombs, who had not just been a Chifley confidant but had been appointed governor of the Commonwealth Bank a few months before the 1949 election. His respect for Coombs would only be enhanced during the next decade and a half. As Menzies remarked upon Coombs's retirement from the bank in 1968:

> You will remember that when I came back into office [in 1949–50] you, as a man suspected of unorthodox ideas, were under a cloud of suspicion by some of my colleagues. The cloud soon disappeared as it became clear to the most prejudiced that we had as a Governor a man of the most conspicuous ability and of the most shining integrity. It remains a matter of great pride for me to have got to know you as well as to have benefitted so much from your great services to our country.[24]

Menzies's team also included Allen Brown, the secretary of the Prime Minister's Department, Brigadier Rourke of the Defence Department, Trevor Swan, chief economist, Prime Minister's Department,

Frank Meere of the Customs Department, and later Roland Wilson, secretary to the Treasury, and John Crawford, secretary of the Department of Commerce and Agriculture.[25] As Martin made clear, the strength which the Menzies government derived from the continuity of the highly talented senior public service which Labor policy had created to meet the crisis of war can 'hardly be over-estimated'. They were intellectually sound mandarins and policy specialists, whom Menzies regarded highly.[26]

All this meant that Menzies kept in place key Chifley policies: Labor's high immigration program (which Menzies had strongly advocated for in his wartime radio broadcasts before the policy was adopted), its development ethos, its Keynesian economics (which Menzies's wartime budgets had first experimented with) and support for public enterprises. At the same time, Menzies did little to upset the post-Federation policy consensus of centralised wage fixing and high tariffs. If anything, arbitration and protection, the foundational Australian institutions, were upheld and advanced.

The department secretary in charge of industrial relations in the 1950s was Harry Bland. Along with the minister, Harold Holt, he maintained close relations with Albert Monk, the veteran and pragmatic ACTU leader. As John Howard recalled: 'Bland's approach—and, so it seemed, the Government's for most of that time—was to use the then industrial relations system to their advantage. The strategy was to recognise the ACTU as the sole voice of employees and in a sense integrate ACTU leadership into the state'.[27] This is significant because, although Labor governments supported the integration of the ACTU into the state, it had previously been unthinkable for Coalition governments to do so.

Nor did Menzies embrace a free trade agenda. As he told Parliament on 21 September 1965: 'The Government is a protection-ist government, and has a firm belief, and well justified in the light of events, in the significance and future of manufacturing industry. I do not need to elaborate that'.[28]

'This was the boldest possible statement of a bipartisan conviction,' remarked Howard. After all, high import tariffs helped keep Australian manufacturing strong and they protected manufacturing jobs. It was a widely held belief because the protectionism appeared to work, given the full employment and the high levels of manufacturing employment at the time.[29]

While Menzies mouthed platitudes about free enterprise, the welfare state became more pronounced. He might have objected to Chifley's government-owned airline monopoly, but Menzies's 'two airline' policy offered private enterprise a far more proscribed role than it had enjoyed before the war. The Commonwealth Bank was not to be Australia's only bank, but it retained significant government support. Canberra as a city and the capital grew in stature and prestige thanks to a healthy injection of government funds. And over time, his government oversaw the transformation of Australia in the great university expansion.[30]

Menzies expanded the role of the Commonwealth government, with spending rising from 14 per cent to 18 per cent of gross domestic product.[31] Social expenditures in the Commonwealth budget had risen under Labor from 31 million pounds in 1942 to 110 million in 1949 thanks in large part to Menzies's support for the social services referendum. According to David Kemp, 'Menzies was happy to see them grow, viewing them as supporting equality of opportunity and acknowledging the humanitarian responsibilities of the state'. Defence spending increases were also a priority.[32]

At the end of 1950, Menzies established the National Security Resources Board (NSRB), which he himself chaired, comprising businessmen and top civil servants to supervise stockpiling and economic planning for development generally and defence in particular. This was in keeping with Chifley's development ethos. In July 1951, Menzies introduced legislation to give the NSRB more power by reimposing, with a few exceptions, the powers enjoyed by the Commonwealth government during the war. This emergency measure greatly alarmed the same government supporters, who feared a return to the wartime controls against which they had fought so vigorously in 1949. When the 1951 budget was brought down, the public servants in the Treasury and the NSRB decreed a sharp increase in taxation and import control through licensing to halt the inflation.[33]

Import licensing had been introduced at the beginning of the war, but after 1945 it had been gradually relaxed until it was confined to imports that cost precious US dollars. The new policy was thus for the government an embarrassing ideological retreat to a major part of the wartime system of direct economic control.[34]

All this had sparked rumblings on the Liberal backbench. In June 1952, *The Sydney Morning Herald* caught the significance of the grim mood. The 1949 election 'threw up on the Liberal side some of the brightest and most earnest young men seen in Parliament for many years'. They were advocates of genuine liberalism, who did not just give lip service to 'free enterprise, desocialisation, a fair deal for private banking, reduced taxation, removal of controls—all the principles so eloquently expounded by their leader'.

According to *The Sydney Morning Herald*:

In the 'glad, confident morning' of the 1950 Parliament, [the parliamentary true believers in liberalism] were full of hope for the future and of trust in the cabinet chiefs.

But they have seen, at first with surprise, and then with growing dismay, party principle after party principle placed in cold storage or thrown overboard. They have seen ministers defer uncritically to the views of socialistic planners, inherited from the Chifley regime …

Now these backbenchers are thinking for themselves, and insisting that the Government take more notice of the party and public feeling, and less of the 'expert' guides who have led it astray.[35]

Liberal intellectuals—from the Melbourne-based Institute of Public Affairs to neo-classical Australian and British economists—also winced at the maintenance of some price controls during the early years of Menzies's tenure. According to Kemp, they lamented that the level of government intervention was choking economic activity by unduly constricting enterprise.[36]

And yet despite all of these concerns, for the most part, both sides of politics strongly supported high levels of government intervention and the social welfare state. Micro-policy areas such as regulation of the financial system, wages policy, import tariff protection and restrictions on competition between producers that governments had implemented over the previous four decades found a widespread policy consensus in Canberra. 'The post-war Australian economy was not a highly flexible and adaptable system,' noted Kemp. 'It was replete with rigidities that were the residue of past election promises and policies, largely reflecting special interest pressures from producers.'[37]

It is true that the Labor Party of the early 1950s sought a bigger economic role for the state than did the Coalition, and that in areas such as housing there was a clear contrast in preferencing public or private ownership. But it's also true that the Coalition showed no inclination to wind back the government's role in the economy through, for example, privatisation, other than the isolated exception of the sale of a part interest in Commonwealth Oil Refineries.[38] This is why Liberals stood accused of being defined as little more than 'anti-Labor'.[39]

Menzies, a Deakinite Keynesian

In embracing an expansionist role for government, Menzies reflected the Deakinite liberal tradition—named after Alfred Deakin, who served as prime minister three times during the early 1900s. This was the belief that high tariff protection, centralised wage fixing, extensive financial regulation, statutory monopolies in certain industries, and a restrictive immigration policy designed to keep out cheap Asian labour would sustain Australian economic development. From Federation onwards, there was little incentive or appetite for major changes in the nation's economic policy. Nor was there any real demand to reform state-funded social welfare that provided a safety net (and it is worth noting that Menzies had even resigned from the Lyons government to protest the abandoning of the National Health and Pensions Insurance Scheme in March 1939).[40]

As George Brandis has argued, Menzies, as was natural for a Victorian Liberal, predominantly hailed from the Deakinite tradition. 'Throughout his post-war prime ministership, Menzies did little to alter the economic architecture ultimately traceable to Deakin's New Protection.'[41] Menzies did rhetorically pick up on many similar themes to George Reid's anti-socialist campaign (particularly during the 1946 and 1949 elections), and his uncle and political mentor Sydney Sampson had been critical of Deakin's closeness to Labor as federal MP for Wimmera (he sat on the crossbench rather than directly supporting Deakin before the 1909 'fusion'), but nevertheless Menzies showed little desire to break free from Deakin's political inheritance.[42]

It should also be stressed that this Deakinite liberal tradition had defined Australia's economic institutional framework long before Keynesianism took hold in public policy-making circles in the 1940s. Keynesianism—named after the British economist John Maynard Keynes—was a natural fit for the Labor Party, because it promoted strong government economic intervention, through deficit financing where necessary, to generate demand and full employment. At the time, it was widely seen to have helped deliver the stable economic expansion of the post-war period in Australia.

But Keynesianism was also a bipartisan endeavour, and Menzies was prime minister during an era in which Keynesian economics was unchallenged. While Menzies championed the virtues of free enterprise, he saw a distinct role for government. As Howard put it, in Australia

> there was a furious argument about bank nationalisation before the 1949 election, but that went to the fundamental question of restricting free enterprise, namely the right of private banks to continue operating—not the government's intervention in the economy so that the conditions in which enterprise operated were as stable and accommodating as possible, which was what Keynes was all about.[43]

Years later, Menzies recognised this mindset. In 1964, eighteen months before his retirement from public life, Menzies declared: 'Where government action or control has seemed to us to be the best answer to a practical problem, we have adopted that answer at the risk of being called socialists'.[44]

In a speech in 1970, four years after he left power at a time of his choosing, he argued:

> The ancient idea that government's only function was to 'keep the ring' while the private enterprise contestants slogged it out has no place in our Liberal philosophy …
>
> On the contrary, we recognise that the state has very wide responsibilities: by appropriate economic and monetary measures to assist in preventing large-scale unemployment; by social and industrial legislation to provide a high degree of economic security and justice for all its citizens. It must have progressive housing policies, accept great responsibilities in such disparate matters as education and transportation, ports and railways.[45]

Conclusion

The Curtin and Chifley governments of the 1940s had prevailed in war and had created the post-war economic structure. Ben Chifley, not unlike Clement Attlee in Britain, used the immediate post-war era to effect profound socio-economic change. He emboldened the welfare state, placed full employment at the heart of government policy, and reaffirmed the central pillars of industry protection, centralised wage fixing, and government regulation that defined Australian economic policy since Federation. Indeed, Chifley's vision was so comprehensive that it was not seriously challenged by Menzies when the Liberal–Country Party Coalition regained power in 1949.

Menzies strongly opposed Labor's attempts at nationalisation of the private banks. As a result, he defeated the openly socialist policy of the Chifley Labor government: if Menzies had failed, the economic history of Australia since the late 1940s would have been fundamentally different, presaging more incursions into nationalisation by the federal government.[46]

However, Menzies's long tenure did not represent any major economic realignment. A creature of his culture, Menzies was a Keynesian, not a disciple of Friedrich Hayek or Milton Friedman. He hailed from the Deakinite liberal tradition; he was hardly a harbinger for the Bert Kelly and John Hyde school of liberalism.

Menzies lived in a different era, and he honoured traditional values and ways of doing things, including not just his much-touted Britishness or Anglophilia, but his deep respect for the public service and Australia's protectionist economic institutions. This commitment to tradition, as Melleuish has observed, comes out clearly in Menzies's famous radio talks of 1942 on the 'forgotten people', described by Menzies as the 'middle class who, properly understood, represent the backbone of this country'.[47]

In defining the relatively new party as Liberal, it was clear he believed in a form of progressive politics. As he put it in *Afternoon Light* in 1967: 'We took the name Liberal because we were determined to be a progressive party, willing to make experiments, in no sense reactionary but believing in the individual, his rights and his enterprise and rejecting the socialist panacea'. He later asserted: 'There was nothing doctrinaire about our policies. If I were to become leader of a great non-socialist party, I must look at every-thing in a practical way'.[48]

Menzies opposed a socialist state that wanted to control society, but he was not a proponent of a dynamic free-market economy, as he made clear during his time in opposition in the 1940s:

> Individual enterprise must drive us forward. This does not mean that we are to return to the old and selfish notions of laissez-faire. The functions of the State will be much more than merely keeping the ring within which the competitors will fight. Our social and industrial obligations will be increased. There will be more law, not less; more control, not less. But what really happens to us will depend on how many people we have who are of the great and sober and dynamic middle-class—the strivers, the planners, the ambitious ones.[49]

All this meant that, in policy terms, as Stuart Macintyre observed, Menzies reaffirmed the Curtin–Chifley technique of civilising capitalism. 'Economic progress secured voters' acceptance of a market economy, while governments in turn accepted a responsibility to intervene in markets and correct their outcomes in the interests of their citizens.'[50]

While the Menzies government did oversee some landmark policy achievements, like the Australia–Japan Commerce Agreement of 1957, the establishment of the Reserve Bank, and the granting of export licences for iron ore, genuine economic policy change did not come about until the mid-1980s. This is when the Aussie dollar and balance of payments crisis sparked a wide range of market-oriented reforms—from tariff cuts and financial deregulation to tax and industrial relations reform—that set out to internationalise the Australian economy and make it more competitive. Australia entered a time of uncertainty made even more troubling because most politicians, including those on the centre-right, had come to believe that the post-war consensus had solved once and for all the underlying problem of modern politics.

The destruction of this conventional wisdom led to a new consensus among both Labor and Coalition parties in support of free trade, privatisation, a reduction of state power, and a bold reassertion of liberal economic principles. This Hawke–Keating–Coalition settlement, like Chifley's, proved enduring, though in different ways. Indeed, it was formalised after the federal election of 1996, when the victorious Liberal prime minister, John Howard (supported by his treasurer, Peter Costello), explicitly accepted and developed the economic and moral insights of their immediate Labor predecessors. In making the case for market reforms, Howard and Costello did not represent any Menzian tradition. For Menzies represented a different tradition of state paternalism, centralised wage fixation, and import tariff protection—even if he left his successors with several of the rhetorical tools necessary to critique state dominance.

CHAPTER FIVE

EARLY THINK TANKS AND THEIR INFLUENCE ON THE MENZIES GOVERNMENT

Andrew Blyth[1]

Introduction

IN THE FIRST volume of this series, David Kemp posed the question, what is the place of the Menzies of 'ideas and principles—in the historiography of his political journey?'[2] Menzies was highly interested in the contest of ideas, as the more than 4000 books surviving in the Menzies Collection housed in the Baillieu Library at the University of Melbourne attest. This chapter aims at filling some of the void which Kemp identified, by examining the manner in which Menzies as prime minister engaged with new sources of ideas coming from outside of the public service, most notably from the advent of research-based policy institutes in Australia. The chapter highlights Menzies's use of external experts, and assesses the influence early think tanks had on the Menzies government. It concludes that while think tanks remained somewhat of a novelty during the Menzies era, Menzies did pay attention to their output, and increasingly experimented with the use of outside experts as his term went on.

Seed sowing

In wanting to leave behind the stresses and struggles of the Great Depression and World War II, Australians in the 1950s sought long-term security, social order, and stability. Stimulated by optimism and growth, this era saw the birth of the 'prosperous society' in Australia.[3] During this period, state intervention in the economy drove economic growth—largely through rapid population development and the transition to manufacturing production. While the decade of the 1940s saw the Australian economy devoting much of its resources to the national war effort; the post-war decades (the 1950s and 1960s)—regarded as a 'golden age'—saw the Menzies government pulling all economic levers at its disposal to sustain the economic boom.[4]

Over the next decade and a half (from 1950), Menzies would be a champion of free enterprise and a believer in Keynesian economics rather than laissez-faire capitalism to support full employment and the welfare state. The principles of Keynesian macroeconomic policy that were adopted ranged from state subsidies for primary export industries to protectionist industry policies. The Menzies government would 'politically manage'[5] the economy, implementing strategies to drive full employment, encourage foreign investment, and pursue an increase in immigration levels.[6] And all of these intricate goals required expertise to manage and fulfil.

As Australia developed and grew, the demands on government increased in range and complexity. Consequently, the public service was forced to change both its structure *and* services offered.[7] It is worth noting that the public service had greatly expanded in both numbers and expertise during World War II partly because of the demands of the war, but also due to the elaborate plans for post-war reconstruction which were drawn up. Keynesianism begat extra public servants and was maintained by them. Hence, the 'mandarins' were placed in a position of dominance that was relatively new in Australian history, and as Tom Switzer's chapter demonstrates, that dominance was not checked by Menzies upon coming to power in 1949.

The increasing demands on government grew not just from Keynesianism and the welfare state, but also the evolving nature of Australian federalism. Fifty years on from Federation, the Commonwealth government's ascendancy in the affairs of the nation was expanding. Increased magnitude, scope, and complexity of government resulted in incremental dependence on professional advice.[8] With the trend towards supplementing personal staff 'evident in all liberal democracies in the post-war period', the task of government and the dilemma of supporting the Executive became more complex. The same driving force which had seen the expansion of the public service would eventually drive a shift from relying solely on their advice.[9]

Origins of Australia's think tank landscape

The Australian think tank landscape has evolved tremendously over the past one hundred years, during which its numbers have steadily grown from three organisations in the 1940s to today ranging from sixty to ninety-five think tanks.[10] Australian think tank analysts Ian Marsh and Diane Stone posit that Australia's think tank industry evolved through three 'waves' (others suggest 'ripples'), each heralding the arrival of a new class of institutes closely emulating the evolution of the British industry.[11] The first wave stretching from pre-World War II until the mid-1970s spawned relatively few policy institutes in Australia. The second wave in the 1970s produced free-market, neo-liberal institutes in increased numbers. The third wave, from 1990 to 2000, is distinguished by the rise of left-leaning think tanks in response to the surge of 'New Right' institutes in the second wave. The fourth wave, associated mostly with the 'Howard era' (from 1996 until 2007), spawned twenty-eight new institutes, regarded as a 'transformational period for the think tank industry'.[12]

Opinion differs on the origin of the first 'think tank' to be established. Canadian academic and think tank scholar Donald E Abelson holds the first think tank developed was the Fabian Society, established in London in 1884.[13] Some academics contend the first think tank in the United States could be attributed to the Russell Sage Foundation, established in 1907, while others argue that the precursor of modern United States think tanks was the Brookings Institution based in Washington DC, founded in 1916. In Britain, its 'modern think tank' equivalent, Chatham House, was established in 1919.[14] The London-based Royal United Services Institute, one of the oldest continuously existing think tanks in the world, celebrated the 180th anniversary of its founding in 2011. With conjecture existing over the form, shape and substance of think tanks, questioning the origins of the first think tank comes as little surprise. What is true, however, is think tanks today are neither the sole domain of the United States nor the United Kingdom but are a rising global phenomenon. The think tank concept was exported to Australia at the start of the twentieth century. In the period we are focusing on for this volume, Australia's pioneer think tanks focused on political science, international affairs, strategic and defence policy, and the economy.[15]

When asked about the influence of think tanks in Australia, esteemed political columnist and author Paul Kelly indicates that they were largely a post-Menzies phenomenon:

> We do not have a culture of think tanks going back over our history the way other countries do. When I started as a political journalist there were virtually no think tanks at all. The focus in a policy sense was the bureaucracy, overwhelmingly. So, two things are happening: we've seen the emergence of quite a number of think tanks over the last three to four decades. And it's an experiment. I think that we're learning how to use think tanks and the think tanks themselves are learning how to operate. We didn't have a think tank culture; this is an experiment. It is a good experiment. I think the results are very mixed and that is only to be expected.[16]

Defining and describing think tanks

Originally the sole domain of military planners meeting to discuss wartime strategy, think tanks have evolved into a diverse collection of policy research and advocacy organisations operating in Western and non-Western countries. Organisational differences and varying activity have traditionally made think tanks difficult for scholars to define. The search for a single definition is a problematic exercise. Diane Stone explains think tanks as being 'relatively autonomous organizations engaged in the research and analysis of contemporary issues independently of government, political parties, and pressure groups'.[17] United States professor and Truman Scholar Andrew Rich describes think tanks as 'independent, non-interest-based, non-profit organizations that produce and principally rely on expertise and ideas to obtain support and to influence the policymaking process'.[18] Leading Japanese think tank specialist Takahiro Suzuki succinctly observed that a think tank is an 'organization that conducts public policy research'.[19] University of Pennsylvania's think tank specialist, and publisher of an annual global think tank ranking survey, James McGann, provides a fuller and more elaborate definition:

> Think tanks are public policy research, analysis and engagement organizations that generate policy-oriented research, analysis and advice on domestic and international issues, thereby enabling policy makers and the public to make informed decisions about public policy. Think tanks may be affiliated or independent institutions that are structured as permanent bodies, not ad hoc commissions. These institutions often act as a bridge between the academic and policymaking communities and between states and civil society, serving in the public interest as independent voices that translate applied and basic research into a language that is understandable, reliable, and accessible for policy makers and the public.[20]

Attempting to define a think tank could be regarded as a futile exercise. While there are contested definitions in the literature, it is generally agreed that think tanks are non-government organisations that combine strategic research with policy advocacy. A summary table produced by McGann is provided below.[21]

CATEGORY	DEFINITION
AUTONOMOUS AND INDEPENDENT	Significant independence from any one interest group or donor and autonomous in its operation and funding from government.
QUASI INDEPENDENT	Autonomous from government but controlled by an interest group, donor, or contracting agency that provides a majority of the funding and has significant influence over operations of the think tank.
GOVERNMENT AFFILIATED	A part of the formal structure of government.
UNIVERSITY AFFILIATED	A policy research center at a university.
POLITICAL PARTY AFFILIATED	Formally affiliated with a political party.
QUASI GOVERNMENTAL	Funded exclusively by government grants and contracts but not a part of the formal structure of government.
CORPORATE (FOR PROFIT)	A for-profit public policy research organization, affiliated with a corporation or merely operating on a for-profit basis.

In summary, think tanks differ in size; operate on a standalone basis or are linked to government ministries, universities, political parties; employ research specialists; specialise on topics; receive different types of financing; aim to inform or influence public policy by engaging in a range of activities. The diversity among think tanks makes it challenging to define exactly what think tanks are (and what they do). While there are conflicting views there is united agreement that the common objective of a think tank is influencing public policy-making.[22] My attention now turns to the Victorian Institute of Public Affairs and its influence on the Menzies government.

Institute of Public Affairs

The Institute of Public Affairs Victoria was established in 1943 during a period of soul-searching for the Australian centre-right discussed elsewhere in this volume, and it has since become an iconic, enduring, and controversial example of the influence that think tanks can wield in Australia. While the name IPA has become synonymous with the Victorian organisation, during the 1940s the Victorian institute was one of several 'Institutes of Public Affairs' founded around Australia with a view towards influencing policy outcomes. Notably there was a New South Wales IPA, which tended to be more economically liberal than its Victorian counterpart that accepted a significant role for the state (perhaps a reflection of the Reidite vs Deakinite traditions of Australian liberalism). According to his *Australian Dictionary of Biography* entry, the Victorian IPA's leading economic thinker Charles Kemp was an 'avid student' of both Keynes and FA Hayek, though he did dissent from 'the more extreme demand-management policies of some of Keynes's Australian disciples'.[23]

The New South Wales IPA also wanted to be directly involved with a political party, in contrast to the Victorian IPA, which made a deliberate decision to remain independent, in effect choosing *to be* a think tank. John Hyde in *Dry: In Defence of Economic Freedom*, recounts that after the 1943 election, the Victorian but not the New South Wales IPA eschewed party-political activism to concentrate on a didactic role. In 1943, Charles Kemp, writing to a member of his Council, proclaimed:

> the political back-biting and sniping is not for our organisation. Leave that to the people who have always done it. I have always looked on the job of the Institute as being to make a really worthwhile contribution to thought and action in Australia. There is plenty of room for it, God knows. The 'sex appeal' methods of business have always failed and will fail again. We want something more solid and enduring.[24]

Kemp had seen the short-lived nature of the United Australia Party, and its predecessors on the Australian centre-right, and he came to the conclusion that his organisation could have a more lasting effect if it stayed aloof from the toxicity of party politics, and instead focused on educating the public and shaping economic debate. The lasting prominence of the Victorian IPA, which has arguably increased since Menzies's day, suggests that this choice of policy activism over party-political activism has proven to be a successful model. Nevertheless, the records of the New South Wales IPA housed in the National Library demonstrate that it too made a significant contribution to policy debate over more than two decades, including advocating for 'decentralisation' and the New States' Movement.[25]

With a nuanced acceptance of a role for the state in the economy, the Victorian IPA embarked on developing economic policies for post-war reconstruction. Espousing the virtues of free enterprise as an alternative to Labor's market controls championed for the post-war economy, the organisation published an eighty-page manifesto, *Looking Forward*, in 1944.[26] The manifesto made the case for independence of business from government; celebrated individual responsibility and initiative; and prescribed what governments should attempt and avoid. The creative power of the manifesto found a supporter in Robert Menzies, then leader of the Opposition in Canberra. On reading the manifesto, Menzies was moved to write to his friend Kemp, saying:

> Last night I read *Looking Forward* of which I understand you are one of the principal authors. It is in my opinion the finest state-ment of basic political and academic problems made in Australia for many years. I feel most enthusiastic about it and would like to see its substance conveyed to the people as widely as possible ...[27]

Drawing on shared beliefs in liberal thought, his relationship with the leadership of the IPA grew and was said to be instrumental in shaping the beliefs and values of the newly formed Liberal Party in 1944, particularly on economic thought.[28] Menzies may have been relieved that the IPA did not try to involve itself directly in the Liberal Party, particularly as he was trying to mitigate a widespread view that the parties of the centre-right were often in the pockets of big business (and many of Melbourne's leading businessmen were founding directors of the IPA, including Sir Walter Massy-Greene, Sir Keith Murdoch, Harold Darling, Geoffrey Grimwade, and Sir Ian Potter). Menzies's pitch to 'the forgotten people' (based on his radio address in 1942) had made clear his concern that an unorganised and unrepresented middle class was being sacrificed for the benefit of well-organised interest groups representing business and trade unions.[29]

With competing voices often at the government's heels—on one hand, the Chamber of Commerce arguing for unrestricted importation of goods, and on the other, the Chamber of Manufactures demanding import controls, for example—Menzies held firm: the purpose of the political process was the balancing and sharing of power. Governing in the national or public interest was to be at the core of the new government. Along with many noteworthy domestic challenges Menzies would confront in his time as prime minister, such as the 1951 'horror budget' (with a 10 per cent income tax increase) and a severe 'credit squeeze' in 1960,[30] he would also face foreign policy milestones, such as committing Australian troops to fight alongside Americans in the Korean War and signing the ANZUS Treaty.

Throughout this period, the IPA continued to disseminate views on industrial and economic policies, garnering a reputation for rejuvenating private enterprise and demonstrating a consistent pattern of emphasising individual responsibility and personal freedom, coupled with independence from state interference.[31] The work of the IPA did not go unnoticed in Canberra. The Menzies Collection demonstrates that Menzies was receiving copies of the IPA's magazine, the *IPA Review*, throughout the 1960s, and that he was even making notes based on his readings.

Addressing the annual dinner of the Institute of Public Affairs a decade after becoming prime minister, Menzies proffered:

> What I liked about the institution of the IPA was that it was designed to get people of moment, of significance in the industrial and business world, to do some clear objective thinking. For after all, gentlemen, a government goes in or a government goes out, but what matters in the country is that there should always be a body of honest, objective thought which means that a great number of leaders of opinion have clear minds and clear long range ideas.

Further:

> I would like to say to George Coles [president], and I would like to say to my friend [Charles] Kemp, that the publications of the IPA have to me, and I don't doubt to many other people, been beyond value because they have always set out to be objective and to be philosophic, to put the matter in the broad, to give us all an opportunity of fitting our thinking into a real pattern.

Concluding his remarks and perhaps hinting at 'think tanks', Menzies proclaimed:

> What we need in Australia, what is needed in all free countries, is a body of men who don't set themselves up to say that the government is always right or that the government is always wrong, because, speaking as one with a fairly long experience in these fields, I know, nobody better, that a government is not always right, that a government can feel that it is right most of the time, and what's more important, always feel that it was honest about what it did, even if it turned out to be wrong, that is as much as any mortal man in public affairs may aspire to.[32]

The dominant position of departments in providing advice was beginning to come under challenge. This was not only because of the government appointing staff from outside the public service, but also because of alternative public policy advice coming spontaneously from non-government sources, such as the IPA. In the Menzies years, ministers both individually and collectively would consult on a regular basis with industry associations. A fair assessment would be that while advocating for such organisations as the IPA in Opposition, it would appear Menzies would keep them at arm's length in office. Perhaps mindful of his earlier statement concerning well-organised interest groups, he would accept (somewhat reluctantly)[33] invitations to speak at annual conferences, but he would rely more on senior members of the public service in government—arguably to his government's detriment. Despite his interest in the work of organisations such as the IPA, Menzies would be seen to listen too much to the public service, which itself had become regarded as isolated from the rest of the country. Menzies's shoulder-to-shoulder approach with the public service was much to the chagrin of his more notable (and noisy) supporters in business, and eventually the Australian public. Menzies did, however, take steps midway through his premiership to reach out to experts for advice. The shifting sands of the relationship between the government and the public service are worth exploring in the areas of higher education and the economy.

Higher education

In December 1956, the Menzies government commissioned Sir Keith Murray, chair of the British University Grants Committee, to head an inquiry into Australia's university system. With three of Australia's original sandstone universities (Sydney, Melbourne, and Tasmania) reaching (or having reached) their centenary, Menzies was looking to the future. Wanting to identify ways for the federal government to contribute to their development, he wrote to Murray, inviting him to 'investigate how best the Universities may serve Australia at a time of great social and economic development within the nation'.[34] Menzies set Murray a cracking pace. He had three months to inquire, deliberate and propose a sustainable path for Australian universities. Murray met the challenge. The 'Murray

Report', presented in September 1957, confirmed Menzies's suspicion of a lack of appropriate facilities, quality of teaching, and a pending explosion in student numbers. Murray's advice was accepted almost entirely in full. As a result of acting on Murray's recommendations, by 1966 there were to be some 95 000 students (about the seating of the Melbourne Cricket Ground) enrolled at Australian universities, an increase of 35 per cent in a decade, including more women; and universities would increase their number from six in 1939 to seventeen by 1973. Menzies's legacy would be to expand educational opportunity, paving the way for an educated middle class.

The Murray Report is a clear example of policy advice coming externally from the public service and directly shaping a key government achievement. Nevertheless, there were specific reasons why Menzies was willing to heed external advice on education when he was less likely to do so in other areas. One was that education was an area of particular interest to Menzies and one on which he had unique and innovative views as outlined in Greg Melleuish's chapter in the last volume.[35] But most importantly, there was no federal Department of Education as the area had traditionally been viewed as a state issue. It would not be until 1963 that Menzies would appoint John Gorton as 'Minister assisting the Prime Minister in Commonwealth activities relating to research and education which fall within the Prime Minister's Department'—partly a result of Menzies's intervention on the 'State Aid' issue of funding independent and Catholic schools. A full education department would come into existence in 1966 following an election promise made by Menzies's successor, Harold Holt.

Economy

Ahead of the 1961 federal election, the drums were beating for Menzies. As domestic economic challenges presented, including the infamous 'credit squeeze' of 1960,[36] business leaders were frustrated by Menzies's almost sole reliance on the federal bureaucracy. He was being urged to listen less to the views of 'interventionist' bureaucrats in Treasury and more to the ideas and views emanating from outside of Canberra. After the election, a one-seat majority served to focus Menzies's mind on the subject.

On 17 October 1962, Menzies, alert to criticisms engulfing his government, announced the appointment of a Committee of Economic Inquiry led by former Colonial Sugar Refining (CSR) chairman and managing director Dr (later Sir) James Vernon. The Vernon Committee was tasked with assessing the government's desire to maintain a high rate of economic growth without prejudicing full employment and price stability. Vernon began his work the following February. The committee would consult widely and the report would be regarded as the most comprehensive analysis of the Australian economy ever undertaken. On its release, one of the country's leading economists, Professor RI Downing, described the three-volume report of the 'committee of economic enquiry' as 'the greatest inquest ever conducted into the Australian economy'. Downing wrote of 'the usefulness of providing a wide basis for a public debate about the issues raised by pursuing a high rate of economic growth', with the report later to be considered 'a milestone'.[37] Menzies held a contrasting view.

The report's most noteworthy recommendation was the 'creation of an advisory council' to review the economy's prospects of growth and to provide a forum of debate.[38] The committee's proposal drew heavily on the workings of the Economic Council of Canada (established in 1963). The Canadian body would prepare an annual review of long-term economic growth prospects; advise on trends in overseas investment; serve as a forum for consultation and communication; and publish research papers.[39] Notably, the council proposed by Vernon was to be purely advisory, its members government appointees (backed by a secretariat), with the government free to reject or accept any advice tendered.[40] Menzies was suspicious.

Fearing a reduction in the government's freedom of manoeuvre, Menzies was enraged at the prospect of his (or any future) government being overridden on economic judgements. He was to have none of it. After a long delay between its presentation to government (May 1965) and its submission to Parliament (September 1965), Menzies rose to his feet in the House of Representatives, charging:

> No government from whatever side of the House it may come, and indeed no parliament, can abdicate its own authority and responsibility for national policy. It will welcome the assistance of experts, but its tasks will take it far beyond the limits of economic expertise. Political policy in a democratic community does not depend upon purely economic considerations ... no government can hand over to bodies outside the government the choice of objectives and the means of attaining them in important fields of policy ...[41]

Menzies 'outburst' on receiving the report astonished not only members of the committee but also members of his own party. The Vernon controversy highlights two possible scenarios: entrenched departments of the public service wielded sufficient power to prevent the establishment of a body cutting across existing channels of advice,[42] therefore limiting the development of new economic institutions and constraining the 'openness' of political processes;[43] and Menzies determined to exert his authority over John McEwen, leader of the Country Party and minister for trade.[44] I suggest a bit of both were at play. Perhaps nearing the end of his premiership and possibly now lacking somewhat in liberal imagination, Menzies, I contend, ignored the evolution of governmental structures and missed a golden opportunity for government reform. The seeds were sown, however, for the tapping of experts and the contestability of advice.

Menzies's legacy

Menzies was a champion of liberal democracy and the contest of ideas. As he put it:

The art of politics is to convey ideas to others, if possible, to persuade a majority to agree, to create or encourage a public opinion so soundly based that it endures, and is not blown away by chance winds; to persuade people to take long range views.[45]

With the creation of policy initially the work of Cabinet ministers (in conjunction with senior officials) the Menzies government came to deal with more and more complex issues. While it had at its disposal an army of public servants (mostly men) delivering 'frank and fearless' advice,[46] it became apparent the public service was no longer the font of all knowledge. What started during the Menzies era was championing reaching outside of the monopoly service provider model and tapping experts for their opinion. In his analysis of the Menzies government, political biographer and commentator Troy Bramston proclaims:

there was a strong central bureaucratic influence over government during the Menzies period. This influence declined in subsequent years due to several factors such as ministers relying less on the bureaucracy, new and competing sources of policy advice, the introduction of personal staff, and structural changes to the bureaucracy that dispersed this power across departments and increased the authority of ministers over public servants. Menzies maintained a close relationship with department heads. He looked to them for policy advice.[47]

Menzies is remembered for running an effective Cabinet process, for being a skilled administrator of government, and party manager. His policies were central to the shaping of modern Australia. In reaching out to experts—both inside and outside of Australia—to aid in shaping policies, the monopoly hold of senior bureaucrats over advice to government was disrupted. I contend that, among the many achievements of the Menzies era, the sowing of seeds for the contestability of advice and the think tank experiment in Australia are among them.

CHAPTER SIX

WHAT LIBERTY FOR THE ENEMIES OF LIBERTY?

Lorraine Finlay[1]

LIBERAL DEMOCRACIES FACE an enduring dilemma. If you are committed to freedom and democracy, then in what circumstances, and to what extent, should you be willing to undermine—or even sacrifice entirely—these core beliefs in order to defeat those who would threaten freedom and democracy?

This is an issue that has confronted Australia in the past, and that we continue to confront today. Whether it be the Menzies-era efforts to ban the Australian Communist Party, the national security legislation introduced following the September 11 terrorist attacks, or current counter-terrorism laws designed to protect Australia from present-day terrorist threats, the same core question arises—what liberty should be provided for the enemies of liberty?

It has been just over twenty years since I submitted my law honours thesis at the University of Western Australia, which examined the constitutional validity of counter-terrorism legislation introduced by the Howard government following the terrorist attacks of 11 September 2001.[2] At the time, the measures being introduced were described by a Parliamentary Joint Committee as being 'the most controversial pieces of legislation considered by the Parliament in recent times'.[3] The then-Attorney General, Daryl Williams, used language reminiscent of that employed during the Menzies-era attempts to ban the Australian Communist Party when he said, 'These measures are extraordinary, but so too is the evil at which they are directed'.[4]

In the course of concluding that there were significant constitutional questions raised by the proposed laws, I noted that while there was no doubt as to the importance of preventing and punishing terrorist acts, 'it is vital however that in a democratic nation national security concerns are balanced with a strong respect for individual rights and freedoms'.[5] That statement remains as true today as it was twenty years ago.

The continued significance of this question points to the value of reflecting on past attempts to find an appropriate balance between national security and individual rights. This paper will reflect on Menzies's attempts to ban the Australian Communist Party as a useful lens through which to consider the question of national security versus individual rights. The issues raised through this reflection are issues that we still confront today, and will have continuing relevance to the leaders of today by virtue of the lessons that can be drawn.

A 'very, very' serious step

On one view, while democracy 'fights with one hand tied behind her back', she nonetheless 'has the upper hand, since preserving the rule of law and recognition of individual liberties constitute an important part of her security stance. At the end of the day, they strengthen her and her spirit and allow her to overcome her difficulties'.[6]

This was the view reflected by Robert Menzies in earlier years, where he actually resisted the idea of banning the Australian

Communist Party on the grounds that 'in time of peace, doubts ought to be resolved in favour of free speech'.[7] In a speech given in 1946, Menzies described it as a 'very, very serious step' in peacetime to 'prohibit the association of people for the promulgation of any particular political views' and that (referring to communism) 'we must not let it be thought that they are such a force in political philosophy that we cannot meet them'.[8]

Menzies's view at this time was that democratic values would triumph over communism if there was an open competition of ideas. For example, in a speech to the Parliament in 1947, Menzies declared that '… I have complete confidence in the basic sanity of our own people. If we deal with these people [the Communists] openly we shall defeat them …'.[9]

The 1940 ban

Of course, Menzies's approach across these years, suggesting that individual rights should be restricted as little as possible consistent with preserving national security, is bookended by the fact that Menzies dissolved the Australian Communist Party on two occasions, first in 1940 and again in 1950. In 1940, the Menzies-led United Australia Party–Country Party government dissolved the Australian Communist Party under the *National Security (Subversive Associations) Regulations 1940* (Cth) on the basis that it was a body that was 'prejudicial to the defence of the Commonwealth or the efficient prosecution of the war'.[10] This was accompanied by the banning of Communist Party publications, and government raids of Communist Party premises.

The ban on the Australian Communist Party and publications was lifted by the Curtin government on 18 December 1942, with Attorney-General Dr Evatt issuing a statement highlighting that the ban had been lifted not because of any sympathy with communist views but rather because of the Communist Party's change of policy since the Soviet Union had become an ally in the war.[11] The regulations were subsequently held to be invalid by the High Court in 1943 in *Adelaide Company of Jehovah's Witnesses Inc v Commonwealth*.[12]

The changing nature of the threat

In the years following the conclusion of World War II, Menzies is on the record as again resisting the idea of banning the Australian Communist Party. But by the 1949 federal election, his position had shifted again. He has been described by some as being 'deeply conflicted' over the question of a ban or even inconsistent with regards to his views on this issue.[13] Others have described his changing position as reflecting 'a Machiavellian belief that divisions within the Labor Party made the issue one with the potential to split the party and thereby destroy it',[14] or as responding to political pressures imposed by a number of allied organisations (including the Returned Services League, Australian Constitutional League, Victorian League of Rights, and the Country Party), which all campaigned in favour of a ban. For example, the Country Party asserted during the 1949 federal election campaign that it 'regards the Australian communist in the same category as a venomous snake—to be killed before it kills'.[15]

This was not an isolated sentiment, with a further example of the sentiment at the time being the editorial in *The Sydney Morning Herald* on 7 November 1947, which stated:

> Communism is cold, harsh and ruthless, and it is building slowly and inexorably to the day when our democratic Government will be superseded by a Godless, tyrannical Communistic dictatorship in Australia ... Any Australian born in this country who embraces Communism is a traitor. There is no half way. There has to be a choice between good and evil, and people must be either loyal or disloyal.[16]

While there is no doubt that Menzies understood the politics of this issue—and it is perhaps no surprise that Australia's longest-serving prime minister was adept at making the most of the political opportunities that presented themselves—it is possible to conclude that the approach taken by Menzies across the years was grounded in values and principle, despite these shifts. My personal reading is that Menzies's core views did not themselves appear to change. He had always consistently recognised the need to strike a balance between national security and individual freedoms, and understood the significance (and undesirability) of limiting those freedoms any more than absolutely necessary in order to preserve the democratic order. Rather, it was his perception of events (including, admittedly, political events) and the nature of the threat being faced by Australia (and the world) that changed—which then, in turn, changed his assessment of where that balance should lie.

In those few years between 1946 and the federal election in 1949 there had been significant developments, both within Australia and internationally, that highlighted the growing influence of communism. Examples in Australia included growing industrial unrest, such as the coal strike that lasted for seven weeks in mid-1949 and an ongoing rail strike in Queensland that was widely believed to be communist-inspired.

The international context was particularly significant, including the communist coup in Czechoslovakia in February 1948, the blockade of West Berlin, and the detonation of the first Soviet nuclear weapon on 29 August 1949. In a public statement in March 1948, Menzies observed: 'Recent events have made it quite clear that Australian communism is treasonable, anti-democratic and destructive. In view of the gravity of the international situation and the vital importance of Australian production and transport, Communist activities can no longer be tolerated'.[17]

The records support the conclusion that Menzies was conflicted over the Liberal Party policy to ban the Communist Party, a policy that had been adopted unanimously by the Liberal Party at a meeting held on 11 March 1948. There were reports at the time that Menzies had been among a group of Liberals who had argued against the policy at the 11 March meeting, and his diaries on a subsequent trip to London highlight his doubts about whether banning the Communist Party was the correct approach.[18]

The 1950 ban

Whatever his private doubts, Menzies took a clear public commitment to ban the Australian Communist Party to the 1949 federal election. In announcing that the Liberals' election platform would include this ban, Menzies emphasised that war with the Soviet Union was foreseeable and that it would have been 'madness to wait until you are at war before you take steps to protect yourself'.[19] He described communism in Australia 'as an alien and destructive pest'[20] and stated that:[21]

> The day has gone by for treating communism as a legitimate political philosophy. Our attitude has been one of great tolerance. We conceded freedom, and were rewarded by a series of damaging industrial disturbance with no true industrial foundation ... the communists are the most unscrupulous opponents of religion, of civilised government, of law and order, of national security. Abroad, but for the threat of aggressive Russian Imperialism, there would be real peace today.

After winning the election in 1949, the Menzies government introduced the Communist Party Dissolution Bill into the House of Representatives on 27 April 1950 as one of its first major measures. The recitals in the Bill sought to describe the nature of the threat being addressed with, for example, one recital describing the Australian Communist Party as engaging in activities or operations 'designed to bring about the overthrow or dislocation of the established system of government in Australia and the attainment of economic, industrial or political ends by force, violation, intimidation or fraudulent practices'.

The Bill targeted three distinct groups. First, the Australian Communist Party was to be declared an unlawful association, meaning that it was dissolved and its property forfeited without compensation. Second, organisations that supported communism or were affiliated with the Communist Party (such as trade unions) could be declared unlawful by the governor-general, which then meant that the organisation would be dissolved and membership of that organisation would become unlawful. It was an offence punishable by five years' imprisonment for a person to knowingly be an officer or member of an unlawful association. Finally, the governor-general could declare a person to be a communist and engaged (or likely to engage) in activities prejudicial to Australia's security or defence, which then meant that person could not hold office in the public service or in industries vital to the security and defence of Australia. The onus of proving that a person was not a communist lay with the person themselves.

There were only limited—and I would suggest overwhelmingly inadequate—safeguards incorporated into the Bill. Reflecting on the law, George Williams has described it as:[22]

> ... one of the most draconian and unfortunate pieces of legislation ever to be introduced into the Federal Parliament. It threatened to herald an era of McCarthyism in Australia and to undermine accepted and revered Australian values such as the presumption of innocence, freedom of belief and speech, and the rule of law.

In a clear demonstration of the dangers of these types of laws, during his Second Reading Speech, Prime Minister Menzies read out the names of fifty-three prominent Australians holding senior office in trade unions or key industries who he claimed were senior communists. He referred to this group as a 'traitorous minority' that threatened the security of the nation.[23] This list had to be corrected a fortnight later with respect to five of those names after it was acknowledged that it contained errors.[24]

During the parliamentary debate considering the Communist Party Dissolution Bill 1950, Menzies addressed the criticism that his proposed law banning communism undermined liberty and democracy by asking, 'After all, what liberty should there be for the enemies of liberty under the law?'[25]

In his Second Reading Speech Menzies acknowledged that the Bill was 'admittedly novel, and it is far-reaching' but described it as 'a law relating to the safety and defence of Australia' designed 'to give the Government power to deal with the King's enemies in this country'.[26] He directly acknowledged his previous opposition to banning the Communist Party, explaining that 'events have moved. We are not at peace today, except in a technical sense' and referenced 'the most threatening events in eastern Europe, in Germany, in East Asia and in South-East Asia'.[27]

The legislation found broad support among key parts of the Australian media at the time. The Hobart *Mercury* described communism as 'no longer to be regarded as a political philosophy. It is a threat to internal and external security. It is an avowed enemy and must be dealt with as such'.[28] *The Canberra Times* editorialised that 'freedom in the accepted British sense' needed to be suspended until it was no longer under threat from the cancer of communism.[29] The Brisbane *Courier-Mail* argued that:[30]

> … if democratic liberty is to be preserved for all who believe in it, it must be defended against enemies who would destroy it. It cannot allow itself to be used for its own destruction, and that is the only use communists have for free speech and other democratic rights.

That is not to say the proposed law was not controversial or criticised. For example, *The Age* in Melbourne warned that the Bill was 'more drastic than many liberal-minded people would have expected'.[31] *The New York Times* warned against 'witch-hunts'.[32] The London *Times* issued a warning that sounds familiar when we consider today's debates around counter-terrorism laws, cautioning that methods which 'imperil fundamental freedoms … once written into the Statute book, may be used in years to come for purposes not remotely to be envisaged now'.[33]

There was also opposition among academics and other prominent Australians. Thirty-two academics from the University of Sydney warned that the 'illiberal' Bill exposed Australia to 'the charge of employing the same tactics as the Communists'.[34] An open letter published in *The Age* on 24 May 1950 from fourteen academics from the University of Melbourne condemned the Bill as 'dangerous and unwise' because it 'departed from the fundamental democratic principles of constitutional and criminal law', and as an example of 'democracy fighting totalitarianism by some of its own methods, and thus undermining faith in the values of democracy without which no democracy can stand'.[35]

Norman Cowper (later Sir Norman), who had previously stood for Parliament as a candidate with the United Australia Party and was closely associated with the Liberal Party, perhaps put it most bluntly in a contribution to *Australian Quarterly* when he wrote, 'Why oppose Satan if we are going to adopt his ways?'[36]

Despite these concerns, the public was in favour of the proposal by a fairly substantial majority. An Australian Gallop Poll in May 1950 found that 80 per cent of voters favoured banning the Australian Communist Party.[37]

The Bill was initially opposed by the Labor Party, with the Opposition leader, Ben Chifley, stating that it 'opens the door for the liar, the perjurer and the pimp to make charges and damn men's reputations and to do so in secret without having either to substantiate or prove any charges they might make'.[38] However, reading the public sentiment and fearing that a double dissolution could be called, the federal executive of the Labor Party directed its members to withdraw their opposition, allowing the Bill to pass. The *Communist Party Dissolution Act 1950* (Cth) became law on 20 October 1950.

The Communist Party Case

Of course, the passage of the Act was not the end of the story. A High Court challenge was launched by the Australian Communist Party, ten unions and communist union officials. Dr Herbert Evatt, then the deputy leader of the Labor Opposition, accepted a brief to appear on behalf of the Waterside Workers Federation. This was a move that the New South Wales president of the Labor Party described as 'ethically correct, professionally sound and politically very, very foolish'.[39]

The subsequent court case—*Australian Communist Party v Commonwealth* ('the *Communist Party Case*')[40]—remains one of the most significant constitutional cases in Australian history. It took twenty-four days of hearings in the High Court, which have been described as 'monumental'.[41] In this case, the High Court of Australia considered the constitutional validity of the *Communist Party Dissolution Act 1950* (Cth), and ruled it to be invalid by a 6:1 majority. The case has been described by constitutional law scholars as 'a celebrated victory for the rule of law'.[42] While all of the judges hearing the case acknowledged that the Commonwealth had the legislative power to protect itself from subversion, the majority found that the Act went significantly further than that, and effectively gave the Executive government the power to 'declare' associations and individuals unlawful, regardless of whether there was any factual connection between those associations or individuals and subversion.

A factual connection was required to bring the law within constitutional powers, but the Parliament had instead attempted through the Act to authorise the government to declare the existence of this connection itself. The Parliament had effectively tried to '... recite itself into a field the gates of which are locked against it by superior law'.[43] As Justice Fullagar stated:[44]

> The validity of a law or of an administrative act done under a law cannot be made to depend on the opinion of the law-maker, or the person who is to do the act, that the law or the consequence

of the act is within the constitutional power upon which the law in question itself depends for its validity. A power to make laws with respect to lighthouses does not authorize the making of a law with respect to anything which is, in the opinion of the law-maker, a lighthouse.

Reflecting on the decision in Parliament only days after it was handed down, Menzies said that while it would be 'foolish to pretend that this decision has not given grave concern to the Government', he had 'no legal criticisms to make'.[45] The High Court decision has been described by George Winterton as one of the most important ever rendered by the High Court in terms of 'its confirmation of fundamental constitutional principles such as the rule of law, its impact upon civil liberties, its symbolic importance as a re-affirmation of judicial independence, and its political impact'.[46]

Double dissolution and referendum

Menzies subsequently called a double dissolution election. This was ostensibly on the basis that the Senate had twice failed to pass the Commonwealth Bank Bill 1950, but in reality the issue that dominated the campaign was communism. The Liberal Party candidate in the seat of Barton—the seat held by Dr Herbert Evatt—was World War II hero Nancy Wake, who campaigned on the slogan 'I am the defender of freedom; Dr Evatt is the defender of communism'.[47]

The Menzies government won the 1951 double dissolution election, and sought to address the High Court's decision in the *Communist Party Case* by amending the Australian Constitution to insert a provision effectively allowing the Commonwealth government to legislate to ban the Australian Communist Party. The question put to the Australian people was, 'Do you approve of the proposed law for the alteration of the Constitution entitled "Constitutional Alteration (Powers to deal with Communists and Communism) 1951"?' Dr Evatt (who was now the leader of the Opposition) described the amendment as 'one of the most dangerous measures that has ever been submitted to the legislature of an English-speaking people'.[48] It is an indication of just how divisive this issue had become that the prime minister retorted that 'The House has just been listening to the most notable defender of communism in Australia'.[49]

The referendum campaign reflected the core question that was highlighted at the beginning of this paper: what is the right balance between national security and individual freedoms? Ivor Greenwood (who was later to serve as a minister in the McMahon and Fraser governments)—described the legislation as 'completely contrary to all that liberalism stands for'.[50]

The referendum was held on 22 September 1951, and was lost. Reflecting on this in 2002, in the context of the later debate over counter-terrorism legislation, Prime Minister John Howard stated that he believed 'the Australian people made the right decision in rejecting the proposal'.[51]

However, it is important not to lose sight of how close this vote actually was. The national Yes vote (that is, the vote in favour of banning the Australian Communist Party) was 48.75 per cent, with only 52 082 votes across the nation (out of 4 821 242 votes cast in total) separating the two sides.[52] It would have taken fewer than 30 000 people in either South Australia or Victoria to have voted Yes rather than No for the proposal to have succeeded, giving the Commonwealth government the power to ban the Australian Communist Party.

Conclusion

While this was effectively the end of formal attempts to ban the Australian Communist Party by the Menzies government, there were still subsequent policy decisions taken by the government to address concerns about communism and to strengthen national security.

Examples include the Royal Commission into Soviet Espionage in 1954–55 (which was set up in the wake of the 1954 Petrov Affair), and Australian foreign policy under Menzies, which was strongly focused on stopping the spread of communism, particularly within Asia.

The fundamental question of how to strike the right balance between national security and individual freedoms did not disappear or become any less important. Indeed, it remains a key issue in Australia today.

Which raises the question: what we can learn from the attempts by the Menzies government to ban the Australian Communist Party? There are two core lessons that can be drawn from the examination of the issue in this paper. The first is that strong public policy requires a combination of both consistent core values and pragmatism. There are inevitably trade-offs and compromises whenever conflicting policy objectives need to be reconciled, and shifting your assessment of the appropriate balance in response to changing circumstances should not necessarily be seen as a sign of philosophical inconsistency. Rather, it is a recognition of reality.

But at the same time, there are limits beyond which core values cannot, and must not, be compromised, lest the very fabric of the nation be irretrievably altered. This is the second lesson, namely that we must be 'wary of laws that undermine the very democratic freedoms that we are seeking to protect from terrorism'.[53]

A key responsibility of any government is to protect national sovereignty and the safety of its people. But ensuring that laws in this area balance the protection of national security with a strong respect for human rights and freedoms isn't a sign of weakness. Quite the opposite. It is a clear indication of the strength of our democracy and our values as a nation.

CHAPTER SEVEN

THE ART OF POWER

Troy Bramston[1]

W HEN ROBERT MENZIES led the Liberal and Country parties
back to power in 1949, he had demonstrated an ability to
master the art of politics, but he had yet to master the art of governing.[2] Menzies had lost power in 1941 when he was effectively
forced out of the prime ministership. Now, in 1949, he was back in
the prime ministerial office. He had to learn how to effectively lead
a government, a Cabinet and a party. How Menzies understood,
gained and applied the art of power was instrumental in his political
success and longevity, and his policy legacy.

Menzies had clear values, principles, and policies that he took to
successive elections, and he could communicate these clearly, often
persuasively. He was a good performer in Parliament. He was an
effective campaigner, and the Liberal Party traded on the respect
and admiration he had earned from voters—although he was not
universally popular—and his command over Labor Party leaders
Ben Chifley, HV 'Doc' Evatt and Arthur Calwell. But campaigning is not governing. Unless a prime minister has a capacity for
executive management and administering institutions—the levers

of power—they can get into difficulty. In other words, mastering the machinery of government and shrewdly managing their relationship with the party room are critical to policy and political success.

In the years between losing the prime ministership in 1941, forming the Liberal Party, leading it to the 1946 election, and then reclaiming government in 1949, Menzies had thought deeply about the levers of power. He had much to learn. He drew on his experience in state and federal politics, consulted with others, read widely, and sought to fashion a new model for a successful prime ministership and government. Menzies considered: how his prime ministerial office was to be structured and how it would operate; how he would lead the Cabinet and his relationships with key ministers; how he would work with the public service; how he would manage the relationship with the Country Party and work with its leaders; and how he would lead the Liberal Party and work with both its organisational and parliamentary wings. The model of executive leadership that Menzies established in these early years after returning to government would be followed for the rest of his prime ministership.

Prime minister's office

On Thursday, 15 December 1949, Menzies travelled to Canberra on an early flight. It was a busy day. He had already spoken to Chifley, the outgoing prime minister, and they met in person for a cup of tea. Menzies met with Allen Brown, the head of the Prime Minister's Department, and invited him to continue in the role. And he met with Governor-General William McKell, who invited Menzies to form a government. The government was sworn in the following Monday, 19 December.

The prime minister's suite was located in the north-eastern corner of Parliament House. There were two smaller offices, for his personal secretary and department head, next to his office. There was a lobby area, several administrative 'cubbyholes' for typists, messengers, and attendants, and a small bathroom. In the early 1950s, Menzies's staff comprised a private secretary, personal secretary, press secretary, three typists, two messengers, and an attendant or two.

His wood-panelled office was adorned with photos of the royal family, cricketers and landscape paintings. A painting by Winston Churchill, *Cap D'Antibes*, a gift from the former British prime minister, was hung in 1955. Hansards and volumes of Shakespeare sat on the shelves. He always used pencils to draft speeches and statements but signed official papers with a fountain pen. He did not like to use the phone, holding it at arm's length from his head, and summoned staff to his office with a small bell. He smoked about half a dozen cigars during the day. In the evenings, he liked to share drinks with staff, MPs and public servants in the Cabinet anteroom.

Menzies usually worked a seventy-hour week. He did not like early starts and rarely arrived at the office before 10 a.m. but routinely worked until about 11 p.m. He read newspapers at The Lodge over breakfast before being driven to Parliament House. He sometimes went home for lunch or dinner, and returned to the office later. His day would begin by meeting with his private secretary, JR 'Bob' Willoughby, who first occupied that post, and set a routine for the remainder of Menzies's prime ministership. Menzies's prime ministerial staff, mostly drawn from the public service, of about eight or nine in the early years, grew to about twelve by 1966.

Several of the senior staff that Menzies employed in these years found him quite unlike the public stereotype of an aloof and arrogant man. William Heseltine was private secretary from 1955 to 1959. Heseltine recalled Menzies being warm, generous, and kind—unlike the man often portrayed by his critics in politics and the media. But he was also shy. One of the implications of Menzies's shyness, Heseltine said, was that he tended to criticise people behind their back. This, however, did not diminish his affection. 'I really loved the old boy and admired him hugely for his great talents both as statesman and politician,' Heseltine said.[3] Tony Eggleton worked as Menzies's press secretary from 1965 to 1966. He recalled his old boss being 'informal' and 'kindly' to staff and public servants. 'Menzies was open to ideas and welcomed advice he may not always agree with,' Eggleton said. The former press secretary admired how Menzies had a political antenna for what the average voter thought. 'He had this strong feeling about the man in the street, the ordinary people, and governing for the majority of the people,' Eggleton said.[4]

Cabinet and ministry

As Liberal leader, Menzies was able to appoint ministers without party room election. Labor Party ministers must win election in the caucus before they can be appointed to the ministry. Wisely, Menzies took into consideration experience, ability, age, and geography, and had to negotiate with the Country Party. All prime ministers look to reward loyalty with ministerial appointments, often favour friends and allies, and identify ability that would assist the government. While Menzies had considerable leeway in choosing ministers, he had to be mindful of several informal constraints on his otherwise unlimited power.

The construction of the first Menzies ministry, in 1949, is instructive. In Menzies's papers is his own handwritten list of appointments.[5] He consulted with Arthur Fadden, who as treasurer would be the most senior minister after the prime minister. Deputy Liberal leader Eric Harrison was given defence and post-war reconstruction. Menzies was magnanimous in victory and offered positions to critics and rivals, including Earle Page, Richard Casey, and Thomas White. Other ministers included Harold Holt, John McEwen, and Enid Lyons as vice-president of the Executive Council—she was not given a portfolio, which irritated her for years after. The only amendment to Menzies's handwritten list was to strike out 'works and housing' from Philip McBride's portfolio and give that to Casey. There were thirteen Liberals and five Country Party MPs in Cabinet.

Menzies was close to his first deputy, Eric Harrison. When Menzies lost the prime ministership in 1941, he named Harrison as one of only three people 'who maintained their resolute friendship' with him and was steadfastly loyal. (The other two were Philip McBride and George McLeay.)[6] He was not as close to Harold Holt, who succeeded Harrison as deputy leader and was long seen as heir apparent. Menzies later recalled that Holt wanted to be 'loved' and judged his prime ministership to be a 'bitter disappointment'.[7] Heather Henderson, Menzies's daughter, recalled that he liked Holt but did not have 'huge respect for him'.[8]

During the second Menzies prime ministership there were two Country Party leaders: Arthur Fadden and John McEwen. The Liberal Party governed in a coalition with the Country Party. Menzies generally got on well with Fadden, the former prime minister who was appointed treasurer, but was alert to his fondness for late night drinking. Legendary public servant Lenox Hewitt told me that Menzies actually had a degree of 'contempt' for Fadden.[9] The prime minister got on very well with Fadden's successor, John McEwen, and would have liked to see him become a permanent prime minister. Menzies thought McEwen was the best minister in his Cabinet. He also greatly admired Paul Hasluck, and preferred him over John Gorton, as Holt's successor. Menzies later said that he had very little regard for Richard Casey and Percy Spender, potential leadership rivals, and regarded them as too ambitious and self-promoting.

In a documentary survey of the prime ministership for ABC TV in 1966, Menzies identified 'the two greatest sources of prime ministerial power' as the capacity to lead and influence 'the creation of policy' in government and being the government's 'chief public relations officer'. Cabinet, therefore, was a key institution for the exercise of power.[10] All prime ministers have advantages in Cabinet meetings, such as the ability to set the time and place for meetings, determine the length, set the agenda, and decide which submissions will be considered, and whether other matters can be discussed.

Prime ministers open and close discussions, decide who gets to speak and when, and their summing-up of matters can be critical.

In addition to these, Menzies had other advantages to employ: his large physical size meant he could be imposing, his undoubted intelligence, his experience in previous cabinets and as prime minister, and his capacity to make a persuasive argument all mattered. And ministers owed a personal loyalty to Menzies given he had appointed them. Enid Lyons argued that Menzies's personal 'aura' and stature had an 'intimidating' and 'inhibiting' impact on other ministers.[11] However, this was not a widely shared view. Despite his dominance, ministers recalled that Menzies did not always get his way in Cabinet. Frank Jennings, who served as Menzies's private secretary from 1963 to 1966, recalled him losing a Cabinet debate to John McEwen. He promptly left the meeting, returned to his office and reached for a volume of Shakespeare to compose himself. Then, after half an hour or so, he returned to the Cabinet meeting.[12]

Nevertheless, Menzies was an effective chair of Cabinet who allowed ministers to have their say and a free rein to work their portfolios, but he could be ruthless with those he judged to be poor performers. The reflections of several of Menzies's ministers indicate his style and approach regarding ministerial meetings and ministers. Doug Anthony—who first met Menzies as a boy—told me that the prime minister was consultative in Cabinet but could be brutal with ministers who were not across their brief. 'He could be difficult, arrogant, and proud when trying to get a decision to go one way or another,' Anthony recalled. 'Menzies used to just make people look like a fool if they were not on top of their portfolio.'[13] Ian Sinclair—the last surviving minister from the Menzies era—recalled that Dame Pattie took a close interest in the development of Canberra. She would not hesitate to complain to her husband about the garbage not being collected, the power going off, or the footpaths not being up to scratch. This would be the number one item at Cabinet the next day.[14] Jim Forbes, the last surviving Liberal minister from the Menzies government, remembered that Menzies's support to ministers in difficulty—as he was when introducing national service—was absolute. '[Menzies] would stick with you,' he said.[15]

Richard Nixon said that to be a good leader, you have to be a good butcher. Menzies was reluctant to sack ministers, although he did remove Billy Kent Hughes and Les Bury for contradicting government policy.[16] Menzies despised Billy McMahon, later referring to him as a 'fool' and a 'worm'.[17] In 1959, Menzies caught McMahon leaking Cabinet secrets and extracted a signed confession. That document, which Menzies kept in a desk drawer, is in the National Archives of Australia.[18] Why Menzies didn't sack McMahon can only be guessed. Perhaps it was because of McMahon's status in the New South Wales division of the party or closeness to the Packer family, or both.

An important innovation in Cabinet governance was the introduction of an outer ministry in 1956. This provided the opportunity to give younger and newer MPs an opportunity to climb the ministerial ranks. But Menzies did little to promote promising MPs such as Bill Wentworth, Jo Gullett, Bert Kelly, Jim Killen, Don Chipp, and Malcolm Fraser. Fraser told me he had asked Menzies that he be promoted to the ministry after the 1961 or 1963 elections, but the PM was unmoved. 'I was getting agitated about not being appointed to the ministry, given I had been there since 1955,' Fraser said. 'I made it clear to Harold [Holt] when he became prime minister that if there was not a spot in the ministry, then I would leave Parliament and make way for someone who could be appointed.'[19]

While Menzies was dominant in Cabinet, he was willing to give ministers a free rein to develop initiatives and then present them for debate and decision. John McEwen negotiated the signing of a trade treaty with Japan. Percy Spender played the critical role in signing the ANZUS Treaty and developing the Colombo Plan. Earle Page oversaw the introduction of the national health scheme. Paul Hasluck took the lead in the development of Papua New Guinea and introducing new governance bodies and local elections. Menzies allowed

Garfield Barwick latitude in developing trade practices legislation and reforming marriage and divorce laws.

There were several policy areas where Menzies took a strong interest and used his authority to win Cabinet support for them. The most important was the development of Australia's university sector and high school education. In 1963, the Menzies government began providing financial assistance to secondary schools in the form of grants for buildings and equipment alongside scholarship schemes for students to attend the final years of schooling or technical colleges. Following the Murray and Martin reports into higher education, the Menzies government significantly boosted funding for universities. Funding increased from $12 million in grants in 1955–57 to $117 million by 1965–66. A scholarship scheme for university and college students initiated by the Chifley government was continued as enrolments dramatically expanded to 95 000 (university students) by 1966, of which three-quarters received some kind of financial assistance.

Towards the end of Menzies's prime ministership, he was out of step on a few issues, although Cabinet ministers did not challenge his authority. For example, Menzies resisted attempts by his own ministers to change the White Australia Policy, expand the Aboriginal referendum, or take a stronger stand against apartheid South Africa. After he retired in 1966, the Cabinet moved swiftly to change course in these areas of policy ossification. Yet it is a testament to Menzies's dominance that he carried the day on these issues when he was probably in a minority.

Parliamentary party

Memories of Menzies's time in state politics and his first prime ministership—which ended in resignation—were never far from mind before the party's 1949 election triumph. The earlier Menzies had poor relations with many colleagues. When Menzies was told by an MP that he did not suffer fools gladly, he famously replied:

'And what, pray, do you think I'm doing now?'[20] He acknowledged that he had to change. 'I might have succeeded better if I had worked less in my office and more in the party room,' Menzies later reflected.[21] John Carrick, who was appointed general secretary of the Liberal Party's New South Wales division in February 1948, told me that there were considerable doubts in party ranks about Menzies's capacity to lead the party effectively. 'He may have been too ambitious, I don't know. But then so was Caesar. Some thought that he was not the right leader,' Carrick said.[22] The upshot was that Menzies recognised the need to work more collegially with others and to be less brusque and overbearing. While leading the Liberal Party to victory in 1949 gave Menzies authority in the new government, he had still to earn and maintain the trust and respect of his colleagues to be truly effective long-term.

The result was that Menzies was utterly dominant in the parliamentary party room after 1949. But Menzies revealed in interviews for a biography that was never written—which I accessed for my own biography—that he did not feel secure in his leadership until at least the 1949 election. Menzies actually resigned as Liberal leader in 1947 and demanded the party get behind him. 'You can't win with Menzies' was a common refrain. Menzies recalled that some in the party wanted to replace him before the 1949 election with Don Bradman or Tom Playford.[23] Richard Casey was often mentioned as an alternative leader.[24] And after 1949, there were reports of a leadership challenge from Percy Spender during 1950–51.[25]

Mindful of how leadership instability often begins on the backbench rather than in the Cabinet, Menzies was attentive to the needs of backbenchers. Any MP who wanted a one-on-one meeting with Menzies would get it with little fuss. Alick Downer recalled that in party room meetings, Menzies listened more than he talked. He allowed backbenchers to raise policy matters and would respond if necessary. But few MPs ever challenged Menzies. The dividend of political success was party room loyalty. He was calm, consensus-driven, and consultative. If challenged in party meetings, he refused to be aroused to anger.[26]

While collegiate and consultative in the party room, Menzies kept a watchful eye over how his ministers were handling their port-folios. Parliament was an important forum for judging ministerial competence. He was, after all, skilled at parliamentary procedure, understood the importance of winning debates in Parliament, and knew how to use the chamber for dramatic purposes. He was a born performer. Accordingly, he also took note of how others performed. At the commencement of Question Time, Menzies would often take a blank piece of paper and draw up a scorecard to rate his minis-ters. At the end of Question Time, Menzies would fold and tear the paper into tiny pieces and then—with a raised eyebrow and slight smile—drop it into the bin so that nobody ever knew what his assessment was.[27]

The Coalition parties

Menzies also understood the importance of party management. He developed effective relations with the Liberal Party organisation and respected the party membership. As Carrick reflected, in the 1940s Menzies had enemies within the party organisation and there were substantial doubts about whether he could lead the party to an election victory and successfully in government. This was another area where Menzies knew he had to change. Menzies's appointment books and correspondence reveal that he was regularly in contact with party leaders about organisational matters, such as campaign strategy, policy development, and personnel. Having been the most important figure in the formation of the party, its structure, philosophy, and character, this interest in the organisational wing of the party was understandable.

Menzies also understood the importance of managing the coalition with the Country Party. He had learned from bitter experience in

Victorian politics and later in federal politics, especially when he was prime minister, the importance of effective relations with the Country Party. An agreement with the Country Party to cooperate with the Liberal Party in government was established before the 1949 election. He had a good relationship with Fadden and an especially strong relationship with McEwen. Menzies respected the Country Party's leaders and their views, and made sure that any disagreements over policy, political strategy, and ministerial appointments were satisfactorily dealt with. Menzies believed compromise was the key to the relationship. When he rejected a Country Party MP being made a minister, another person was found. When McEwen had a strong objection to a matter of policy, an alternative way forward was agreed. Ian Sinclair, a minister in the Menzies government and later Country Party leader, said compromise was the key to the relationship. 'Menzies was the chairman, and McEwen was the managing director,' Sinclair recalled. 'If there was ever a problem, they were always resolved between the two leaders.'[28]

Public service

Menzies respected the public service. He kept on many of the senior public servants who had worked for the Curtin–Chifley governments, such as Brown. John Bunting took over from Brown in 1959 and continued as head of the Prime Minister's Department until Menzies's retirement in 1966. It has become a cliché, but Menzies did welcome and encourage frank and fearless advice from public servants. He looked to departmental heads for advice on policy, asked them how ministers were handling their portfolios, and asked for their opinions on each other.

The Prime Minister's Department, which was first established in 1911, steadily grew as a coordinating and leadership agency within government, and was tasked with specific responsibilities. It continued to expand its influence in government during Menzies's prime ministership, which helped to consolidate Menzies's prime ministerial authority within government. The department also played a key role in better organising and supporting Cabinet meetings with more formal processes for setting meeting agendas, the submission and circulation of papers, and the recording and following-up of decisions. Menzies was given briefings on every other submission by ministers, which undoubtedly strengthened his authority in Cabinet meetings.

Conclusion

Menzies appreciated the virtues of Cabinet government. He worked collegially with ministers and government MPs. He was a good administrator of government who was disciplined and focused, and had an efficient personal office. He was a good party manager and understood the importance of striking a good relationship with the Country Party. And he respected the public service. Like any prime minister, he endured setbacks and had to reverse course occasionally on policy, but he always learned and improved in the job—this is the mark of any good politician.

After Menzies informed the UAP party room and then the joint party room of his decision to resign as prime minister late in the evening of 28 August 1941, he joined his private secretary, Cecil Looker, in the corridor. Menzies put his arm around Looker's shoulders and said, 'I have been done'. With tears in his eyes, he then quoted a Scottish ballad:

> Ile lay mee downe and bleed a-while,
> And then Ile rise and fight againe.[29]

He did rise again. His success the second time round was largely due to his mastering of the art of politics *and* power.

CHAPTER EIGHT

MENZIES, EVATT, AND CONSTITUTIONAL GOVERNMENT

Charles Richardson[1]

M Y THEME IN this chapter is the role that Robert Menzies played in Australia's constitutional development, and particularly in the form taken by parliamentary government. I propose to look at some of the key events in the middle part of Menzies's career that bear on constitutional questions, using as a foil the views of Herbert Vere Evatt, whom he faced across the chamber for many years but who was also a noted constitutional scholar. Menzies and Evatt represent alternative traditions in Australian constitutionalism—roughly speaking, 'imperial' versus 'progressive'—but the difference, as we shall see, is not all that it might appear. By placing their political practice in a context of constitutional theory I hope to offer some food for thought on the interplay between the two.

So first of all, what is parliamentary government? The basic idea is that executive power is in the hands of ministers who are appointed by and govern in the name of the head of state, but are responsible to Parliament; they are appointed on the basis of their ability to command a parliamentary majority. The system therefore depends on a balance between three centres of power: the head of state, the ministers, and Parliament. Parliamentary government evolved gradually over centuries in England and has now spread around the world; as the legal historian SB Chrimes puts it, 'The English Constitution is remarkable ... in having been exported wholesale, often more or less *en bloc*, to distant lands, and imitated in greater or less degree by numerous foreign States near and far'.[2]

Usually the head of state is either a hereditary monarch or an elected president (with either direct or indirect election). But in Australia, although we have retained the monarch as a ceremonial head of state, the effective head of state is neither of these, but a viceroy: a governor-general (federal) or governor (state), who represents the monarch but is an appointed official, with neither the predictability of hereditary succession nor the democratic mandate of election.[3] So in what we might call a viceregal system, in addition to the three-way balance of forces involved in parliamentary government, there is a four-way interaction between the government, the viceroy, the monarch, and the 'home' government; in our case, the government of the United Kingdom.

The imperial relationship

By the time that Menzies and Evatt were born—and they were born in the same year, 1894—the first of these, the three-way balance, was pretty much settled. There has been some movement at the margins,[4] but fundamentally a prime minister today, whether in Britain or Australia, stands in the same relationship to Parliament and monarch (or viceroy) as Gladstone and Salisbury did in Queen Victoria's day. The second set of relationships, though, which are distinctive to a viceregal system, have changed a great deal.

When the Australian Federation was established in 1901, it and other British possessions of a similar status (known collectively as the dominions, although Australia never used that title) were regarded as self-governing but not fully independent of Britain. They were part of the empire, and the imperial government—that is, the British government in London—had an ill-defined overall responsibility, particularly for matters concerning foreign affairs and defence. That included the power to pass overriding legislation and to veto legislation passed in Australia.[5] As AV Dicey remarked in 1914, 'The Commonwealth of Australia itself is, as regards the Crown and the Imperial Parliament, nothing but a large self-governing colony'.[6]

The status of the governor-general reflected that. He (they were always men, of course) was appointed by the monarch on the advice of the British government—it appears that at first the Australian government was not even consulted. In addition to his duties under the Australian Constitution, he was seen as the representative of the British government. Australia had no diplomats of its own; the first high commissioner to Australia from the UK was not appointed until the 1930s, and as late as 1939 Menzies was still fighting a rear-guard action against appointing Australian diplomats.[7] Instead, Australia communicated with Britain via the governor-general.

World War I revealed some of the shortcomings of these arrangements, and during the 1920s there were discussions between Britain and the dominions that ultimately led to an imperial conference in 1926, followed by the passage of the Statute of Westminster in 1931. These redefined the imperial relationship, in a way intended to ensure that Britain and the dominions were 'autonomous Communities within the British Empire, equal in status, in no way subordinate one to another in any aspect of their domestic or external affairs, though united by a common allegiance to the Crown, and freely associated as members of the British Commonwealth of Nations'.[8]

At the time the dominions divided into two groups: Canada, South Africa, and Ireland, on the one hand, were assertive about their independence and sought to upgrade their status. On the other hand, Australia, New Zealand, and Newfoundland were less forward and more relaxed about constitutional issues—they were, in DL Keir's words, 'less anxious to undertake the delicate task of re-defining the constitutional system of the Empire'.[9] The Statute of Westminster, which was an Act of the British Parliament, required adoption by this latter group in order for it to take effect there, and this became a political issue in Australia in the 1930s.[10] By that time, however, Menzies and Evatt were significant players, so we need to say something about them.

Menzies and Evatt

Other contributors to this volume have had a lot to say about who Menzies was. I would pick out four things that I think are important:

First, he was a royalist: this is well known—indeed, these days it is perhaps the most well-known thing about him—and it persisted throughout his career. In John Nethercote's words, 'His faith in the Crown was not simply formal and professional; it was deeply personal as well'.[11]

Second, he was an anglophile; his devotion to Britain deepened, if anything, as he grew older. Saying that is not to question his loyalty to Australia, but rather to stress that (like many Australians of that era) he saw no conflict between British and Australian patriotism. As Tom Switzer remarked at the conference, he was 'a man of his time'.

Third, although he believed in monarchy he was also a Whig: to quote Nethercote again, 'By education and experience Robert Menzies was steeped in the traditions of responsible parliamentary government mainly as developed at Westminster'.[12] He identified with Parliament in its struggles with the crown: when he visited Britain for the first time, in 1935, he referred in his diary to Oliver Cromwell as 'the man whose sword and character made England a free country'—not something that a Tory would ever say.[13] And this wasn't only a feature of his youth; even in his memoirs, published in 1967, you can see him give a thoroughly Whiggish interpretation of the reign of George III.[14]

Fourth, and obviously (but the obvious things are often the ones we neglect), he was in politics as the leader of a centre-right party. Whatever his instincts might be on a particular issue, in general terms, when there was a contest between progress and reaction, his was the party of reaction. He may not personally have been a reactionary—in many respects he clearly was not—but he was on the side of those who were and his calculations always had to take that into account.

What to say of Evatt? He was a distinguished lawyer, a High Court judge at the age of thirty-six (still the youngest ever appointed) and later leader of the Labor Party for most of the 1950s. He was also the author of the standard work on viceregal powers, *The King and His Dominion Governors* (first published in 1936). The Labor Party's self-image, which Evatt's book partly reflects, held it to be the progressive or democratic force in constitutional matters, supporting Australian independence. But Evatt's book is by no means an anti-imperial tract. His main argument is that regal and viceregal powers are poorly defined, and that the conventions that govern them should be made explicit and enforceable, either by the courts or by the legislature.[15] He is conscious of the problem that if British control is excluded then the viceroy could have too much independence, leading to a loss of democratic accountability.[16] He is also mindful of the problem of the viceroy's insecurity of tenure, which we'll come back to a bit later.

Fundamentally Evatt was a rationalist, always looking for clarity and transparency, whereas Menzies had more of the conservative's instinct for mystery, of the power of things unknown or unseen. Paul Hasluck, who worked for Evatt for a number of years in External Affairs, said that 'What he liked did him far more credit than what he disliked but too often he let his dislikes take control'.[17] Robert Murray, the historian of the Labor split, called him 'a clumsy colossus', who 'combined extremes of naïveté and labyrinthine cunning'.[18]

So, to return to the 1930s and particularly to the Statute of Westminster. In 1934, Menzies had moved to federal Parliament and become attorney-general in the government of Joseph Lyons, and in 1937—six years after it had been passed—he brought in a Bill that would have Australia adopt the Statute of Westminster. He portrayed it as a relatively minor piece of housekeeping, but it was not proceeded with—apparently due to dissension on his own side.[19] Instead it waited until 1942, after war had broken out, when Menzies was in Opposition. Evatt had left the High Court to enter Parliament and was now attorney-general and foreign affairs minister, and he introduced a similar Bill.

Again the non-Labor side was divided. The debate is just outside our period, but it makes for a very interesting read, because it sees Menzies caught half-way between Evatt and the more doctrinaire imperialists in his own party. He explained his position in the debate and in a subsequent radio broadcast.[20] There he denied that adoption of the Statute would affect Australia's status, saying that the relevant provisions 'became law at the end of 1931, and needed no adoption by Australia'. But although he said that the remainder involved 'relatively minor technical questions', he 'quarrel[ed] with the language that was used': 'to endeavour to put into written form a relation part of whose strength rested upon its very vagueness and want of definition, was a cardinal blunder. There was a living spirit, and we endeavoured to imprison it within the four corners of a legal formula'.

Menzies had a further objection that he phrased as being about ambiguity, but what he really objected to was the idea of the separate status of the crown in right of the different dominions. He denied that the king could 'be at peace and at war at the same time in relation to the same foreign power'—echoing the argument of DL Keir, who had said that a situation where 'the King may receive and be obliged to act on mutually inconsistent counsels … comes very near to being an absurdity'.[21] But it was an absurdity that people were learning to live with, as indeed we still do. Even at the time Ireland had succeeded in remaining neutral in the war, having previously taken the lead in pushing to the limit the powers embodied in dominion status.

Menzies never really reconciled himself to this state of affairs; nonetheless, he conceded that 'in our Empire relations we have by no means reached either finality or certainty'. And unlike some Opposition speakers he avoided any suggestion of deep disagreement with the government, saying only that 'having regard to the misunderstandings which do arise on this question, it would have been wise to impose some delay upon the passing of the Adoption Bill'.

The McKell appointment

But the Bill passed, the war was won, and Menzies returned as leader of the Opposition. In 1946, the prime minister, Ben Chifley, announced the appointment of a new governor-general: William McKell, previously the Labor premier of New South Wales. It was long-standing Labor policy that the governor-general should be an Australian: back in 1930 (before the Statute of Westminster but after the Balfour Declaration), Prime Minister James Scullin had personally confronted George V in London, insisting on the appointment of Isaac Isaacs.[22] But Menzies was strongly critical of the McKell appointment; moving a motion of no confidence on the issue, he said that Labor had chosen 'to force upon His Majesty, by depriving him of any other choice, one who in the nature of things will be regarded by Australians generally not as a representative of the King but as a representative of the present Prime Minister'.[23] He implicitly threatened to have McKell dismissed if the Liberals won the following election.

And in the debate he was able to quote Evatt in support of his position. Evatt thought that it was a good thing for the monarch to appoint an Australian and to act on the advice of Australian ministers, but in *The King and His Dominion Governors* he had worried that if the monarch has no discretion in the matter, then incoming governments will find it convenient to have the current viceroy dismissed and replaced by their own nominee, and that therefore 'the office of Governor-General will become a mere reflection of the existing Dominion administration, and consequently … no exercise of any reserve power will take place'.[24] So Menzies argued that 'if all parties in this House believed the Governor-Generalship was simply a political "plum" to be handed out to some party colleague in Australia—then, of course, with every change of government the appointment of the Governor-General would be terminated and some other politician put in his place'.[25]

Evatt declined to rise to the bait. He defended the government's record but ignored the constitutional question. (The no confidence motion, of course, was defeated on party lines.) The McKell episode, however, ultimately shows Menzies in a better light. Having made his political point, once McKell was in office he was courteous and correct to him and they worked together well. As AW Martin says, 'In due course Menzies came to follow this elementary courtesy with genuine respect for McKell's dignity and complete impartiality'.[26]

Menzies in government: Four cases

Then in 1949 Menzies returned to power. I want to look at four episodes from this period, although we'll have time to consider the last two only briefly.

First is the double dissolution of 1951. The Chifley government in its last term had reformed the Senate voting system, producing the more evenly balanced Senate results that we are used to today. That meant that Labor retained a substantial Senate majority (34–26) after the 1949 election, because half of the senators had been elected under the unreformed system in the Labor victory of 1946. That Labor majority proceeded to give the Menzies government some trouble with its legislation, although it did so cautiously because it was reluctant to give him an opportunity for a double dissolution. For that reason it eventually allowed through the legislation to dissolve the Communist Party, which was later struck down by the High Court.

But in the case of another Bill, the Commonwealth Bank Bill 1950, the Senate, after first passing it with amendments that were unacceptable to the government, then, when it was presented a second time after the required three-month interval, delayed debate on it for some weeks, referring it to a select committee. There was some doubt as to whether this amounted to a 'failure to pass' within the meaning of section 57 of the Constitution; Colin Howard later pointed out that 'failure to pass is a non-event and it is not easy to say when a non-event has happened'.[27] Menzies, however, formed the view that it did and asked Governor-General McKell to approve a double dissolution.

This is a classic case of where the viceroy is often said to have an independent discretion, and Menzies's admirers have pointed out that he recognised that and did not try to coerce McKell. 'In his advice recommending the dissolutions, [Menzies] emphasised that this was an occasion when the Governor-General had to act on his own discretion: the Prime Minister's advice, in this instance, was not advice which it was obligatory for the Governor-General to accept.'[28]

But if you look at the actual advice, which Menzies eventually tabled in Parliament some years later,[29] that discretion is somewhat illusory. Yes, Menzies told McKell that he had to make up his own mind on the question of whether the legal requirements of section 57 had been met—that is, whether the Senate had 'failed to pass' the Bill:

> In the course of our discussion, I had made it clear to His Excellency that, in my view, he was not bound to follow my advice in respect of the existence of the conditions of fact set out in section 57, but that he had to be himself satisfied that those conditions of fact were established.

That, however, was the only discretion that he admitted.

Menzies knew that in the previous case of a double dissolution, in 1914, the prime minister had given advice in terms of the general parliamentary situation, not just the specific Bill at issue. Times had changed since then. He gave advice on that point as well as a backup, but he did not concede that McKell was entitled to consider it, 'having regard', as he put it, 'to modern constitutional developments'. And he gave no hint of a suggestion that once McKell was satisfied that the legal requirements for the double dissolution had been made out, he had any right to form his own judgement about whether it was a good idea or not. And McKell, despite his Labor background, accepted Menzies's advice.

Although Labor was understandably unhappy with the double dissolution, which cost it control of the Senate, Menzies's practice was completely consistent with the lessons that Evatt had drawn from his analysis of the 1914 double dissolution. The key one was 'That so long as the conditions mentioned in Section 57 are complied with, the Governor-General will grant a double dissolution to Ministers who possess the confidence of the House of Representatives'.[30] As John Howard, a source by no means unsympathetic to Menzies, puts it, McKell 'was sworn to observe the conventions of his office, which required him to take the advice of his PM, unless it were manifestly wrong—which, in this case, it clearly was not'.[31]

The second noteworthy occasion came the following year, with the selection of McKell's replacement as governor-general. He had served for the customary five years (in fact he ended up serving six), but while Menzies repented of his personal hostility to him, he did not let that stop him reverting to the practice of making it a British appointment rather than an Australian one. 'Menzies' initial hostility to ... McKell, had soon waned and the two became good friends. But the Prime Minister still steadfastly held that the Governor-General should be an Englishman'.[32] So he travelled to Britain in 1952, when Queen Elizabeth was new to the throne (she had not yet been crowned), to consult her. There was something very Whiggish in his patronising attitude to the queen, reminiscent of Lord Melbourne and Queen Victoria.[33] But the result of their discussions was the appointment of another Englishman, William Slim, a military hero of World War II.

Howard's comment on the Slim appointment is 'That was where the practice of appointing British citizens to the post should have ended, but Menzies would do it twice more'.[34] In 1960, Lord Dunrossil took the job, and after he died in office, Viscount De L'Isle was appointed in 1961—neither of them previously known for any connection with Australia. Menzies maintained his accustomed deference to Britain and to the monarchy; in Nethercote's words, Slim, Dunrossil, and De L'Isle all 'met a criterion Menzies considered essential for the appointment: the Queen knew them'.[35] Events had moved on, but Menzies was still defending the unity of 'the empire', or at least its last constitutional remnant.

Eventually Menzies accepted the need for an Australian governor-general with the appointment of Lord Casey, his former foreign minister, in 1965, the year before his retirement. But he stuck to his guns on the primary ground on which he'd criticised McKell's appointment, namely that he was a serving politician at the time. On that basis he was privately critical of the appointment of Hasluck in 1969, saying that it 'violates every principle which I stated quite clearly at the time of the McKell appointment'.[36] But whether by this time he cared more about the principle itself or the need to preserve his own consistency is impossible to tell.

My third case takes us back to December 1953, after Slim had taken up the job and before the queen's first visit to Australia. Menzies introduced the Royal Powers Bill, to give the queen the ability, while in Australia, to exercise in person powers that were given by statute to the governor-general.[37] Sub-clause 2(4) stated blandly that 'references to the Governor-General or the Queen shall be read as references to the Governor-General, or to the Queen, acting with the advice of the Federal Executive Council'. This could easily have been an occasion for a general discussion about reserve powers and the constitutional role of the monarchy. But it wasn't.

Instead, it was a sign of how much consensus there was on these topics, and a complete contrast to the 1942 debate on the Statute of Westminster. Menzies gave a very brief second reading speech, which occupies only a single column in Hansard. Evatt, now Opposition leader, spoke a bit longer in reply and gave a somewhat garbled account of the background, but he supported the Bill—as well he might, since it was a small step towards his goal of codification.[38] And that was it. The Bill passed through all stages without further debate.

Finally, we come to 1955. Menzies and his government had narrowly survived the 1954 election, then Evatt's misjudgements had led to a catastrophic split in the Labor Party, and Menzies seized the opportunity for an early federal election to win a more substantial majority. This was just the sort of request that Hasluck later argued the governor-general had a discretion to refuse: he is 'not obliged to grant', as Colin Howard put it, 'a general election based on no better grounds than political advantage'.[39]

But while Menzies explained to the House of Representatives his version of why an election was necessary, he gave no indication that he had felt any need to justify it to the governor-general, or that he thought Slim had any discretion in the matter at all.[40] And Slim, of course, followed his advice, as has every governor-general since. No doubt it was not Menzies's intention to turn the governor-general into a mere rubber stamp, but his practice, allied to his long tenure of office, clearly contributed to that trend.

Some lessons

What lessons can we draw from all of this? I shall mention four.

First, politics is hard. Time and again, politicians, especially in government, find themselves having to say and do things that sit poorly with the doctrines that they have espoused in the past.

That tends to be especially the case for those who have some taste for intellectual speculation. As we have seen, Menzies and Evatt were both in that position at times, but that doesn't necessarily make them hypocrites. They were doing their job.

Second, as some of the other contributors have suggested, Menzies is both more complex and more interesting than you might think from the caricatured version of him that is often presented. Although, as I said, he was both a monarchist and an anglophile, he found ways to reconcile those things, more or less convincingly, with an Australian patriotism and a very serious commitment to parliamentary government. The fact that he clung to the imperial idea well past the time of its relevance may have tarnished that achievement, but it remains significant.

Third, Australian constitutionalism has an importance that goes beyond this country. Although we remained a monarchy (as we still do), the role of the viceroy was an important precedent for how a republic might operate in a way that was different from the separation of powers model used in the Americas. Together with the other dominions, Australia showed, through both federal and state experience, that parliamentary government could develop peacefully and work effectively even without either a hereditary monarch or an elected head of state. Prior to World War II, parliamentary republics were almost unheard of: now there are dozens of them, and anyone with experience of Australia's constitutional arrangements can immediately understand how they work.

Fourth, the problem that Evatt drew attention to, of the insecurity of tenure of the viceroy, is still with us. It was of course an underlying presence in the crisis of 1975, when John Kerr felt he needed to act quickly and secretly for fear that otherwise he would be dismissed. A monarch, or for that matter an elected president, would have some security in their position and therefore not be subject to the same pressure.[41] Evatt's worst fears have not been realised—incoming governments have not thought it necessary to wipe the slate clean by getting themselves a new governor or governor-general—but the problem has not been solved.

The fact that we have managed to live with such problems can be put down to the fact that our political class most of the time have shared a commitment to playing by the rules, and also a broad agreement on what those rules are. And for that, both Menzies and Evatt deserve a share of the credit.

CHAPTER NINE

THE FORGOTTEN PEOPLE BY THE SEA? LIBERALISM AND THE SUBURBANISATION OF THE CENTRAL COAST OF NEW SOUTH WALES DURING THE 1950s

Christopher Beer[1]

OMMONWEALTH POLICIES DURING Menzies's prime minister-ship profoundly affected Australia's cities and regions. Some places were spectacularly changed: Canberra was developed as a national capital and massive engineering projects transformed the Snowy Mountains and the Ord River. Other policies shaped more general investment in the built environment and the movement of people, and thus affected everyday life in cities, towns, and the bush. Within this wider context, the chapter considers the early post-war Menzies government (1949–54) from the perspective of a particular region, that of the Central Coast of New South Wales. In doing so, it examines the changes the region saw in association with federal policies, with a particular focus on its suburbanisation. It will also assess how national electoral politics played out in this community.

Regional history as a practice sometimes suffers from perceptions of parochialism or idiosyncrasy. However, Australian historiography has been greatly enriched by explicitly regional studies, or studies otherwise deeply linked to particular places. For example, the 'world of the Sixty-Nine tram' in Janet McCalman's *Journeyings* can be read as a hybrid local history of 'Melbourne's middle-class heartland, from St Kilda Beach to Cotham Road, Kew' as much as its ostensible subject matter of examining the life courses of a certain generation.[2] Eric Rolls's examination of the 'million wild acres' of the Pilliga region in northern New South Wales effectively narrated much broader Australian social, economic, and environmental histories, as did WK Hancock's study of the Monaro, and more recently Grace Karskens's history of the Hawkesbury River.[3] Studies of regional polities have also added to our understanding of wider political trends and tensions such as, for example, those of the marginal federal electorate of Eden-Monaro.[4]

Several aspects of the Central Coast during the 1940s and 1950s potentially engender broader interest. Like the nation as a whole, it grew substantially during this period. Sitting between Sydney and Newcastle, the region's population increased from around 29 000 people at the 1947 census to more than 38 000 at the 1954 census. Physically similar to Sydney's Northern Beaches, the Central Coast is characterised by numerous long white sand surf beaches, bounded by sandstone cliffs and headlands, and backed by low rising hills. While there had been clearing through to the 1940s, including to enable citrus growing and other agriculture, rainforest was (and remains today) visually prominent, with Gosford, Woy Woy, Wyong, Terrigal, and The Entrance being the only towns of any size. Referencing the region's environmental appeal, the report of the Commonwealth's National Population Inquiry of 1975 noted that between 1947 and the mid-1960s, the Central Coast and the Gold Coast were exemplars of a trend among Australian-born persons of migrating to certain 'highly desirable residential areas', notwithstanding some of these places not having much in the way of traditional commercial or industrial employment.[5] As such, it can be understood as one of the leading localities of 'seachanging', which was among one of the most important transformations of Australian life during the second half of the twentieth century.[6] The region's growth can also be seen as a case study of the wider mid-century proliferation of outer metropolitan development encouraged by all levels of government, and which remains a core image in the popular iconography of the Menzies era.[7] The electoral marginality of the region at a federal level is a further point of interest. Geographically, it formed the core of the Division of Robertson. Won by the Liberal Party from Labor at the 1949 general election, it was retained at the 1951 and 1954 general elections, but its electors also declined to support the government's 1951 referendum proposals to restrict communism.

A liberal urbanism of enabled, revealed choices

The immediate post-war years saw a flurry of public interest around the reform of Australia's cities and the potential decentralisation of population to regional areas. While many powers relating to urban and regional development were in the hands of state or local governments—for example, around town planning and transport planning—the Commonwealth did much to shape how cities and other places changed. Australia's overall population increased substantially through federal policies encouraging large-scale European immigration. What was quipped as a 'milk bar economy' of individuals and families chasing their material desires replaced the austerity of the 1930s and the collective consumption of the war economy of the 1940s.[8] Among its other guises, in Australia's cities this saw the emergence of mass automobility and associated new built forms, including shopping centres surrounded by parking, and drive-in cinemas.[9] However, its most significant manifestation was a major expansion of home building and ownership. In *The Measure of the Years*, Menzies proudly noted that 'When I add that of all the dwellings in Australia over forty percent were built [during his term of government] it will be realised that on the housing front we would claim a notable record of achievement'.[10]

The conceptualisation of home was, of course, central to Menzies's 'The Forgotten People' broadcast of 1942 and its positing of 'homes material, homes human, and homes spiritual'[11] as touchstones of the middle class whose status he saw as fundamental to the fate of the nation—'what really happens to us will depend on how many people we have who are of the great and sober and dynamic middle class—the strivers, the planners, the ambitious ones'.[12] The speech did not meditate explicitly on the cities where most Australians lived then, and moreover hints at agrarianism in places. Nonetheless, Menzies made very clear statements on the desirability of the widespread ownership of real estate. In broad terms he drew a contrast between 'landless men [who] smell the vapours of the street corner. Landed men smell the brown earth and plant their feet upon it and know that it is good'.[13] His image of property that ordinary people might reasonably aspire to aligned with a suburbia of detached single-family houses: 'one of the best instincts in us is that which induces us to have one little piece of earth with a house and a garden which is ours … into which no stranger may come against our will'.[14]

A substantial literature has examined how the Menzies government acted upon these sentiments in office in what later became framed as the pursuit of a 'property owning democracy'.[15] While the Australian rate of home ownership was already high in international comparison at the end of World War II, the combined effect of Commonwealth and state policies was to push the ownership rate even further, from around 50 per cent in the 1940s to a peak of 73 per cent in 1966.[16] In the immediate post-war years, governments massively intervened in the housing market, including through providing discounted loans to veterans and finance to cooperative building societies, while also selling public rental housing to tenants. By the mid-1950s, Commonwealth subsidisation programs were responsible for about a third of all owner-occupier finance.[17]

While, as John Murphy points out, the endurance of the long boom was only fully clear in retrospect,[18] the Menzies government's full employment policy and other aspects of its economic management encouraged financial confidence among a wider proportion of the population. As well as encouraging more people to take on mortgage debt, in combination with prevailing social mores, it also underpinned the period's 'marriage boom' and 'baby boom' that saw urban populations increase further and historically high proportions of people living within nuclear family households.[19]

In this context, the Central Coast's experience reflected both choices structured by the Commonwealth as well as the decisions of ordinary households vis-à-vis the market opportunities and cultural shifts of the era. The historiography of the 1950s sometimes portrays it as a time when dreams from earlier in the century were finally realised. As elsewhere along the Australian coast, the early twentieth century saw an overly optimistic burst of subdivisions in the region.[20] Notwithstanding the rise of a distinct national beach culture, sales remained slow from the 1910s to 1940s as connections beyond the areas around train stations on the Sydney–Newcastle line remained fraught. In effect, the Menzies era saw a local land glut converge with newly enabled demand, particularly as improvements to rail services, the Sydney–Newcastle highway, and local roads progressed. The region's land market spanned a range of price points, but a substantial proportion of blocks were affordable for a very large spectrum of households pursuing desires to have a space of one's own near the ocean. While waterfront sites always attracted a premium, a block of land away from the water might typically be priced at £50 in the 1950s,[21] or roughly 5 to 10 per cent of male annual earnings.[22]

A building boom consequently ensued, with the number of dwellings in the region increasing from 8600 in 1947 to nearly 18000 in 1954. Notably, around three-quarters of dwellings were owner-occupied in 1954, a rate somewhat higher than the New South Wales average.[23] Moreover, around a third of the dwellings appear to be second homes ('weekenders'),[24] reinforcing a picture of the region embodying a widening state of affluence.

While demand for residential property in the region can be seen as driven by a general upswell in interest in outer metropolitan and coastal land, the region's incoming residents were somewhat different from those of other suburbanising areas. A disproportionate number were retirees, with 21 per cent of the population in 1954 being aged sixty and above as opposed to 13 per cent across New South Wales as a whole.[25] Different localities within the region were associated with different groups within that category. For example, the attractive beach-side suburb of Terrigal was noted by a consultant town planner engaged by Gosford Shire as attracting younger (and possibly wealthier) retirees. Woy Woy was identified as another concentration of retirees, if generally older.[26] As the region's first main stop on the rail line from Sydney it was also linked with families with employment connections to the railways. A local historian interviewed in a *Sydney Morning Herald* profile of the region suggested that these 'workers had built fibro garages on plots on the Woy Woy sand plain. They would take up a door one week, a window the next, an outdoor dunny and a dingy, building on to the garage'. Thereafter, 'at the end of their working days, the holiday house became the home'.[27]

Long-distance commuters were a separate distinct cohort. While transport connections between the Central Coast and Sydney improved after World War II, journeys to or from the metropolis still took approximately two hours each way in the mid-1950s. Nonetheless, an assessment from that time suggested that 10 per cent of the region's workforce—or about 1000 persons—travelled daily to Sydney from Gosford, Woy Woy, and the region's smaller stations.[28] Although there were various schemes to encourage industrialisation in the region, such commuting only increased over time. Along with people travelling from beyond the south and west of the main body of Sydney (that is, the Illawarra and Blue Mountains regions), this cohort were early practitioners from a growing group of Australian households willing to trade travel time for access to property ownership and lifestyle opportunities over the latter decades of the twentieth century. Notwithstanding the growing proportion of Sydney's population being born overseas, the region's population remained predominantly Australian born, with Gosford's town planner noting that people from the United Kingdom or the Netherlands were the only significant foreign-born groupings.[29]

Taken together, the Central Coast's growth during the Menzies government can be viewed as a liberal urbanism of revealed choices enabled across all levels of Australian federalism. While the period saw a general expansion of town planning at a state and local government level across Australia, this did not seek to preclude the region's development even though it was not initially seen as a place where suburbanisation was to be encouraged. Gosford Shire's engagement of a town planner reflected a desire to more effectively manage growth, rather than halt it. The local federal member for most of the Menzies government, Roger Dean of the Liberal Party, meanwhile sought to facilitate popular support for a growing population. For example, in 1951, he gave a speech to the Gosford Rotary Club lamenting that 'Australians as a whole seem to possess a feeling of distrust to all foreigners and regard some of them with suspicion', including even Britons. However, he noted that

> the Government will continue to bring new settlers here and will continue to do what it can to place them in employment and supervise their early entry into the community ... It is our job to assist the New Australian when he comes to live in our area and help him to understand our ways of life.[30]

Prefiguring debates that would come to dominate the region's politics in later decades, he also publicly spoke about the need for development to be sensitive to environmental values, telling a meeting of the local flora protection society that he was 'impressed by their aims' and that he 'wished the society every success and assured it of his cooperation'.[31]

On the margin

The region's federal electoral history, and the wider career of Roger Dean, provide further perspectives on the Menzies government and the 1940s and 1950s. As well as standing on the cusps of land and ocean and town and country, the Division of Robertson was won and held by narrow margins at the general elections during this period.

While the Division of Robertson was created at Federation, its boundaries had changed substantially by mid-century. Originally an inland electorate encompassing central western New South Wales localities such as Mudgee and Dubbo, by the late 1940s it had comprehensively moved to the coast. As shown in Figure 1, its northern

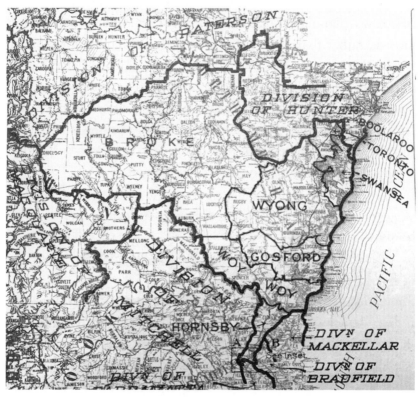

Figure 1: The Commonwealth electoral Division of Robertson, 1948.

boundary touched Newcastle and the Lower Hunter region, while at its other end it extended into Sydney's Upper North Shore, taking in Hornsby and abutting the divisions of Bradfield and Mackellar.

The Australian Labor Party took the seat at the 1943 election before it was won by Dean and the Liberal Party in 1949 with 21 617 first preferences to the incumbent's tally of 18 236.[32] Dean won it again in 1951 with a similar margin (22 804 to 19 406)[33] but had to rely on the redistribution of 1077 Communist Party preferences to win with a two-party preferred margin of 282 at the 1954 election.[34] Notwithstanding this support for the Liberal Party, the No vote at the 1951 referendum to give further powers to the Commonwealth to control communism was 17 226 versus a Yes vote of 14 595, making Robertson one of seven New South Wales seats held by the government rejecting the government's proposals.[35]

Contests in individual electorates are, of course, typically affected by a range of factors. Roger Dean's initial success perhaps partially reflects the broader success of his party in 1949, but he nonetheless held the seat as some of that support later ebbed nationally and saw it lose seats elsewhere on the edges of Sydney.[36] In an interview for the Commonwealth Parliamentary Library, Dean himself partially ascribed the 1949 result to his Labor opponent not campaigning particularly hard, that is, '… he gave me the impression that he was just going through the exercises of form. And he [assumed he] would continue to be the member'.[37] As a local member, Dean appears to have been conscientious and generally viewed as competent by his constituents.

Aged thirty-five at the time of his entry to Parliament, Dean was born into a Newcastle manufacturing family and spent five years with the army during World War II, serving as a lieutenant in northern Australia and the Pacific.[38] Upon his return he became active in the Liberal Party and, in his telling, gained pre-selection for Robertson as an external compromise candidate.[39] While he was not a resident of the region prior to his election, his wife's family had historically been a significant local landowner, and they subsequently moved to Gosford.[40]

Dean's career was not spectacular in the sense that he never became a minister or otherwise achieved national prominence, although during his time in Parliament he served on various committees and was described as a 'favourite son' of his party.[41] After leaving Parliament he was appointed as the Commonwealth's administrator of the Northern Territory (1964–70) and Australia's consul-general in San Francisco (1970–74).[42]

As the holder of a marginal seat, Dean recalled his electorate receiving frequent visits from the prime minister, both during election campaigns and at other times. Menzies purportedly once joked that the only features of the division of Robertson were 'pigs, passionfruit, poultry and pensioners'.[43] Ahead of the 1949 election, Menzies addressed a conference for New South Wales and Queensland Liberal candidates held at Toowoon Bay, emphasising a range of messages to take to voters, including around inflation, tax reduction, petrol rationing, imperial loyalty, and coal industry reform, summarising that 'The Socialists pose as radical reformers and cast us for the part of Tory reactionaries. We are in fact the radical party, and the Socialists are the reactionaries'.[44] Newspaper coverage of the 1954 election noted that Menzies spent a block of time holding public meetings in Robertson and the neighbouring division of Paterson where the party believed its candidates 'could be in trouble'.[45] Later in the 1950s, the region similarly served as Menzies's first stop on a 'meet the people' tour of northern New South Wales. After meeting Dean at Gosford, it was reported that the prime minister 'sipped whisky and soda' at the Terrigal Apex Club and gave a speech warning of the risks of centralising powers with the Commonwealth, before attending a garden party elsewhere in the electorate.[46] More broadly, Dean considered Menzies 'a very good friend in many ways' who was 'extraordinarily good company … when travelling'. He also recounted that Menzies and

Dame Pattie 'were very good to our children', including bringing them toys when they visited.[47] However, certain strains also came with the job. Alongside the burdens of regular travel to Canberra and circuits of meetings with constituents across an expansive electorate, Dean recalled that he was also asked by the prime minister more than he'd have wished to host visiting dignitaries, leveraging the attractions of his electorate and its nearness to Sydney.[48]

Dean's various public statements and his later reminiscences suggest that his popularity stemmed from his electorate generally being comfortable with his party's orthodoxies, alongside his willingness and ability to give recognition to particular issues of importance to the people of the Central Coast.

As already noted above, Dean spoke to his constituents in favour of the federal government's immigration program. More broadly, his international outlook was mixed, balancing a sense of Australian Britishness against an active interest in constructive engagement with Asian countries. When asked in the 1980s, he cited Menzies's work in the 'maintenance and development of the concept of British Commonwealth of Nations' as one of his government's two main achievements (the other being the economic development of Australia, broadly construed).[49] In later life, he still saw a desire to 'keep up' Western European migration, while allowing more diverse immigration than previously. That said, he also spoke with pride about having a Vietnamese 'foster daughter', as well as hosting Vietnamese and Malaysian Colombo Plan students.[50]

Dean's general political philosophy was similarly consistent with the broader directions of the Menzies government, combining rhetorical advocacy for markets and property while denouncing communism and socialism. In a 1954 newspaper article, Dean was reported as telling a public meeting in his electorate ahead of the general election that 'there can be no neutrality on May 29', warning that:

> socialism is still the main objective of the ... [Labor Party] ... One
> of the greatest diseases that can permeate the Australian way of life

is the socialist objective and this means control of him [i.e. ordinary Australians] by compulsory unionism. Control of his physical way of life by means of rationing and by a break in his initiative and spirit.

In contrast, he pragmatically put forward that: 'We Liberals believe that while it may not be perfect, the system of free enterprise is the best base that society has yet contrived upon which to plan a progressive community and a prosperous and healthy nation'.[51]

Forthright anti-communism can also be found in earlier statements, including ahead of the 1949 general election where he was reported as saying 'throughout the electorate' people were 'frightened to speak freely' due to fears of communist reprisals, arguing 'this evil must be destroyed for all time as it is undermining our democratic way of life'.[52] Such comments were broadly consistent with a lively local politics of anti-communism in Robertson, including, for example, Gosford Shire Council refusing the Eureka League (a communist youth organisation) permission to use a council campground for an event,[53] or one beach suburb mothers' club excluding communists from its membership.[54] Dean was nonetheless conscious that he walked a fine line with some of his constituents, including, as previously noted, to the extent that his re-election was once reliant on communist preferences. He estimated that he required around one third of the votes of the region's coal-mining communities and saw it as his duty to visit mines and go below ground. Indeed, looking back from the 1980s, he expressed a view that 'in no way in those days did I blame ... the miners going on strike in the hope of getting better working conditions' (though he made a careful distinction with any grievances in relation to pay).[55] At the same time, he suggested more broadly that 'the Australian people as a whole are a free enterprise people. I don't necessarily say they're Liberal or Country Party or whatever. But they are a free enterprise people'.[56]

Beyond identity positioning around liberal enterprise and its antithesis, Dean was also involved with bridging the Menzies government with local economic concerns in other, more mundane, ways. He chaired a parliamentary committee inquiring into certain material shortages during the period.[57] He sought to manage farmers' expectations around the development of export markets for eggs.[58] He chastised the state (Labor) government over trading hour controls as a form of regulatory capture at the expense of the majority.[59] During a period of drought in the late 1950s, it was reported that he 'asked the CSIRO to start rain-making experiments over the Central Coast'.[60] While these efforts may not have led to major substantive changes in the lives of the people of Robertson, his *Sydney Morning Herald* obituary described him as a 'kindly, generous and pragmatic man, known as a "gentle furnace"', who energetically represented his region without making waves.[61]

Homes coastal

The suburbanisation of the Central Coast during the Menzies era thus underscores certain aspects of the latter's historiography but also offers counterpoints. While some have argued that the affluence of the early 1950s was somewhat tentatively experienced, the region's experience shows that widespread home ownership had already been achieved in places by the middle of the decade and that indeed second home ownership was also not uncommon. While international migration clearly transformed many parts of Australia, this co-existed in places like the Central Coast with localised population growth driven predominantly by internal migration. Moreover, this internal migration was not necessarily linked with industrialisation or resource extraction but with an emergent economy within which the production and trading of real estate products and lifestyle-linked intangibles were major drivers. This local economy was not centrally planned but sprung from a set of enabled, revealed choices of ordinary households. During the ascendency of Australian beach culture its shoreline and hinterland were viewed as places where recreationally and environmentally richer lives might be experienced by more people. While Australians generally did not worship the ocean as such, the period saw proximity to the sea as something of a widely accepted spiritual good.[62] To play with Menzies's formulation of homes, the region's 'homes coastal' combined human, spiritual, and material elements in distinct ways.

The Central Coast's political history also provides nuance to other wider themes. Its electors rejected constitutional change to restrict communism, but anti-communism was also a genuine local political movement. From 1949 and through the 1950s, they returned a Liberal Party federal member of Parliament who combined vociferous opposition to communism with empathy for improving the employment conditions of miners. While Dean did not have a particularly distinguished career during his time in federal Parliament, Frank Bongiorno's observation in another regional political history, that 'democracy … often happens under the radar: among ordinary people, and their not so very extraordinary representatives', also resonates here.[63] To understand the politics of the 1940s and 1950s, it is important to look at how its themes and debates played out in different communities, including those which generally did not attract the interest of the national media. Dean's successive electoral successes with the voters of the Division of Robertson serve as a reminder that the constituency for the liberal democratic Australia offered by the Liberal Party included 'forgotten people' by the sea, mostly living lives of neither great privilege nor great disadvantage, both like and unlike other suburbanites.

Finally, the region's 1950s suburbanisation embodied important changes to Australia's political geography that would become increasingly significant as the century progressed. As in other places, the making of new suburbia created another battleground on the edge of a major city for the two main national political parties. After Dean's tenure the Division of Robertson was held by the Liberal Party until 1969, before returning Labor representatives until 1996 when the incoming Howard government picked up the seat again. However, along with housing, transport, and social services being important issues as elsewhere in middle Australia, the region was notable for continuing growth in the importance of environmental politics and associated positioning of its elected representatives, including at a federal level. In effect, environmentally influenced migration during the 1950s provided a base for later mass environmental politics. The region was also notable for its concentrated plenitude of aged persons, whose wider emergence as a distinct, sometimes pivotal electoral constituency across Australia is another twentieth-century phenomenon whose local effects merit further exploration. While the suburbs of mid-century Australia have been frequently characterised as culturally uniform, the Central Coast's homes coastal show that some households, given space, were willing and able to make new domestic value choices during the Menzies era in ways that prefigured the national politics of latter decades.

CHAPTER TEN

MENZIES AND ECONOMIC MANAGEMENT, 1950–54

David Lee[1]

Introduction

THE HALLMARK OF the Menzies government's economic policy during the years from 1950 to 1954 was its acceptance of the Keynesian principles of macroeconomic management developed in the early Menzies and the Curtin and Chifley years. Consolidation of a unified government after 1950 enabled the Menzies government to achieve a considerable measure of stability in the 1950s. Nevertheless, differences between the Treasury and the Commonwealth Bank, and the limitations imposed by the balance of payments resulted in a 'stop-go' pattern of economic activity in the 1950s. Although the Coalition parties had campaigned on ending economic controls, the government was pragmatic in deciding to maintain some of them. The introduction of a comprehensive regime of import licensing, which lasted throughout the 1950s, is the most salient example of this pragmatism. The real ending of the wartime era of economic controls would not come until the abolition of import licensing in February 1960.

Menzies, Chifley, and the 1949 election

Between 1945 and 1949, Robert Menzies pursued a skilful campaign against the Chifley Labor government's retention of wartime economic controls and its attempted nationalisation of the private trading banks.[2] Many of the Chifley government's controls were concomitant with Australia's financial, economic, and trading relationship with the United Kingdom. The mother country, virtually bankrupted by the war, had been forced to borrow three billion dollars with strings attached from the United States.[3] One of the US conditions of offering the loan was a requirement for Britain to make sterling convertible with the dollar as early as 1947. Another was an agreement to negotiate downwards the preferential tariffs established with British Commonwealth countries in the period since 1932.

Australia was in a stronger financial position than Britain at the end of the war.[4] US lend-lease aid and American military spending in Australia during the war had resulted in buoyant overseas reserves. Nonetheless, Australia was a member of a currency bloc, the sterling area, that consisted of Britain and countries in its empire that traded in sterling. Britain, moreover, was Australia's largest export market and Australia had limited opportunities, besides wool, to export to the United States for dollars.[5] Consequently, Australia had to rely on Britain's central reserves to finance essential requirements that could only be sourced from North America. Australia's pound was not readily convertible with the dollar, and Chifley was forced to retain import licensing, a wartime measure, for goods imported from North America and the 'dollar area'. Likewise, export controls were placed on commodities, such as butter, which were rationed to ensure that Australia retained enough supplies to export to Britain.[6]

In 1947, the British found convertibility of the dollar and sterling to be an impossible undertaking. Its overseas reserves would have been exhausted and its economy wrecked. Britain reintroduced currency restrictions and restricted imports from North America.

Chifley was sympathetic to Britain's plight and promised to help. He intensified Australia's import controls on goods from the dollar area in late 1947, and in 1949, he laid the groundwork for rationing of petrol, which was sourced from the dollar area, by persuading the states to delegate their power over its distribution to the Commonwealth. Before he could establish the scheme, the shortage of petrol was producing chaos.

In September 1949, after the British Labour government devalued sterling, Chifley devalued the Australian pound by the full 30 per cent to protect Australia's export trade with Britain and the value of its external reserves. In the following month, after Victoria had joined the other states in delegating power to control the distribution of petrol to the Commonwealth, Chifley introduced the *Liquid Fuel Rationing Act*. Menzies opposed the measure and promised 'to make it our business to get it in adequate quantities'.[7]

Petrol rationing became emblematic of Menzies's campaign against Labor's 'socialistic' and controlled economy. In his campaign speech on 10 November 1949, Menzies sketched a platform of scaling back government intervention and encouraging the free enterprise economy. He declared that:

> Every extension of Government power and control means less freedom of choice for the citizen. Government activities are monopolist. Monopolies exclude choice. No choice for the producer. No choice for the employee. No choice for the customer. The abolition of choice is the death of freedom.[8]

Menzies, delivering a campaign speech on behalf of the Liberal and Country parties, promised to raise dollar loans to help alleviate such shortages as of petroleum, to restore the Commonwealth Bank board as the governing body of the Commonwealth Bank, to introduce child endowment for the first child in every family and to establish compulsory military training. Chifley stood on his record. He stressed his government's achievement of full employment and the measures taken to buttress Australia's position against adversity abroad. It had built up Australia's reserves to £450 million, he reminded Australians, reduced government debt, negotiated long-term contracts for primary products, kept interest rates low, and created large reserves of public construction works.

The Labor prime minister did not match Menzies on child endowment for the first child, mainly because the Arbitration Court was at the time considering a basic wage application from the trade unions.[9] Weariness with wartime controls, impatience with industrial disputes such as in the coal industry and the concern of many about Labor's socialist objective saw the Australian electorate give the Coalition parties a decisive mandate. At the election on 10 December 1949, the Liberal and Country parties together achieved seventy-four seats to Labor's fifty-seven.[10]

The Cabinet and the public service

The Cabinet that Menzies assembled after the election included loyalists from his earlier period in government: Eric Harrison, minister for defence, George McLeay, minister for shipping and fuel, and Philip McBride, minister for the interior. But it also included those critics and their sympathisers who had ended his first stint as prime minister in August 1941.[11]

From the Country Party were Arthur Fadden, deputy prime minister and treasurer, John McEwen, minister for commerce and agriculture, Larry Anthony, postmaster-general, and Earle Page, minister for health. From the Liberal Party were Percy Spender, minister for external affairs, and Harold Holt, minister for national service. Also in Cabinet were Thomas White, whom Menzies had passed over in 1939, and RG Casey, who had been a rival for the leadership in 1939 and sent to Washington as minister to the United States. The latter now returned to the Cabinet as minister for national development. Newcomers included the Sydney lawyer Howard Beale, minister for information (later supply), and Neil O'Sullivan, a Catholic from

Queensland who led the government in the Senate and served as minister for trade and customs.[12] One of Menzies's great successes was to meld critics and loyalists from his earlier government with the newcomers into an effective and generally harmonious ministry.[13] The key ministers in managing the economy were Menzies, Fadden, McEwen, O'Sullivan, and Holt.

Adapting plans inherited from Chifley, Menzies set up a Cabinet secretariat to service the entire Cabinet system, ministerial and official committees, and Commonwealth–state and international conferences. He made this new secretariat responsible for arranging Cabinet meetings, circulating agenda, memoranda, and other documents, ensuring that departments were carrying out decisions, and keeping and indexing Cabinet records. This initiative meant that the records of decision-making at the highest levels of government 'would henceforth be coordinated at the centre, under the authority of the prime minister'.[14]

Unlike Chifley, Menzies did not take on another portfolio besides that of the prime minister, and he was less interested than his immediate predecessor in economic management. But he did agree to the transfer of the Economic Division of the Department of Post-War Reconstruction to the Prime Minister's Department, thereby inheriting able economists, including AS Brown, the permanent secretary of his department, and John Bunting, who would succeed Brown in that position in 1959. Menzies developed a close relationship with Brown, nicknaming him 'Bruno', or sometimes 'Le Brun', in contrast with 'Le Noir', his name for the Country Party's formidable John 'Black Jack' McEwen.[15]

Menzies gave the new Economic Policy Division the task of providing him with its own thoughts as well as background briefing material on economic and other matters. This sort of briefing was entirely new in the Prime Minister's Department, for it introduced public servants other than those directly linked with a particular item into Cabinet processes.[16] As the years passed, this development saw the Prime Minister's Department evolved as an 'independent source of advice to the prime minister and as an agency of inter-departmental co-operation'.[17]

The Treasury, led first by GPN Watt and, from 1951, by the strong-willed economist Roland Wilson, was the main source of the government's economic advice.[18] But it was not the only source. HC ('Nugget') Coombs, formerly director-general of the Department of Post-War Reconstruction and Australia's pre-eminent Keynesian, was chairman of the Commonwealth Bank from 1949 to 1958. Although Coombs had been close to Chifley and the former prime minister's main economic adviser, Menzies held Coombs in high regard and encouraged his offering advice to the Treasury and the government.[19]

Other key economic advisers were John Crawford, a relatively young agricultural economist promoted over the heads of more senior officers by Menzies and McEwen to be permanent secretary of the Department of Commerce and Agriculture. Crawford would be instrumental in working with McEwen under Cabinet's overall direction to oppose the US plan to bring wool under a system of international control in 1950 and 1951. Frank Meere, a senior officer in the Department of Trade and Customs, who became comptroller-general and permanent secretary in 1952, was another key official in the making and administration of economic policy during the Korean War period.

Meere was part of the top-level delegation that accompanied Menzies to Washington shortly after the outbreak of the Korean War. In August 1950, the Australian delegation with Meere's assistance secured from the International Bank for Reconstruction and Development (the World Bank) a $100 million development loan, the largest credit extended by that institution to that point.[20] The credit covered the development and expansion of electric power facilities, water conservation works, railways, agriculture and land settlement, mining, smelting and refining, iron and steel and engineering, and other industries. The dollar loan and the Korean War economic boom of 1950–51 enabled the government to maintain its election promise to dispense with petrol rationing and provided substantial assistance to the government's program, led by McEwen, to boost Australia's agricultural productivity.

Menzies and Keynesianism

Menzies and the Coalition came to power on a plan to free up the economy from socialistic controls. There were, however, significant obstacles in the way of achieving this objective. One was the need for continuing exchange controls, given that sterling would not become fully convertible with the dollar until the end of the 1950s. Menzies also had to retain restrictions on imports from hard currency countries and then to extend them to all countries in 1952 to defend the balance of payments.

Another constraint on the government's economic freedom of action was the relatively narrow range of Australia's exports. In the 1950s, these were overwhelmingly rural; there were few manufactured exports and, before the mining boom of the 1960s, mineral exports, principally lead and zinc, amounted to a relatively small proportion of total exports.[21] Commodities such as wool, wheat, dairy products, and meat were subject to fluctuations in prices, seasonal variations, and stiff competition from competitors. Australia had the advantage of imperial preference and long-term contracts with the United Kingdom, but the bilateral trading relationship was skewed in Britain's favour until its renegotiation by McEwen and Crawford in 1956.

European countries such as France and Germany adopted protectionist agricultural policies, as did the United States, which in 1954, passed Public Law 480, a law authorising a 'food for peace' program that involved giving away surplus crops owned by the US government as an instrument of foreign policy during the Cold War.

The program undercut Australia's wheat exports to countries such as India. Australia had markets in Britain and some of the continental European countries, but the United States offered few opportunities for Australian exports. The Chinese market had been closed off with the advent of the People's Republic in October 1949; the war-devastated Japanese economy was only at the beginning of its post-war ascent; and the rest of Asia had been affected by wartime occupation or political turmoil.[22]

A final constraint on economic policy was the government's decision to introduce compulsory National Service to prepare an expeditionary force to be sent to the Middle East in the event of a global war.[23] To help it balance the civilian and military economies, the government set up at the end of 1950 a National Security Resources Board.[24] One of the recommendations of the board was to restore control over capital issues under the *Defence Preparations Act 1951*.[25] Jodie Boyd and Nicola Charwat have persuasively argued that Menzies used the Act to facilitate peacetime access to capital issues controls under the Constitution's defence power and thereby to reassure the government's supporters that turning to direct economic controls was not a vindication of the 'socialism' that it had promised at the 1949 election to oppose.

In September 1950, the government committed Australian forces to the US-led effort to defend South Korea against an invasion by communist North Korea.[26] All this meant that Australia was placed in a position of advanced defence preparedness for the duration of the Korean War from 1950 to 1953. The doubling of defence expenditure in that time presented a serious challenge to the government in balancing the requirements of the civilian and military sectors of the economy.

In the civilian economy the major challenge was inflation, which had been steadily accelerating from the late 1940s. On coming to power the Menzies government inherited pent-up public demand for goods that were in short supply. With the partial relaxation of the wartime controls of the 1940s, these two factors combined to accelerate the rate of inflation. In its first year in office, inflation was exacerbated by a very large wool cheque, basic wage 'prosperity' loadings, war gratuity payments, and loan conversion payments.[27]

A hallmark of Menzies's post-war government was the embrace by ministers and senior officials of 'Keynesian' principles of economic management. Deriving from the ideas of English economist John Maynard Keynes and his followers, Keynesianism involved following the policy of maintaining high employment and controlling inflation by varying interest rates, tax rates, and public expenditure. As economic historian Selwyn Cornish has shown, however, there were important differences among Menzies's economic advisers. Coombs and the Commonwealth Bank were decidedly more 'Keynesian' than the Treasury under Watt and Wilson.[28]

The bank under Coombs advised the government to raise interest rates to moderate inflation. The Treasury, which was more concerned with encouraging long-term economic growth, at first discouraged these ideas. Moreover, in its first budget in 1950, the government abandoned a proposal for a 30 per cent wool tax. It decided on a lesser measure—that 20 per cent of the price obtained for wool should be paid to the Treasury until income tax became payable on the wool proceeds—and merely to balance the budget.[29] The delay in taking decisive action against inflation in 1950 meant that it had to take more stringent measures in 1951. By the middle of that year, inflation had reached what Treasurer Arthur Fadden called a 'virulent stage'.[30] Retail prices were rising at the rate of 25 per cent per year and average earnings by 30 per cent per year, and bottlenecks in coal, steel, building materials, transport, and power were hampering production. Labour was universally short and its turnover high.

The government brought down drastic anti-inflationary measures between July and October 1951. The level of public works, state and federal, was pegged; capital issues controls were further tightened and, most significantly, the government budgeted for a large surplus.

Fadden's 1951 budget of £927 million Commonwealth expenditure raised revenue amounting to £1042 million and a record surplus of £115 million. The tax increases in the budget amounted to £115 million: from an increase in personal income tax of 10 per cent, increases in company tax, drastic rises in indirect taxes on a wide range of non-essential goods, and hikes in excise, which sent up prices of beer, spirits, wine, tobacco, and cigarettes.[31] Economic historian Greg Whitwell described Fadden's 1951 budget, the so-called 'horror budget', 'as an event of major significance in Australia's budgetary history. For the budget represented the first explicit use of fiscal policy for anti-cyclical purposes. The budget was Keynesian in practice, principle and spirit and openly so'.[32]

The Labor Opposition launched an immediate attack on the higher rates of taxation. On the other hand, Sir Douglas Copland lauded the 1951 budget as a 'landmark in public finance'.[33] The reaction of the press was mixed. In Melbourne *The Argus* gave cautious approval and *The Age* was mainly factual and non-committal.[34] *The Financial Review*, however, described the budget as a 'punitive expedition' and the 'road to ruin' for the government and the economy, and *The Daily Telegraph* in Sydney commented that: 'As things stand, Sir Arthur has run the risk of bringing down a Budget which may turn out to be more suited to last year's problems than to meet contemporary tends'.[35] *The Sydney Morning Herald* was the strongest of all press critics in calling on backbenchers to 'prevail on the Government, in its own as well as the national interest, to cut the commitments responsible for the crippling tax increases, before it is compelled to do so by sheer force of circumstances'.[36]

Despite this criticism, the effect of the government's policies was to cut down the overall demand for goods which had been excessive since the war; to enforce greater concentration of public works activity on more essential projects; and to restrict expansion of private industry, considering the requirements for defence and development. Economic historian Paul Tilley has argued that Menzies and the Treasury managed to achieve in the 1950s a measure of relative stability, politically and economically, 'perhaps for the first time since Federation'.[37] Nonetheless, the differences between Treasury and the Commonwealth Bank on economic policy led to something of a 'stop-go' pattern, with the economy suffering small rises in unemployment in the early and mid-1950s and a larger one in the early 1960s. Apart, however, from the 1960–61 period, the level of unemployment was never high enough to damage the electoral prospects of the government.

The wool boom

By 1950, the position of wool had improved markedly from its position in the 1930s and early 1940s. At the end of World War II, fearing the continuation of low wool prices after the war, the United Kingdom and the wool-growing dominions had set up the U.K.–Dominion Wool Disposals (the Joint Organization) to liquidate stores of wool accumulated in wartime without unduly depressing wool prices. From 1947, as the 'New Look' spread from America to other Western countries, it became fashionable for women to depart from austere wartime conditions and wear fuller length woollen skirts. Spurred on by post-war economic recovery and longer hemlines in the West, worldwide demand for wool rose and so did wool prices. In these more buoyant times, the Joint Organization was able to complete in six years what some had expected would take twice that long.

In the couple of years immediately before the outbreak of the Korean War, consumption of apparel wool exceeded production. Because the accumulated stocks of the Joint Organization could fill the gap, the problem created by unusually high consumer demand was masked.[38] With the outbreak of war in Korea in June 1950, however, the imbalance between the demand for and supply of wool became glaring. In August 1950, not long after the outbreak of hostilities in Korea, the United States responded to the wool problem—its high price and the need to obtain more wool for military purposes.[39] Specifically, the United States proposed the suspension of wool auctions until agreement on a system of international allocation of wool could be achieved.

In the latter part of 1950, the Menzies government persuaded the Americans not to put in place any special measures, even pre-emption, to meet US wool requirements.[40] Menzies and his advisers set about preparing the Australian argument (for free trade and *laissez faire*) against any revisiting of this position.[41] The government's argument was that, except during a wartime situation, the maintenance of public auctions was essential to the well-being of the Australian wool industry. For Australia, price control and public auctions were incompatible: it would not be possible to operate any effective system of wool allocations while still maintaining effective public auctions.

In July 1951, Menzies took the decisive step of sending Crawford, as the most senior Australian official concerned with wool, for discussions with the Americans. When Crawford arrived in Washington, Australia was on the back foot. This was at a time when the Australian government was devoting much diplomatic effort to persuading the United States to sign the ANZUS security pact with Australia and New Zealand.

Some Australian diplomats were worried that if Australia did not bend to the American will on wool, then the negotiation of the ANZUS Treaty might be jeopardised. The Americans were arguing trenchantly that the failure to allocate wool supplies through some means other than uncontrolled auctions would endanger the military situation and that the failure to impose ceiling prices for wool threatened economic stability in the United States. With Australia now on the defensive and being portrayed as a country shirking its obligations to the 'free world', Crawford went on the attack. He explained that wool was a billion-and-a-half dollar industry that represented an economic force in Australia almost exactly equivalent to the entire farm bloc in the United States. The American demand to suspend wool auctions, he charged, was 'tantamount to asking an anti-Socialist Government in Australia to adopt a form of socialised marketing of our greatest single industry against the will of that industry'.[42]

At the end of July 1951, Crawford was able to report that 'the atmosphere is now much calmer and the Americans have realised that they need to expound their case by something better than vague generalities'.[43] Nevertheless, with the Americans, now supported by the British, determined to press ahead with a plan for wool ceiling prices, Menzies and the Cabinet decided to act emphatically and unilaterally. On 22 August 1951, Menzies issued a statement, that the government 'had reached the conclusion after full considera- tion that the review of statistics and other factors affecting or likely to affect the world wool market did not provide grounds for the adoption of any special wool distribution measures or for action to regulate wool'.[44]

Import licensing

The wool boom ended abruptly in the latter half of 1951. In the 1940s, Australia's balance of payments position had steadily improved, and in July 1951, Australia's international reserves reached a high of just over £800 million. But in the latter half of 1951, occurred a sudden and precipitate fall in the level of Australia's reserves, caused by a decline in the value of total exports and a large increase in the value of imports. Australia's international reserves fell from £843 million to £362 million. Fadden in his budget speech for 1952–53 described this fall as 'quite without parallel in previous experience'.[45]

In the period of fixed exchange rates under the Bretton Woods system, countries could only alter their exchange rate (that is, appre- ciate or depreciate currencies) with approval from the International

Monetary Fund to remedy a 'fundamental disequilibrium'. Australia had only recently depreciated in 1949, and Cabinet had little appetite to depreciate again and take further value out of the Australian pound, which Menzies had promised to restore. Other options—such as cutting back defence expenditure, or the immigration program inherited from Chifley or the ambitious plans for development such as the Snowy Mountains Hydro-Electric Scheme—were equally unpalatable. The solution to the problem taken by Menzies was to turn back to the wartime remedy of import restrictions.

On 6 March 1952, Cabinet decided 'to impose overall import restrictions in the interests of conserving London funds ... and that the licensing system should be begun, in a matter submitted orally by ... [Frank] Meere'.[46] This was a significant intervention insofar as the decision applied to non-dollar goods, including imports from Britain, as well to goods from the dollar area. Although restrictions on dollar goods had been accepted as a fact of life, it had not been necessary since the 1930s to restrict goods from sterling sources for balance of payments reasons.[47] Import licensing was discouraged by the emerging 'rules-based order' of multilateral trade but was permitted in special circumstances under the transitional provisions of the International Monetary Fund and the General Agreement on Tariffs and Trade.

Menzies, in announcing the scheme, observed that it was not intended to set up a permanent licensing system. He and other spokesmen hoped that the restrictions would be temporary. Public servants, however, were more cautious in believing that import restrictions would be needed for some time. They were right to be cautious because the import licensing regime lasted for the rest of the 1950s and would only be dismantled in February 1960.

After 1952, the Menzies government's operation of the licensing system took on something of a 'stop-go' character. In the period from April 1953 to March 1955, import controls were slightly relaxed. But in the second half of 1954, when Australia's international reserves again fell steeply, the government tightened them once more in the period from April 1955 to July 1959. In 1956, Menzies arranged for the creation of a unified Department of Trade by merging the old Departments of Trade and Customs and Commerce and Agriculture. McEwen became the minister for trade and Crawford his departmental secretary, and they administered the import licensing system after 1956. By the late 1950s, the import controls were becoming unpopular in the business community and in branches of the Liberal and Country parties, especially after allegations of bribery and corruption in the system were aired in the press. In 1960, the new federal treasurer, Harold Holt, persuaded Cabinet to dismantle the controls as a primarily anti-inflationary measure. This year marked the beginning of the more liberal economic order to which Menzies aspired in 1949.

Conclusion

Menzies's post-war government from 1949 to 1954 achieved a considerable measure of stability in managing an economy on a semi-war footing. The operation of the government was facilitated by reforms to the Cabinet secretariat and the Prime Minister's Department and Menzies's adept harnessing of the experience of the public service in the age of the 'mandarins'.[48] The government's Keynesian economic policies contributed to a period of unparalleled economic stability, albeit that differences between the Commonwealth Bank and the Treasury produced something of a 'stop-go' pattern. This pattern was exacerbated after 1952 when the balance of payments had to be protected by a comprehensive import licensing regime. Lasting eight years, import licensing was ratcheted up and down in a similarly stop-go fashion to the government's macro-economic policies.

Menzies had come to power in 1949 promising a new era of free enterprise, and he achieved successes in ending petrol rationing, obtaining dollar loans, and forestalling American intervention in the wool industry. But the controlled economy lasted for another decade. Two later measures, the 1957 Commerce Treaty with Japan and the 1960 abolition of import licensing, together with the extraordinary mining boom of the 1960s, ushered in a new, more open era for the Australian economy.[49] As a later secretary of the Treasury, John Stone, described the end of import licensing:

> I think it was one of the most important decisions in the post-war period because it really was a kind of watershed in putting the war … behind us. It might seem strange putting the war behind you 15 years after the event, but that is what really happened.[50]

A PRUDENT AND URGENT MEASURE: THE FOUNDING OF THE AUSTRALIAN SECRET INTELLIGENCE SERVICE

William A Stoltz[1]

THE USE OF spies and secret agents is as old as civilisation itself. Different cultures and political systems have had their own norms and traditions regarding the role of this profession. In Australia's case, its spies owe their lineage to the British tradition, which is encapsulated in a portrait of Queen Elizabeth I, known as the Rainbow Portrait. In the painting, Elizabeth I wears her dress replete with embroidered eyes and ears. After years of assassination attempts, foreign wars, and civil sectarian unrest, Elizabeth is flaunting that she sees and hears all.

Indeed, in her efforts to secure her crown Elizabeth was supported throughout her reign by one of the most sophisticated secret services in history, set up by her secretary of state, Sir Francis Walsingham. While much has changed since the Elizabethan era, there are features of Walsingham's secret service still embodied in modern spy services of the British tradition, including the Australian Secret Intelligence Service (ASIS) and the British Secret Intelligence Service (SIS), also known as MI6.

Walsingham's spy network existed to serve the crown first and foremost, with intelligence designed to support the decision-making of the head of state and protect her power. Further, Walsingham's operatives were given permissions and immunities to carry out otherwise illegal activities that only the monarch could authorise. Their mandate to exist came from the monarch's executive authority, not from the legislative power of Parliament.

For Elizabeth, as today, secret services carried out two related, yet distinct, sets of activities: the stealing of secrets to create intelligence, and the conduct of activities to secretly shape and disrupt external events. The former we call espionage, the latter is typically referred to as covert action.

These things remain broadly true today: ASIS's primary 'customer' is Australia's prime minister and their Cabinet, i.e. those executives of Australia's government who must make ultimate decisions affecting Australia's security and foreign affairs. Further, a legislated mandate is only a relatively new feature for ASIS. For the first fifty years of its operations, it existed on the basis of executive orders and even today it is highly subject to executive direction. And, like Elizabeth's network, ASIS has two functions, ASIS's two hidden hands: one with which to steal secrets and another with which to shape events abroad.

Even prior to Federation in 1901, Australia's governments had engaged in espionage overseas. This was primarily through commissioning officials and expatriates already operating in the South Pacific to collect commercial secrets and other intelligence about the non-British European powers operating in the region.[2]

Australia's first federal governments would be similarly interested in the activities of other powers operating close to Australia's shores. The New Hebrides was of particular concern for the government of Alfred Deakin, Australia's second prime minister. Deakin leveraged the Commonwealth's commercial agents in the Pacific to gain insights about French settlers and military positions in the islands and to help argue for a greater British military presence in the Pacific.[3]

A decade later during the Great War, because Australia had no dedicated external affairs department or established intelligence agencies, Australia's contribution to intelligence was conducted via the military. Following this, through the 1920s, Richard Casey, who would go on to help create ASIS, was embedded in the UK Cabinet and Foreign Offices as Australia's representative in London.

Casey would see first-hand how SIS intelligence from well-placed human sources improved the policy decisions of Britain's Cabinet, including in wartime. Casey was also envious of Britain's ability to secretly shape international events using what he called their 'black arts': covert actions to distribute propaganda, change foreign governments, and deploy paramilitary units abroad.[4]

Such was Casey's purported access to the British government, that he claimed some documents were marked as only for distribution to 'KCC': King, Cabinet, and Casey.[5] Although examples of documents marked in this way are yet to be identified.

Australia's approach to secret statecraft became more sophisticated in World War II, particularly in the Pacific theatre in areas occupied by Imperial Japan. The Allied Intelligence Bureau (AIB) was set up as a joint organisation to pool Australian, British, Dutch, and American intelligence resources operating in the Pacific. Much of its activities were targeted against Japanese forces operating in what today is Indonesia, Malaysia, Timor, and Papua New Guinea.[6]

AIB comprised sections focused on special military operations, sabotage, human intelligence, rescuing POWs, and propaganda.[7] Alfred Deakin Brookes—the grandson of Alfred Deakin—served with AIB in the sections focused on propaganda and sabotage behind enemy lines. As will be discussed, Brookes would go on from AIB to be the first director-general of ASIS.

Alongside Richard Casey, Alfred Brookes would be another important advocate for an Australian Secret Intelligence Service. Following the war and his service with AIB, Brookes worked on the staff of HV Evatt, including during UN efforts to establish Indonesia as a separate state.[8]

It was during this time that Brookes proposed the idea of an Australian Secret Service directly to Evatt, but to no avail.[9] At a similar time, in October 1947, Dick Ellis, SIS's lead intelligence officer in the Far East, also visited Melbourne and Canberra to lobby the Chifley government to set up a standalone agency. He was similarly unsuccessful.[10]

The truth was that Chifley and Evatt had a difficult relationship with the British and American intelligence communities. This was particularly due to the revelation in 1948 that Australia's departments of External Affairs and Defence had been thoroughly infiltrated by Soviet agents.

In 1947, decryption of intercepted Soviet diplomatic cables by the CIA indicated that the Australian government had been infiltrated. Soviet communications referenced the acquisition of top secret Allied material that indicated it had been acquired by Australian sources.[11] In January 1948, the CIA's director of intelligence briefed President Harry Truman on the compromise of the Australian government, stating: 'there is a leak in high government circles in Australia, to Russia ... The British Government is now engaged in extensive undercover investigations to determine just where, in the Australian Government, the leak is'.[12]

An MI5[13] delegation visited Australia to address the issue, but the full origins of their investigations were hidden from Australian officials. To outline the leak, the MI5 delegation met with Prime Minister Chifley and Evatt who was both attorney-general and external affairs minister. They explained the urgent need for reform of Australia's counter-espionage capability that MI5, SIS, and the CIA believed was required. They principally believed Australia needed a dedicated domestic security service.[14]

Chifley and Evatt expressed initial scepticism that the leak had arisen from Australia. Evatt felt that the British were exaggerating the seriousness of the situation and Chifley expressed reluctance to undertake the institutional reform requested, which would require a more rigorous vetting of public servants. Indeed, Chifley only agreed to the reforms—which would create ASIO—after it was threatened that without the changes, Australia would be cut off entirely from the exchange of top secret information.

In recently declassified SIS and CIA correspondence from the period, officials expressed concern about whether Chifley and Evatt regarded the challenge of Soviet espionage seriously enough. Of Evatt, they were worried about his ability to direct ASIO as attorney-general while also being in charge of external affairs—the department most at risk of espionage. Suspicions that Evatt's own office had been infiltrated endured for years.

Conversely, SIS and CIA officials expressed hope that Robert Menzies's newly created Liberal Party would be elected in 1949, believing them to be more favourable partners. There is also some evidence to suggest that Menzies and other senior Liberals were made aware of the Soviet infiltration prior to coming to government and prior to being officially briefed on the matter by ASIO in 1950.[15]

Had this been known to Chifley and Evatt it would have confirmed the suspicions they, as Labor men, had long held about the British intelligence services. After all, they regarded the British services as being populated by the same type of entitled patricians who had flung Australia's working men against German machine guns in the Great War and who in World War II conspired with Churchill to withhold Australia's Middle East division from returning to the Pacific.

While the Chifley government was setting up ASIO[16] and grappling with SIS, MI5, and the CIA over Soviet infiltration, Menzies and Casey were laying the groundwork for the 1949 election campaign, which would place a strong emphasis on anti-communism and national security.

By 1947, Casey had returned from overseas and was the federal director of the Liberal Party; he would also eventually be preselected for La Trobe. In his capacity as federal director he employed Brookes in October 1947 as 'a specialist officer on the staff of the Federal Secretariat, to deal with foreign affairs, imperial defence and subversive activities'.[17] These were doubtless strange things for a political party to employ someone for, but they make more sense when considered against the Liberal Party's wider agenda for the 1949 campaign.

Banning the Communist Party of Australia was one of the Liberal Party's central campaign commitments, and the proxy wars and geopolitical tensions of the early Cold War placed foreign affairs, if not front of mind for voters, definitely at the forefront for Menzies, Casey, and other Liberal candidates who had held leadership positions throughout World War II. Liberal Party research reports from the time reveal a strong interest on the part of the wider party in foreign affairs and the risks of communist interference in Australia and its neighbours.[18]

While preparing these reports and working closely with Casey, Brookes would later express his desire to be pre-selected as a Liberal Party candidate for a Melbourne seat at the 1949 election, although this did not come to pass.[19]

We know that immediately after Menzies's election victory, Brookes advocated directly to Casey and Menzies to set up ASIS in 1950.[20] But it is quite possible that Brookes lobbied for ASIS prior to the election win and while employed by the party. He had been forward leaning in putting the idea to Evatt several years earlier, and it is almost inconceivable that he and Casey, if not Menzies, wouldn't have discussed in some way the idea of an Australian secret service prior to the election.

It raises the question: Could the establishment of ASIS have been a secret election policy, determined by the party leadership but not foreshadowed with the electorate?

Whether Menzies or Casey became firmly settled on the idea prior to being in government, or discussed it more widely within the party, is thus far unknown. However, it is fair to say that establishing ASIS was a distinctly Liberal Party policy. Not just because of Casey and Brookes's enthusiasm for the idea, but it is difficult to conceive that Chifley's government would have set up ASIS if they were re-elected. The poor relationship of Chifley and Evatt with the British intelligence community but also Evatt's multiple rejections of proposals to create an Australian secret service are evidence of this. While a future Labor government may well have set up ASIS, it simply would never have happened while Evatt held the attorney-general's and external affairs portfolios.

As mentioned, the idea to establish ASIS should be conceived of in the context of a wider agenda of national security reform undertaken by the Menzies government, which included the goal of banning the Communist Party but also preparing Australia for World War III.

Upon being elected, Casey was appointed as Menzies's minister for national development—not external affairs, as one might have assumed given his experience and passion for world affairs. That portfolio went to Percy Spender. So, Casey's subsequent leadership within Cabinet for setting up ASIS is on face value a little strange. However, in this portfolio, one might think of Casey as the minister responsible for preparing Australia for the contingency of a third world war between the communist and Western blocs. At the time of the Menzies government coming to power, the Malayan Emergency is taking place to Australia's near north, and the Korean War would break out shortly after in June 1950.

Rehabilitating Japan was also still a huge focus for Australian, British, and American foreign policy, and suspicion of what future path Japan might take was still present, as demonstrated by Australia's initial reluctance to sign the Treaty of San Francisco with Japan. In this post-war period nuclear weapons were proliferating and advancing at great speed, including through extensive testing in Australia's own territory.

Australia's capacity to deal with its changing world required the rapid development of its fuel security, port infrastructure, mines, and manufacturing, all of which fell into the National Development portfolio under Casey. So too did policy consideration for Australia developing nuclear technology and infrastructure—remembering at this time Australia's option to adopt nuclear weapons was still a distinct possibility. The focus of this portfolio on developing Australia was also not just about Australia's own security, it was about its contribution to allied efforts to shape the Asia-Pacific region. As Casey would explain, 'the building up of our economic strength is the best contribution we can make. We are one of the main support areas'.[21] This is demonstrated by correspondence Casey had with Bill Donovan—founder of the CIA—writing in 1950 on behalf of American businesses. Donovan wanted Casey to develop the Blair Athol coal reserves in Queensland.[22] His argument to Casey was that Australia needed to prioritise the development of coal mines to provide secure energy supplies to the developing Japanese economy. This would ensure Japan's post-war industrialisation but would also keep it from needing Chinese or Russian coal and falling into their political orbit. Therefore, by virtue of his portfolio as well as his past interests, Casey was fixed on the issues of strategy and geopolitics closely affected by secret intelligence and covert activity.

The importance of establishing ASIS to Menzies's national security agenda is evidenced by the fact that on the same day Menzies introduced the Bill to ban the Communist Party of Australia he met with Casey, Percy Spender from external affairs, Philip McBride from Defence, and Brookes to discuss how to take the idea of introducing ASIS to the full Cabinet.[23] Shortly afterwards Casey briefed Cabinet on the proposal using the unfolding Malayan Emergency as illustrative context for the need for Australia to main tools of covert statecraft.[24] He described how with a communist insurgency so close to Australia's borders and impacting a Commonwealth territory, there was an urgent need for secret intelligence and covert options to anticipate and intervene in unfolding events.

To reinforce his case, Dick Ellis, SIS's head of Far East operations, was present to take Cabinet's questions on the work of SIS in the region and how ASIS would be of use to the wider British Commonwealth. Cabinet ultimately agreed to explore how the agency should be set up with support from SIS. Shortly afterwards, Brookes was dispatched to the United Kingdom to observe and learn how SIS operated and was structured.

At this stage in 1950, the exact scope of work and structure of ASIS was still contested within the public service. The Department of Defence was initially of the view that any special operations function should rest with the military;[25] while External Affairs was resistant to the need for foreign intelligence, believing their diplomatic reporting to be sufficient for the insights government needed.[26]

In 1950, Menzies wrote to the UK prime minister, Clement Attlee, saying:

> I have decided to establish a Secret Intelligence Service which, when organised, will operate in South East Asia and in Pacific areas adjacent to Australia. Recent developments in Asia and our 'near north' make this a prudent and urgent measure. Knowledge regarding this scheme has been restricted to the fewest possible here and for added security, I have chosen to write rather than cable. I trust that the establishment of an Australian Service may in some small measure reduce the onerous world-wide commitments of the United Kingdom.[27]

While it would be a small, boutique agency, ASIS nevertheless reflected the focus of Menzies's wider foreign policy, which was decidedly on the preservation of British power in the Asia-Pacific, and the centrality of British power to the Cold War struggle in the region. In this sense, ASIS was envisaged as an 'empire' agency that would plug in to and support the intelligence needs not just of Australia but the wider British Commonwealth. Behind this was Australia's larger aspiration to lead in the formulation of Commonwealth strategic decision-making as it related to the region.

Adding more to the intelligence picture would lend valuable decision-making leverage for Australia. As Menzies stated, 'our decision [to create ASIS] was made in the light of the grave developments in Asia and in accordance with the policy that Australia should assume a larger share of responsibility for Commonwealth Defence in the Pacific Area,'[28] In addition to his correspondence with Attlee, in January 1951, Menzies visited London and dined with the head of SIS, or 'C', Sir Stewart Menzies, at Australia House. There is no apparent record of their conversation.

While Menzies and the Cabinet had decided in principle to establish ASIS, the structure and scope of the Service were contested for a year or so. The key contested details were:

- Should ASIS be responsible for covert action, or should this rest with Defence?
- Should it operate under a 'foreign service act' as Percy Spender initially suggested?[29]
- Who should be the responsible minister? The minister for defence or for external affairs?
- Should ASIS use 'diplomatic cover'?

These issues were resolved, temporarily at least, when Casey took over as minister for external affairs in April 1951 and pushed for a final decision on the form ASIS should take. The consensus decision emerged that the defence minister, in consultation with the external affairs minister and prime minister, via a special sub-committee of Cabinet, would be responsible for authorising ASIS's activities. ASIS's officers would operate with diplomatic cover, including British cover, but its budget would be provided by the Defence portfolio.

With Casey having helped iron out the finer details, Menzies finally created ASIS through an order of the governor-general's

Executive Council on 13 May 1952—not via an Act as Spender had encouraged. Alfred Brookes was made the first director-general of ASIS at just thirty-two years old.

Creating ASIS in this way, via an executive order not an Act, meant that the prime minister had it signed into being without informing Parliament. This not only reflected the high secrecy of the service but also the often unilateral way Menzies wielded the executive power of the prime ministership when it came to national security decisions. Menzies did not regard it as necessary for ordinary members of Parliament to know that an Australian secret intelligence service had been established. Indeed, given his suspicions of some members of the Labor Party he may not have trusted them with such knowledge.

However, creating ASIS without legislation had the potentially unlawful result of the government concealing the service's funding in the Defence budget to keep it secret from Parliament.[30] Alongside the executive order creating ASIS, Menzies issued an accompanying top secret directive or charter, explaining in more detail the agency's functions. While ASIS now operates under a piece of legislation— the *Intelligence Services Act*—its director-general still receives these classified directives from the PM.

In his first top secret directive to Brookes in 1952, Menzies outlined that the purpose of ASIS would be the collection of 'secret intelligence'—espionage, on overseas targets—and the carrying out of 'special operations' that 'afford no proof of the instigation of the government'—what we describe today as covert action.[31] Importantly, the directive also instructed that ASIS would work closely with SIS, and that Brookes would have direct access to relevant Cabinet ministers, essentially allowing him to go around departmental secretaries.

ASIS's operations started small in 1952, initially with nine officers, but it had extensive access to SIS's intelligence products and 'stations' in the region.[32] ASIS would eventually establish stations of its own: the first being in Jakarta, Tokyo, and Bangkok, with another office in Australia for 'debriefing' returning expats. For ASIS's covert action function, SIS helped by dispatching stores of weaponry and other equipment as reserve stocks for ASIS's imagined 'wartime' special operations.

Casey would initially revel in being in charge of the agency. On his travels abroad, SIS found Casey to be the most frequent and enthusiastic visitor, and he often hosted visiting SIS and CIA officers at his farm in Berwick, Victoria, where it is rumoured he allowed ASIS to use his airstrip for unregistered 'black flights'.[33] If nothing else, in letters to one another, Brookes and Casey have an extensive discussion about the appropriate locks for Casey's aircraft hangar.[34]

As ASIS expanded, it created a covert radio station in Kowandi in Darwin in 1953, in order to connect into SIS's 'Diplomatic Wireless Service'. This was used to receive encoded communications and, over time, support the interception of neighbouring countries' signals.[35]

By 1954, ASIS had nineteen intelligence officers and twenty-two supporting staff. Its close relationship with SIS was added to with the first CIA liaison officer assigned to ASIS.[36]

Despite the steady growth of ASIS, Brookes would run into trouble with his bureaucratic counterparts almost immediately. These principally included Frederick Shedden, secretary of Defence, Alan Watt secretary of External Affairs and Arthur Tange, deputy secretary of External Affairs. The main issues at play were responsibility for ASIS's funding and its use of diplomatic cover.

As alluded to, ASIS had a somewhat confusing structure. It resided in the Department of Defence under the cover of the 'Central Plans Section' and had its funding hidden in the Defence budget.[37] But its officers were to work abroad out of British and Australian embassies and high commissions, while using diplomatic cover, but often only being accountable to SIS officers.[38]

Initially this structural separation from ASIS was looked at as a good thing by the mandarins of External Affairs who wanted little to do with ASIS, but this would quickly change.

Brookes was a remarkable man: his experiences of Australia's region during the war made him incredibly worldly for his age. He was confident, cool under pressure, and charismatic. Many of the features of an effective spymaster. However, his desire for swift action meant he chafed against the hierarchy of the civil service, and his preference for relying on his personal relationships with Casey and Menzies put him offside with those departmental secretaries who were technically his superiors.

For example, in his contest with Defence and External Affairs, Brookes directly complained to Menzies about the institutional rivalry. Brookes explained to Menzies that ASIS's relationship with Defence and External Affairs had degenerated into 'a generally unfriendly and petty atmosphere'.[39] He sought the PM's intervention by asking that instead of being placed under Defence, ASIS simply be made directly responsible to Menzies. However, due to the concerns of Watt and Tange over ASIS's use of diplomatic cover, it was moved to External Affairs in 1954.

Another issue for Brookes was his relationship with Casey. Casey and Brookes's personal relationship is perhaps one of the closest to be observed between a minister and an agency head. Theirs was the correspondence of two close friends—one the elder mentor to the other—and very frequently Casey turned to Brookes for policy advice on topics well outside of Brookes's purview as DG ASIS.[40]

Brookes also volunteered advice to Casey on how to engage with Casey's UK and US counterparts without consulting External Affairs. In this context Brookes would write an extraordinary letter to Casey in 1955 on his view of what the ideal role of a secret service should be in the public service.[41]

Against the backdrop of the Cold War confronting Australia, Brookes believed that ASIS should be the central agency for setting national security and foreign policy. He argued that Australia needed a stronger capacity to deploy economic and psychological warfare against communist-aligned states and that only ASIS was equipped to build this capacity. Brookes was not sparing in his criticism of the wonks in Defence and External Affairs who looked down on intelligence and covert action, saying to Casey: 'It is important to gradually cure the thinking of the toffee-nosed orthodox that there is something queer and "unpleasant" about those willing to forgo the fruits of office and engage in jobs which, intellectually and sometimes physically, might be a little dirty'.[42]

The final straw, however, came in 1957 when Brookes took the extraordinary step of flying to Washington DC to meet with US Secretary of State John Foster Dulles and his brother, the director of the CIA, Allen Dulles, without first engaging with his counterparts in External Affairs and Defence. Among other things, he discussed with the Dulles brothers the sensitive and politically charged issue of potentially using Australia as a base for long-range nuclear missiles. It is ambiguous how much Casey knew or approved of this engagement. It is entirely possible Brookes was dispatched at Casey's insistence to broker this sensitive proposal without the wider knowledge of the bureaucracy.[43]

Regardless, this engagement was seen by Watt and Shedden as an irrecoverable act of roguishness. It appears that at this time Casey also became less favourable towards ASIS's operations. Brookes would explain in later years that Casey appeared to have become terrified that an ASIS agent using diplomatic cover would be exposed and that, as the minister responsible, it would lead to Casey's removal from office.[44]

In May 1957, while Menzies was absent for surgery, a number of Cabinet ministers including Casey met with Shedden and Watt and decided to abolish ASIS.[45] It is not clear if Menzies's absence was directly exploited to expedite their plot. What proceeded was a flurry of activity by ASIO, SIS, and the CIA in Canberra, London, and Washington to prevail upon Menzies and save ASIS at the eleventh hour.

The DG of ASIO, Colonel Charles Spry, an old friend of Brookes, argued vehemently to keep ASIS, but with important restructuring that included the sacking of Brookes as head. This decision troubled Spry greatly as he owed his own appointment to Brookes, who had recommended him to Menzies in 1950.[46]

Meanwhile, Australia's ambassador in DC—Casey's old rival, Percy Spender—was informed by the US State Department of their grave concern at Australia's decision. The CIA lobbied Casey directly against disbandment.

The strongest lobbying came from the SIS. The vice chief of SIS, Sir James Easton, came in person to Canberra for a five-day blitz of Australia's politicians and senior public servants, and he attended to Casey at Berwick. The message from SIS and the CIA was that without ASIS Australia could not expect privileged access to their top secret intelligence.[47]

The intelligence relationship was still recovering from the Soviet infiltration of the 1940s and a trusted Australian secret service along with ASIO were seen as pivotal to rebuilding trust and access for Australia. So it was that Menzies overturned his colleague's decision and ASIS was saved, but not with Brookes at the helm.

The story of Menzies's creation of ASIS reveals a government contending with many of the same issues concerning secret statecraft that Australia's government still grapples with. Covert action and espionage are controversial tools of statecraft for a liberal democracy. For Menzies, they were seen as tools to find influence and advantage in a fast-changing, uncertain, and hostile world dominated by the Cold War. Today, our outlook is not too dissimilar, given events in the South Pacific and further afield.

Menzies leaned heavily on executive authority to create and oversee ASIS, but today the pendulum has swung to legislating these things in more detail. Nevertheless, security agencies with extraordinary powers, like ASIS, are still subject to the judgement and discretion of Australia's most powerful executive leaders, just as was Walsingham's secret service to the Queen in the Elizabethan age.

Recognising ASIS as a tool of British power in the Asia-Pacific and an asset for the Commonwealth also adds complexity to our typical view of post-war Australian foreign policy as being derivative of America.

The modern day separation of intelligence and policy is very far from Brookes's view that the 'clandestine services', as he called them, should be at the centre of policy-making.

Finally, what this study of ASIS's creation shows is that studying Australia's secret statecraft is possible and indeed it is sorely needed because today, like in Menzies's time, hidden tools of shaping and understanding the world are again critical to achieving national advantage in a contested era.

CHAPTER TWELVE

AN INNOVATIVE REALIST: PERCY SPENDER'S ACHIEVEMENTS IN THE LIBERAL TRADITION OF AUSTRALIAN FOREIGN POLICY

David Furse-Roberts[1]

I N HIS BID to return to the prime ministership after eight years in the political wilderness, Robert Menzies delivered his election speech on 10 November 1949. Projecting his blueprint for Australia to a captive Melbourne audience, he set forth the foreign policy agenda he intended to execute once in office. In a nod to both continuity and innovation, Menzies declared:

> We advocate a close co-operation between the Commonwealth and Empire and the United States of America, with which we have and hold in common all those basic faiths and traditions which a free and democratic world so much needs. In our own corner of the world, we have special interests and responsibilities. We shall therefore support and practise a 'good neighbour' policy in the South West Pacific.[2]

Once in government, this foreign policy vision would be given effect by Sir Percy Spender (1897–1985), one of Menzies's most senior Cabinet colleagues. In keeping with the theme of Robert Menzies's 'coming to power' in 1949, this chapter will discuss the keynote achievements of his first minister for external affairs. In particular, it will examine Spender's contribution to formulating the 1950 Colombo Plan, brokering the ANZUS Treaty and negotiating the Japanese Peace Treaty. With Spender helping to erect these three key pillars of Australia's early post-war foreign policy, it will be concluded that he was an innovator and reformer who nonetheless stood in the conservative realist tradition of the Australian centre-right.

After Robert Menzies returned to the prime ministership at the end of 1949, Percy Spender succeeded HV Evatt as minister for external affairs from 19 December 1949 until 26 April 1951. Although his seventeen-month tenure in the portfolio was relatively brief, he was arguably one of Australia's most consequential ministers for foreign affairs since World War II. What made Spender's record as minister noteworthy was not simply his concrete policy achievements, but his successful blend of reformist innovation with conservative realism. To be sure, his attachment to Australia's historic links with the British Commonwealth and United States, together with his preference for bilateral ties over multilateral relationships, placed him squarely in Australia's centre-right tradition of foreign policy. Yet he also brought a far-sighted, reformist approach to deepening Australia's engagement with its own region of the Asia-Pacific. As Professor David Lowe appreciated, the highly travelled Spender had 'a highly developed sense of geopolitics and of change in the Asia-Pacific region'.[3] In an age where Asia was still widely looked upon with suspicion by Australians and their leaders, this distinguished Spender from many of his contemporaries on the conservative side of politics and would form the basis of an enduring legacy.

Equipped with an insight into the region

Percy Claude Spencer was born in the inner Sydney suburb of Darlinghurst on 5 October 1897. Educated at Fort Street High

School, he matriculated to the University of Sydney where he earned a Bachelor of Arts and a Bachelor of Laws with First Class Honours and the University Medal. In 1923, he was admitted to the New South Wales Bar and set up chambers in Phillip Street where he specialised in commercial law and even co-authored a textbook entitled *Company Law and Practice*. In 1935, he took silk and at thirty-eight became the youngest King's Council in the British Empire at that time. Following his successful career at the New South Wales Bar, Spender set his sights on federal politics. Contesting the Sydney seat of Warringah in 1937 as an Independent, he won it convincingly against the sitting United Australia Party (UAP) member, Archdale Parkhill, on ALP preferences.

While Percy Spender was elected to federal Parliament as an Independent, he joined the UAP in 1938 led by Prime Minister Joseph Lyons. With Robert Menzies assuming the prime minister-ship for the first time in 1939, Spender's potential was recognised when he was appointed acting treasurer in November 1939 and then treasurer from March to October 1940. In the Treasury portfolio, he favoured a Keynesian, interventionist approach to managing the economy, which he believed was justified in wartime circum-stances.[4] After serving as treasurer, Spender served as minister for the army from 1940 to 1941 before the Curtin Labor government came to power.

Despite his prominence in Menzies's Cabinet, Spender remained something of a maverick within UAP circles. Not only had he 'rolled' the highly prominent Parkhill, but his individualist streak was evi-dent in his initiative to produce his own series of World War II radio broadcasts to rival those of Menzies's 'Forgotten People' (1942).[5] Moreover, Spender continued to serve on the Advisory War Council even after the UAP decreed its members could no longer serve on the body. His refusal to follow the party directive got him expelled from the UAP in 1944. Thereafter, Spender published his own book on Australian foreign policy in 1944 and in 1945.

For all his independence of thought, Spender was evidently of the view that he was best placed to contribute to policy and public life by remaining a team member of the Australian centre-right once it had a viable political vehicle. Accordingly, he followed Menzies into the new Liberal Party of Australia, birthed at the Albury Conference in December 1944. Despite having supported interventionist measures in wartime, Spender's philosophical instincts were essentially Liberal. In his speeches, he stressed the primacy of the human spirit and focused on the individual and freedom of choice, while expressing an antipathy towards socialism and centralised bureaucratic planning.[6] In particular, he deplored communism as a threat to the survival of freedom, democracy, and Christian civilisation.

With the return of Menzies to the prime ministership in December 1949, Menzies appointed Spender as his minister for external affairs. To better appreciate the innovative contributions Spender made to Australian foreign policy in the early post-war years, it would be helpful to traverse some of the background experiences and influences that informed his outlook on foreign affairs.

Uniquely for a conservative politician of his era, Spender's primary international exposure had been in the region of Asia at a time when his contemporaries, most notably Menzies, typically made their first overseas trips to Britain. During his career at the Bar in the 1920s and 1930s, Spender had essentially discovered Asia as a tourist, visiting Hong Kong, the Philippines, Hawaii, Singapore, Malaysia, and Indonesia. As Lowe noted, 'Spender's cruises as a tourist brought an awareness of geography, and at least some sensitivity to the social and economic conditions in the region'.[7] It was this first-hand experience of Asia that equipped Spender with an insight into the region and the need for a post-war Australia to forge closer ties with its Asia-Pacific neighbours. On his appointment as external affairs minister, Spender made his approach to Australian foreign policy clear on 2 January 1950:

I indicated immediately that my intention was to examine and strengthen Australia's relationship with her neighbours in South East Asia. Australia, I said, should make her primary foreign relations effort in Asia and the Pacific. Geographically Australia is next door to Asia and our destiny as a nation is irrevocably conditioned by what takes place in Asia. This means that our future to an ever-increasing degree depends upon the political stability of our Asian neighbours, upon the economic wellbeing of Asian peoples and upon understanding and friendly relations between Australia and Asia.[8]

This vision guided Spender in his efforts to tailor the 1950 Colombo Plan, calculated to advance Australia's security interests in the region and to address specific areas of need in Asia-Pacific nations. More than any other consideration, Spender's farsighted predisposition to the Asia-Pacific would distinguish him as a reformist innovator on the Australian centre-right.

The other factor that shaped Spender's outlook was of course the advice he received from the Department of External Affairs (DEA). When the Menzies government assumed office from 1949, the department was led by the secretary, Dr John Burton, who had reviewed Australian relations with Asia. Although he did not serve long as secretary following the defeat of the Chifley Labor government, his impact on the trajectory of Australian foreign policy proved far-reaching.[9] One of the key strands of Burton's thinking was 'the growing interdependence of Australia and South East Asia'.[10] Conscious of both the spectre of communism and the shift to decolonisation in the region after the war, Burton envisioned that Australia could play an effective role in establishing 'stable, moderate and friendly governments' in South-East Asia, which would serve as a security buffer between Australia and mainland Asia. Burton held that the best way for Australia to exert political influence was by fostering economic development in the region through expanded trade and the provision of economic and technical assistance.

In addition to the leadership of Burton, the department's vision for engagement with the Asia-Pacific was influenced by the input of William Macmahon Ball, a political scientist based at the University of Melbourne. In 1948, Macmahon Ball led a six-week 'goodwill' tour of Asia, visiting major cities across Indonesia, Malaya, Burma, Thailand, China, Indochina, Singapore and the Philippines. The purpose of the tour was to investigate the region's aid requirements while making contact with senior Asian diplomats.[11] Receptive to their feedback, Macmahon Ball noted that 'Asian leaders recognised their need for outside economic and technical assistance'. Despite misgivings about Australia's restrictive immigration policies, these regional leaders appeared well disposed to Australia, with a relative lack of fear or resentment. Most crucially, Macmahon Ball recognised that the key to cultivating such goodwill lay in targeting Asia's youth, particularly students and vocational trainees. Foreshadowing the purpose behind the Colombo Plan, Macmahon Ball observed that:

> To win the friendship and goodwill of the students and technicians is to win the goodwill of people with great political influence ... Goodwill towards these people must become a national habit, built on respect for the racial sensibilities and national aims of our neighbours.[12]

Such an objective was evidently adopted by Spender as he sought to give effect to it in formulating the strategy and focus of the Colombo Plan. His willingness to be influenced by public service and academic advice was not unique in a Menzies government, which had made the self-conscious choice to hold onto most of the department heads it inherited from Chifley, but it does reflect Spender's open-mindedness compared with some of his more conservative colleagues and successors.

Birthing the Colombo Plan

As innovative as Percy Spender's Colombo Plan initiative was in the early post-war world, it was by no means conceived in a historical

170

vacuum. The notion of Australia developing a regional scheme to provide aid to its neighbours in the Asia-Pacific had been entertained by the preceding Labor governments of John Curtin and Ben Chifley. Serving as minister for external affairs in both, HV 'Doc' Evatt envisioned a more prominent role for Australia in the Asia-Pacific realm. Daniel Oakman noted that after Britain announced India's independence in 1947, Evatt saw his chance to elevate Australia's regional presence.[13] On 26 February 1947, the external affairs minister told Parliament that the time had come for Australia to formulate an 'appropriate regional instrumentality' for South-East Asia and the Western Pacific.[14] Drawing on advice from Burton and other senior DEA officials, Evatt successfully created a consultative regional forum for the Pacific. Launched in February 1947, the South Pacific Commission provided a mechanism for Australia, France, the Netherlands, New Zealand, the United States, and the United Kingdom to promote development in Pacific Island territories.[15] Comprised wholly of Western powers, Evatt's commission did not necessarily represent a forerunner to the Colombo Plan. Nevertheless, it embodied a similar mission and focus to facilitate aid and development in the Asia-Pacific.

Succeeding Evatt in the portfolio from December 1949, Spender inherited the same DEA that had advised his predecessor. Through reviewing departmental briefs, it was evident that Minister Spender likewise adopted Burton's pattern of thinking and brought this to the 1950 Colombo Conference that spawned the Colombo Plan. Just prior to attending Colombo, Spender articulated Australia's plans to give effect to the conference's deliberations:

> We can offer valuable assistance to the newly formed governments of South East Asia ... we can offer advice and assistance in financial and industrial matters, and supply much-needed industrial equipment and finished goods. By concerted action, we ... can help the countries of South East Asia to develop their own democratic institutions and their own economies and thus protect them against

those opportunists and subversive elements which take advantage of changing political situations and low living standards.[16]

Attended by the foreign ministers of eight Commonwealth countries, including Spender, the Colombo Conference of January 1950 aimed to address the economic and security needs of South and South-East Asia in the face of burgeoning communism in the region. The participating nations included Australia, Britain, Canada, New Zealand, South Africa, India, Ceylon (later Sri Lanka), and Pakistan.

Contributing to the conception of the Colombo Plan at the conference and leading the drafting process, Spender proposed that the distribution of food and raw materials be part of the Commonwealth's regional aid program for South and South-East Asia. In addition, Spender called upon the governments represented at Colombo to make credit available for 'essential productive purposes' in the region.[17] The beneficiaries of this aid would be Pakistan, India, and Ceylon to begin with, followed by non-Commonwealth countries, including Nepal, Thailand, the Philippines, and Indonesia. While the conference conceived the Colombo Plan, the initiative itself would assume greater form with the inclusion of more countries and the adoption of new programs, including student exchanges allowing promising students from the region to study at Australian universities.

In Spender's eyes, the Colombo Plan served both a geostrategic and humanitarian purpose. At the same time as helping to fortify Asia-Pacific nations against communism and thereby buttress Australia's own security in the region, Spender envisioned the plan as a 'co-operative effort to raise living standards, combat disease, eradicate pestilence, provide a better life for millions of people and advance their social welfare'—hence strategic realism was mixed with a genuine hope and desire for progress.[18] Another feature of the Colombo Plan was that such aid would be rendered on a 'mutual obligation' basis, whereby 'recipient countries should, to the extent of their ability and means, also be donor countries'. According to Spender, this 'served to promote national self-confidence and good relations between all participating countries' and it arguably fitted in with a traditional centre-right opposition to creating cultures of dependence.[19]

Although Spender's contribution to the conception and early formulation of the Colombo Plan at the 1950 conference was critical, it is important to acknowledge that he was by no means its sole architect. The contributions of the British foreign secretary, Ernest Bevin, were significant as were the inputs of JR Jayewardene, the Ceylonese minister for finance, and Ghulam Muhammad, the representative of Pakistan.[20] Jayewardene, in particular, appreciated the cooperative dynamic of the Colombo Plan, remarking that the purpose 'of raising the living standards of the largest mass of people ever attempted in man's long history' is a task organised 'not by one state alone, but by the co-operative endeavour of a large number of independent States'.[21] Muhammad, meanwhile, proposed that 'a serious and sincere beginning should be made at once in dealing with the problems of the area' if 'hope was to be revived in the hearts of millions in Southeast Asia'.[22] Notwithstanding the collaborative efforts of all participating nations, Spender's role was prominent in being assigned the chief drafter of specific measures for the conference to consider and eventually implement.

The other dimension that Spender brought to the conception of the Colombo Plan was the engagement of the United States as a potential partner, given its geographical position in the Pacific and its close alliance with Britain and the Commonwealth through shared history, values, and wartime experiences. Warmly disposed to Australia's ally in the northern Pacific, Spender spoke regularly of the United States sharing 'a common heritage and way of life'.[23] Accordingly, he appealed to the Americans for their active cooperation in an Asian aid program such as the Colombo Plan. The United States was initially slow to respond to Spencer's overtures, but by November 1950, the Americans decided to associate their own aid proposals with the Colombo Plan Committee.[24] Formally admitted to the Colombo Plan in February 1951, the Americans joined on the condition that the scheme remained informal, exploratory, advisory, and consultative.[25]

Brokering the ANZUS Treaty

The resolve of Spender to engage the United States leads on to his second signature achievement as external affairs minister, where he negotiated the terms of the 1951 ANZUS Treaty. With Spender long recognising the receding influence of Britain in the Pacific, he maintained that some kind of security pact with America would be essential for both Australia's protection and the containment of communism in the Pacific. Addressing the nation in August 1950, Spender proclaimed that: 'Australia must seek to revive the close working association with our American friends which existed during the war. This relationship should, in due course, be given formal expression within the framework of a Pacific Pact'.[26] As with the Colombo Plan initiative, the concept of a security pact in the Pacific was not entirely new, having featured in the foreign policy of Spender's Labor predecessor. In 1944, Evatt had attempted to strengthen Australian and New Zealand strategic and territorial interests in the Pacific with the formation of the bilateral ANZAC Pact, also known as the 'Canberra Pact'. Conceived in the midst of the Pacific theatre of war, the agreement envisaged a 'system of world security' based on a zone of defence 'stretching through the arc of islands north and north-east of Australia to Western Samoa and New Zealand's possessions of the Cook Islands'.[27] The ANZAC Pact differed from the ANZUS Treaty in that it was a non-military alliance which did not include the United States, yet it provided the diplomatic framework for a security partnership between Australia and New Zealand.

Desiring to draw the United States into an enlarged Pacific security pact, Spender's pursuit of the ANZUS Treaty raised the ire of Australia's oldest and closest ally, Britain. Despite the 'special relationship' between the United Kingdom and the United States, the British lamented the ceding of their hegemony in the Pacific to the Americans, and the proposed ANZUS Pact was yet another reminder that its empire was fading. From the UK perspective, ANZUS signalled to the world that Britain was no longer capable of protecting Commonwealth countries in the Pacific and potentially put its colonial possessions of Hong Kong, Singapore, and Malaya in jeopardy.[28] While recognising the US as a benign force that would augur well for peace and security in the region, the UK resented its exclusion from a security pact between its North Atlantic ally and two of its former colonies in the Pacific. The British foreign secretary, Herbert Morrison, remarked that 'we are most certainly a pacific power' and 'it would not have been unwelcome to us if we were included in the proposed pact'.[29]

Given the natural affinity and warmth between Australia and the United States, it would be easy to assume that Spender's brokering of the ANZUS Treaty would have been a forgone conclusion, but this was far from the case. Spender first raised his proposal for a US–Australia–NZ pact with President Harry S Truman in September 1950. Truman was sympathetic to the idea in principle and agreed to discuss it with his secretary of state, Dean Acheson, but the secretary doubted the necessity of such a pact given his view that Australia was not at risk of a hostile attack.[30] The US envoy, John Foster Dulles, was even less receptive and suggested that Australia's security needs could be met simply by America retaining its troops in Japan.

With wartime hostilities still fresh in the public consciousness, this resolution was clearly unacceptable to Spender and eventually a compromise between him, Dulles, and Assistant Secretary of State for Far Eastern Affairs Dean Rusk amounted to an in-principal acceptance of the Australian proposal for a Pacific pact. The other factor that brought the Americans around to accepting Spender's proposal was the entry of Maoist China into the Korean War in October 1950.[31] In February 1951, Dulles arrived in Canberra to discuss the pact proposal with Australians and New Zealanders, and after further negotiations, a draft security treaty was finally agreed, which largely resembled the form of the final ANZUS Pact. In the drafting of its terms, Ralph Harry of the DEA played a key role in Spender's negotiating team. With the US Senate approving the draft, the ANZUS Treaty was signed at a ceremony at the Presidio in San Francisco on 1 September 1951 by Percy Spender and his New Zealand counterpart, Carl Berendsen. Speaking at the ceremony, Australia's external affairs minister remarked on the diplomatic and geostrategic significance of ANZUS:

> The Treaty about to be signed on behalf of the three countries expresses in formal language, the close ties of fellowship, understanding and comradeship between us. But it is much more than that. It marks the first step in the building of the ramparts of freedom in the vast and increasingly important areas of the Pacific Ocean … This Treaty, directed to regional security in the Pacific, fashioned within the framework of the Charter of the United Nations, and dedicated to its high and noble purposes, takes the first step towards what we hope will prove to be an ever widening system of peaceful security in this vital area.[32]

The treaty was planned to enter into force on 29 April 1952. Australia, New Zealand, and the United States were now allied formally and agreed to respond to mutual dangers in the Asia-Pacific region.

Considering the tortuous path of its negotiation, the objections of Britain, and even the initial coolness of Menzies himself, the brokering of the ANZUS Treaty was a credit to the tenacity and skilled diplomacy of Spender. According to Andrew Kelly, the ANZUS Treaty 'was one of the most impressive achievements by any Australian foreign affairs minister'.[33] Shortly after its signing, the long-serving secretary of the Department of Defence, Sir Frederick Shedden, congratulated the minister for external affairs on negotiating the security pact. In a personal letter to Spender, Shedden praised it as 'a great and historic achievement' and remarked that it 'must be a source of immense personal satisfaction to you as the negotiator of it'.[34] Reflecting on his lengthy prime ministership, Menzies saw ANZUS in a similar light 'as one of the major achievements of his administration' and 'the keystone of our Pacific structure'.[35] With Spender appreciating the merits of ANZUS long before Menzies, it underscored the degree to which the external affairs minister was arguably more disposed to the US than his prime minister, positioning Spender closer to the famously pro-American outlook of Harold Holt than that of his anglophile predecessor in The Lodge. It also speaks to Spender's optimism, which balanced and complemented his realism; he could see the potential in a 'superstructure built on a foundation of jelly', even when others had their doubts.

Negotiating the Japanese Peace Treaty

Closely related to Spender's brokering of the ANZUS Treaty was his negotiation of the US-initiated Japanese Peace Treaty of 1951. Desiring to bring a post-war Japan into the Western alliance against communism, President Truman sought to mend wartime hostilities and negotiate a peace settlement with the Japanese. As Spender pointed out, the notion of a peace treaty with the Japanese was first stressed by General Douglas MacArthur in February 1947.[36] The Americans were keen to forge a peace treaty with the former enemy for strategic and geopolitical reasons as well as diplomatic goodwill. With the onset of the Cold War giving rise to a realignment of Western powers against the Soviet Union, the US appreciated the strategic importance of having a West-aligned Japan onside. Dulles claimed that if the Soviet Union gained control of Japan and Germany, the chances of peace, or victory, in the event of a future war, would be greatly diminished.[37] With the interests of the Pacific in mind, Dulles also said that the US was keen to hear the views of Australia, the Philippines, and Burma on the peace treaty and any concerns about Japanese rearmament.

On his visit to Australia, Dulles raised America's Japanese peace proposal with Spender in the same Canberra meeting of February 1951 that produced the draft ANZUS Pact. Reflecting Australian sentiment at the time, Spender had reservations about the peace proposal, particularly its lack of guarantees against Japanese rearmament in the proposed peace terms.[38] From Australia's perspective, the treaty needed to contain restrictive provisions against Japanese rearmament as well as long-range economic controls and conditions pertaining to atomic energy, industrial war potential, and the prohibition of military forces as distinct from purely internal police.[39] According to Spender, it was Australia's view in 1950 that the risk of a remilitarised Japan was too real to be disregarded for the sake of any advantages of a 'soft peace treaty' without any safeguards.[40] The external affairs minister was supported by the Australian high commissioner in London, Eric Harrison, who likewise warned of the temptation for Australia to 'slip into an easy treaty'.[41] With the possibility of Japan's military resurgence at the forefront of Australian leaders' minds, Harrison held that Australia needed security against future Japanese aggression.

As far as Spender was concerned, Australia's position was clear: 'we had to do all we could to insist that Japan would not be allowed unrestricted freedom to re-arm'.[42] Yet despite the insistence of Australia, the Americans were unmoved, possibly fearing that if Japan were to be subject to the kind of restrictions proposed by Australia, it could erode the goodwill of the North Asian nation towards such a treaty. Given, however, that the negotiations of the ANZUS Pact and Japanese Peace Treaty were interlinked, Spender was pragmatic enough to view the peace treaty in the broader context of procuring Australia's security in the Pacific through ANZUS, noting that:

> ... a Pacific Pact would make Australian policy on a peace treaty
> with Japan less difficult to handle. There was, I stressed, a real fear
> in Australia, of the people of Japan again falling into the hands of

a militaristic clique bent upon aggression. But if Australia could rely upon America, the risk would be much reduced and public misgivings abated.

In essence, the shortcomings of the peace treaty could be outweighed by the benefits of procuring a security pact with the US in the Pacific.[43] Accordingly, Spender assured Dulles that Australia would give its assent to the Japanese Peace Treaty, and Spender represented Australia at its signing in San Francisco on 8 September 1951.

Unlike the ANZUS Treaty, Australia's decision to support the Japanese Peace Treaty was contentious and went against domestic public opinion. The ALP Opposition voted against it and in a Morgan opinion poll, 67 per cent of Australians also opposed a peace treaty with Japan.[44] Spender was not insensitive to Australia's national interest and in negotiations with Dulles, he suggested that Japan be subject to rearmament controls that could help give Australians peace of mind.[45] The US declined to adopt Australia's suggestions, yet Spender was a realist, who accepted the peace treaty as a necessary step to buttressing the peace and security of the post-war world. Indeed, Australia's signing of the Japanese treaty was a decision Spender did not live to regret. In his 1972 memoirs, *Politics and a Man*, the former external affairs minister described the treaty as 'perhaps the wisest and most magnanimous accorded [to] a defeated nation in modern times'.[46] He appreciated the wisdom of Dulles, who desired no repeat of the mistakes of Versailles in 1919 which had embittered a vanquished foe in Germany. In contrast to the thinking behind the post-World War I treaty, Spender agreed with Dulles that a 'harsh repressive peace would only light the fires of vengeance that could be no foundation of a stable peace'. To avoid any future prospect of embittering Japan, Spender believed it was eminently wise to offer peace terms that the Japanese could accept with dignity. With Dulles's farsighted attitude towards the former enemy vindicated with the emergence of an irenic and constructive post-war Japan, Spender credited the Japanese Peace Treaty as

'Dulles' greatest achievement'.[47] However, it should also be noted that the speed with which Spender made the Australian government acquiesce to Dulles's plan arguably played an important role in fostering the goodwill that would lead to the 1957 Australia–Japan Commerce Agreement—hence it was a Spender achievement as well.

An innovator yet a realist

Spender's contribution to the Colombo Plan, ANZUS, and the Japanese Peace Treaty reflected the broader view of the Menzies government that Australia's post-war focus needed to be on the Asia-Pacific. To this end, Spender's priority was forging closer ties with both the United States and Australia's neighbours in South-East Asia but in a way that would not detract from Australia's historical ties with Britain and the Commonwealth. After setting forth his vision to engage more closely with the Asia-Pacific, he assured Parliament on 9 March 1950 that:

> The British Commonwealth can be not only an organisation with which we feel proud to be associated with but an instrument for our security and prosperity. If the Commonwealth can be kept together and work together, and can cooperate as a Commonwealth with the United States and Western Europe, it means an overwhelming force in support of peace.[48]

Foreshadowing the thinking behind AUKUS several decades later, Spender favoured a working alliance between the US and the British Commonwealth of which Australia would be an integral partner with close ties to each.

Pivoting Australia's foreign policy towards the Asia-Pacific region so strategically in the aftermath of World War II, Spender was well ahead of domestic popular sentiment when Eurocentrism and antipathy towards Asia still lingered. In 1950, when Asian cultures still appeared alien and exotic to most Australians, Spender was resolved to advance mutual understanding between Australia and its Asia-Pacific neighbours. Yet in his cooperation with the US and the British Commonwealth, he also built on a long tradition of Australian foreign policy dating back to Alfred Deakin and the first decade of Federation. As prime minister, Deakin was loyal to the British Empire but also made overtures to the United States, helping to convince President Theodore Roosevelt to send the US Navy's Great White Fleet to visit Australian shores in 1908.

Thus, while Spender was an innovator and reformer, his approach to foreign policy was in the conservative realist tradition of the Australian centre-right. In contrast to the more multilateralist approach of his Labor predecessor, HV Evatt, Spender was somewhat circumspect towards the United Nations and favoured the development of bilateral relationships, believing that such partnerships with the United States and the British Commonwealth could better serve Australia's national interests and objectives.[49] In his landmark 'Statement on Foreign Policy' speech to Parliament on 9 March 1950, Spender had cautioned:

> Let us recognise how fatal it would be for Australia's future if our foreign policy rested solely on an affirmation of faith in the United Nations. There is a distinction between wholeheartedly supporting its principles—which we do—and believing that all its members will find in the foreseeable future common agreement on the application of those principles.[50]

In what would become even more apparent in the ensuing decades of the UN's operation, he was attuned to the reality that not all member states would abide by its principles, however agreeable these were. Accordingly, he believed that Australia could not rely upon the UN alone and must foster robust bilateral relations, holding that 'where the United Nations is manifestly unable to protect Australian interests, it is the duty of the Government to follow simultaneously a policy of making supplementary arrangements among those we know to be our friends'.[51] To this end, his contribution to Australia's forging of closer ties with both the US through ANZUS and

Asia-Pacific neighbours via the Colombo Plan defined his legacy as external affairs minister. Importantly, as a senior member of Menzies's first Cabinet after World War II, Spender's efficacy in the External Affairs portfolio also reflected the considerable freedom Menzies was willing to afford his ministers to innovate and drive government policy.

CHAPTER THIRTEEN

OVERSEAS STUDENTS IN AUSTRALIA: BEFORE AND AFTER THE COLOMBO PLAN

Lyndon Megarrity[1]

O NE OF THE myths of Australian history is that the overseas student program in Australia began in 1951 with the Colombo Plan.[2] In fact, Australia was a destination for overseas students from the early twentieth century onwards, when the pros and cons of expanding the international student presence began to be a part of the national conversation. Such conversations became more insistent in the post-war period as Asian nationalism transformed the geopolitical situation and Australia's place in the world. In many ways the Colombo Plan student program was a continuation of the sponsored student schemes developed during the 1940s. This chapter will contextualise the Colombo Plan student program within the broader history of Australia's involvement with international education. It will also show how the Menzies government expanded the sponsored overseas program through the Colombo Plan and was able to strategically capitalise on the presence of Asian scholarship students in a way that the preceding Chifley government could not or would not.

Overseas students in Australia: The first four decades

At the dawn of Federation, at least some non-European students were residing in Australia. They included the children of Chinese, Japanese, and Indian merchants, storekeepers and farmers, along with those of Pacific Island labourers. Early Commonwealth legislation, however, reduced the number of non-Europeans gaining access to the Australian education system. Most Pacific Islanders were deported and a dictation test for prospective non-European immigrants was introduced to deter Asian migration.[3] Temporary non-European visitors were nonetheless allowed into Australia under the category of students. The majority of students arriving in the first half of the twentieth century were from Asia, but some Pacific Islanders, notably from Tonga and Nauru, gained entry, mostly studying at secondary level.[4]

The first formal policy decision on overseas students was the Watson Labor government's 1904 decision to relax regulations relating to the entry of Indian and Japanese merchants, students, and tourists. The new regulations allowed Japanese and Indian visitors to enter Australia for educational purposes. They were exempt from the dictation test but had to apply for a certificate of exemption from this test after twelve months.[5]

The 1904 regulations for Japanese and Indian students were widely publicised, but responsible ministers remained tight-lipped about the fact that from around this point onwards, they were also quietly allowing temporary entry for Chinese students as well.[6] Wanting to avoid alienating the small but assertive Australian–Chinese business community, but also committed to the White Australia Policy, which was marked by anti-Chinese prejudices, successive Commonwealth administrations found it difficult to develop a cohesive Chinese student policy. This is reflected in the 1912 comments of Josiah Thomas, external affairs minister in the Fisher Labor government:

> When I first came here [to the External Affairs Department] I found that quite a number of young Chinese had been permitted to come to Australia in order to go to the schools ... Most of them were young children from 11 to 14 years of age, and the idea was that they would remain in Australia for three or four years, and then return to China ... but the thing began to grow until it looked like assuming large proportions. Then I decided to shut down on it.[7]

The Fisher government subsequently introduced regulations for students in which Chinese students were only eligible to enter Australia if they were aged between seventeen and twenty-four, and could only remain in the country for six years.[8] By 1920, however, the age restrictions had been removed and students could stay as long as they needed to complete their studies.[9] As Home and Territories Minister George Pearce noted, it was recognition that:

> There are good grounds for believing that ... Chinese students now being trained in Australia will play a prominent part in promoting trade between China and Australia in the future. If the Commonwealth Government decided to discontinue altogether the concessions granted to students, such action would ... react detrimentally on the trade relations which business men in Australia are now endeavouring to build up.[10]

Such views mirrored comments made by Asian and Western observers over several decades.[11] Commentators such as the 1930s Chinese Consulate-General Dr Pao urged Australia to reap the potential economic benefits of a policy of generously encouraging overseas students to enter the country:

> Dr Pao said that America and England had long realised that Chinese students returning to their own countries were potential trade ambassadors. Australians, he said, should realise their best friends in the East are the Chinese who have returned from Australia.[12]

While Australia's exports to China had reached a value of £1 973 862 in 1934/35,[13] the Commonwealth government was not inclined during the inter-war period to prioritise Asian overseas student policy; it fluctuated between restricting and loosening conditions of entry based on age limits.[14] It is unlikely that there were more than a few hundred mainland and ethnic Chinese studying in Australia in any given year during the 1920s and 1930s.[15] In any case, Australia remained economically and culturally focused on its ties with Britain, and Commonwealth politicians presumably wished to minimise suspicion that they were not taking the White Australia Policy seriously.

Aside from setting and enforcing immigration conditions, Australian governments had little practical engagement with non-European overseas students. However, during the inter-war period, some church-based groups filled in the gap. One such example was Miss Sears of the Presbyterian Women's Mission Union, who ran a school for Chinese nationals in Little Bourke Street, Melbourne, emphasising English language and singing.[16] Subsequently, the University of Western Australia offered at least one specified scholarship for an Indian student to study Agricultural Economics, with the successful candidate for 1939, SM Thacore, selected by the Australian Christian Movement.[17]

However, it was Australia's responsibility for administering Nauru on behalf of the British Phosphate Commission which may have begun the Commonwealth's shift from regulating overseas student entry towards actively influencing the direction of the overseas student program. From 1923, the Australian administration financed the entire provision of education for Nauru people from phosphate revenue, using some of these funds to send a small number of islanders to Australia to undergo formal training in teaching, wireless telegraphy, book-keeping, and other work during the inter-war period.[18] Scout Commissioner Harold Hurst hosted several of these trainees in the 1930s and 1940s while they completed their studies at Geelong educational institutions.[19] Subsequently, when the Pacific war postponed the repatriation to Nauru of Islanders who had studied in Geelong, Commonwealth officials became involved with their welfare.[20]

Significantly, Austin Bernicke (ca 1908–77) of Nauru was selected by the Australian administration in Nauru to become the first Pacific Islander to attend university in Australia. He is likely to have received official funding and support.[21] After studying at Melbourne University between 1931 and 1934, Bernicke returned to his homeland without completing his degree. He gained work as a pathologist and later superintendent at Nauru's General Hospital. Bernicke was also heavily involved with Nauruan politics from the 1950s until his death in 1977.[22]

Australian government policy towards overseas students before World War II was ad hoc and reactive. However, much of the rationale for maintaining an overseas student presence, including international goodwill, promoting potential trade benefits, and supporting the creation of elites within developing countries was already present, although only faintly articulated.

Overseas student policy during the Chifley years

The Chifley Labor government of 1945 to 1949 grasped the geopolitical significance of emerging Asian nationalism and paid increasing attention to the diplomatic aspects of the international student presence. There were only about 300 non-European students in Australia by 1947, partly a reflection of overcrowding in Australian tertiary institutions as returned service personnel retrained for new careers.[23] Despite misgivings about limited tertiary facilities, the Chifley years saw the modest beginnings of Australia's active involvement in administering overseas student scholarship schemes.[24]

Influenced by the British Council[25] and the United Nations Educational, Scientific, and Cultural Organization (UNESCO), the Department of External Affairs organised two major scholarship schemes during the 1940s. These scholarships were designed to spread goodwill towards Australia within Asia.

The most important Chifley government scholarship scheme was the South-East Asian Fellowship Scheme, begun in 1949. In order to partially meet its commitment to UNESCO's worldwide program of post-war reconstruction assistance, the Australian government announced in 1948 that it would spend £60 000 on scholarships.[26] Under the South-East Asian Fellowship scheme, Australia committed itself to providing short-term training in Australian institutions for students from war-torn South-East Asian countries. The emphasis was not so much on gaining qualifications; rather, the scholarships were designed to assist with the development of skills which would be of use to national development and reconstruction.[27] The fellowship came to an end in 1956 after training fifty-seven students.[28]

Apart from the UNESCO-inspired fellowship scheme, the Australian government also initiated a small international scholarship on its own behalf. Cabinet decided in 1948 to award three scholarships a year to South-East Asian students to study in Australian universities. The total cost was to be £5000 per annum. As the prime minister stated:

> It was considered that the provisions of opportunities in Australia for the students concerned would give further practical evidence of the goodwill of the Australian people towards the peoples of the countries concerned, such as India, Pakistan … [and] Indonesia.[29]

It can be strongly argued that these two post-war scholarship schemes were the 'trial run' for Commonwealth educational policies and practices now traditionally associated with the subsequent Colombo Plan sponsorship program of the 1950s. Like the Colombo Plan, for example, the students and their fields of study were nominated by the country receiving the aid. While the Commonwealth's education officials do not appear to have been as heavily engaged in monitoring South-East Asian scholarship and fellowship holders as they later did for Colombo Plan students, they nevertheless provided some support. Commonwealth Office of Education officers assisted scholars by meeting them on their arrival, arranging accommodation, helping them settle in and making themselves available should the student require further advice.[30] The Australian government was also quick to respond to the demands of scholars to learn more about Australia to help them adjust to the new environment. In February 1950, all twenty UNESCO-related scholarship holders attended a Summer School at Sydney University, in which they learned about 'Australia's Rural Background' and 'Australia's Concepts of Standards of Living and Social Services' through lectures, discussions, films, and visits to museums and other institutions. This intensive approach to learning about Australian culture was adopted, in a modified format, for arriving Colombo Plan students during the 1950s and 1960s.[31]

In the 1940s, however, Asian irritation with the device of using scholarships as a diplomatic gesture while firmly keeping the immigration door shut overshadowed publicity given to Australian educational aid. The Chifley government's attempt to portray itself as a friend to emerging Asian nations was frustrated by Immigration Minister Arthur Calwell, who interpreted the White Australia Policy with all the finesse of 'a buffalo in a china shop'.[32] During 1948, for example, fourteen Malays and Indonesians were deported from Australia after living in the country since World War II, and in some cases, marrying Australian citizens. Such incidents provoked a rush of negative publicity in Singapore, Malaya, and Thailand.[33] Many Australian newspapers also embarrassed the Chifley government by putting a human face to Asian individuals facing deportation, such as North Queensland potato farmer Frank Jang, whose white farming colleagues lobbied the federal government and Opposition to allow him to stay.[34] Although no friend of Asian scholarship schemes, Australian Country Party leader Arthur Fadden neatly highlighted the ineffectiveness of the South-East Asian Scholarship scheme as a means of expressing Australian regional commitment: 'As these coloured scholarship holders will be forever debarred from re-entering Australia by the operation of the white Australia policy, the goodwill value of this gesture will be completely nullified'.[35]

The Colombo Plan

Nevertheless, when the Menzies government came into power, it retained the former government's commitment to sponsoring overseas students. Furthermore, Menzies's minister for external affairs, Percy Spender, played a major part in initiating a new British Commonwealth aid scheme, which included a generous scholarship component: the Colombo Plan. Spender's development of the Colombo Plan initiative was no doubt influenced by the attitudes and internal discussions of major public servants, many of whom served both the Chifley and Menzies administrations, including William John Weeden (Commonwealth Office of Education) and John Burton (Department of External Affairs).[36] Indeed, momentum to expand the sponsored student program had been growing since the late 1940s. Involved with Australia's official support of UNESCO from a very early stage, Weeden claimed in later life that one of his achievements was 'the five UNESCO scholarships, which Chifley agreed to, and which led to the Colombo Plan with many [scholarships] because it was the Australian [UNESCO] delegation that said, "Why don't we offer scholarships between Commonwealth countries?"'[37]

It is likely, however, that the UNESCO delegation and the Department of External Affairs were independently thinking along similar lines. In 1947, when a letter to the prime minister from the United Kingdom high commissioner asking if Siamese (Thai) students could be trained in Australia was sent to External Affairs for its opinion, the secretary of External Affairs, John Burton, argued that

> The proposal for Commonwealth Scholarships should not stop short at Siam ... no such scholarships should be granted unless Australia is also able to offer similar scholarships initially to India, the Republic of Indonesia and the Philippines and, perhaps later, to certain other Asiatic countries.[38]

By December 1949, External Affairs was arguing that 'Australia should give whatever political and economic assistance she can to help maintain stability in South-East Asia and increase resistance to Communism',[39] and, by implication, the generous provision of scholarships was a potentially useful part of this objective. Through educational assistance to Asia:

> Australia can earn valuable goodwill and at the same time foster a better understanding of Australian conditions and ways of life ... All countries of the [South-East Asian] region are taking full advantage of the present limited programme of Commonwealth Government scholarships and fellowships tenable in Australian training institutions ... this programme could usefully be extended and greater numbers of trainees accepted[.][40]

It is likely that such advice influenced Spender's ideas when he met with other Commonwealth foreign ministers in Colombo during January 1950. Partly as a result of Spender's leadership at this conference, the Colombo Plan for Co-operative Economic Development in South and South-East Asia was established by the British Commonwealth to assist with the economic development of member nations in Asia. Commencing operations in 1951, the plan also involved non-Commonwealth countries such as the United States, Vietnam, and Indonesia. Aid was given through a process of bilateral agreements between the donor and recipient.[41]

In sharp contrast to the Chifley era, the Menzies administration was able to successfully promote itself as an educational donor of goodwill within the Asian region. The new government symboli-cally overturned a number of Calwell's notorious decisions on the deportation of individual Asian immigrants such as Frank Jang and Lorenzo Gamboa, earning the Liberal administration some respect within South and South-East Asia.[42] The incoming Liberal regime was hardly enlightened in relation to racial matters, but perhaps its 'newness' as a political force meant that it was not so associated with the 1940s immigration scandals and could therefore achieve more through international education policy under the Colombo Plan.

Between 1951 and 1965, Australia spent over £58.5 million on the Colombo Plan, including over £17 million on technical assistance such as student scholarships. A total of 5908 students were accepted to study in Australia under the scheme during this time.[43] Thanks partly to the intense publicity devoted to it by both the Australian government and the press, the student program was the component of the Colombo Plan which received the most public attention.[44]

Numerous former Colombo Plan students subsequently obtained government leadership positions, but it is hard to quantify the influence their time in Australia had on the regional outlook of Asian leadership groups.[45] It can be argued, however, that the Colombo Plan was one means by which the perception of Australia as a British outpost near Asia became seriously challenged. For instance, the positive experiences of Colombo Plan scholars and trainees assisted in making Australians appear less racist in the eyes of Asia's professional and official elite. Walter Crocker, official secretary of the Australian High Commission in India, told External Affairs Minister Richard Casey in 1953 that part of the value of the Colombo Plan was that students who arrived in Australia anticipating that they would encounter extreme racial prejudice were powerfully and pleasantly surprised by the 'friendly reception they have met with there [in Australia]'.[46] Such beneficial people-to-people encounters may have helped smooth the waters for the increased Australian trade with Asia over the next few decades. The rapid growth in private Asian students studying in Australia during the 1950s and 1960s may also have been partly inspired by positive Colombo Plan publicity.[47]

Further, despite repeated complaints regarding the reputed anti-Asian prejudices of landladies and others,[48] by 1954 there was a growing domestic acceptance of the Colombo Plan as an example of Australian generosity of spirit towards the Asian region. This was exemplified in a letter to *The Age* by Mrs MG Swinburne of Surrey Hills in Melbourne:

> It has been our privilege to give part-board to three Asians who are here studying under ... the Colombo Plan ... We find that to know these students better is to regret very much that we are debarred by our own immigration law from any chance of having them as our real next-door neighbours.[49]

The experience of hosting temporary Asian visitors helped Australians make the transition from White Australia principles to a broader acceptance of multiculturalism as racialist immigration policies were dismantled from 1966 onwards.[50] In 1954, however, there was still a long way to go down this path. The Menzies government remained vocally supportive of the White Australia Policy, which Immigration Minister Harold Holt praised as having 'played an important part in the building up of the Australian nation'.[51] Furthermore, a report of a 1954 official ceremony farewelling one group of Indonesian Colombo Plan students and welcoming a new group highlighted the limitations of Australia's engagement with Asia in a way which still resonates today:

> Two of the visitors, in perfect English, acknowledge their recognition in speeches well above the average standard of those commonly heard in the adjacent House of Representatives, and every one spoke sufficient English to make his way quite comfortably in Australia. By contrast, not a single Australian present was able to speak to the guests in their own tongue, although the majority were associated with the working of the Colombo Plan.[52]

Conclusion

Around twenty thousand Colombo Plan scholars and trainees studied in Australia between 1951 and the first half of the 1980s, by which time the Australian government was prioritising other aid scholarship schemes.[53] The official rationale for the phasing out of

Colombo Plan scholarships is unclear, but it is likely that as the British Commonwealth became less significant as a focal point for Australian foreign policy, the Colombo Plan may have seemed an anachronism at a time of increased Australian nationalism.[54] Scholarship programs to assist Asian and Pacific scholars to study in Australia have remained a significant part of Australian education aid, and they still reflect the ideals of the Colombo Plan—chiefly, the advancement of goodwill and diplomacy.

Furthermore, in 2014, Australia's sponsored overseas student program was complemented by the nostalgically named New Colombo Plan (NCP), which supported 'Australian undergraduates to study and undertake internships' in the Indo-Pacific.[55] Introduced by a Coalition government, the NCP has continued under the Labor government elected in 2022. According to the Department of Foreign Affairs and Trade, 'This two-way educational exchange [that is, the NCP and sponsored overseas students studying in Australia] underpins Australia's bilateral relations with the region ... by building enduring institutional and people-to-people links'.[56] Fine words. But the notion of youthful Australian and Indo-Pacific scholars as goodwill ambassadors is much less prominently featured by the Australian media than it was at the height of the Colombo Plan. Since the Commonwealth began to markedly reduce funding to universities in the 1990s, the role of fee-paying international students in maintaining the financial health of the higher education sector has received excessive public attention. The challenge for today's politicians, educators, and policy-makers is to move beyond this narrow market vision and create an inspiring policy narrative which stresses the potential goodwill and cultural enrichment that overseas students can bring.[57]

The Colombo Plan student program was one of the remarkable success stories of the Menzies years. It contributed to the economic development of emerging Asian nations and remains a potent symbol of Australia's shift towards regional engagement with Asia during the latter half of the twentieth century. But it did not emerge from a vacuum. Australia has had an overseas student program since the 1900s, and the ideas of regional goodwill and the development of trade links through hosting international students were being discussed by commentators at an early stage in the nation's history. However, it was only the rise of Asian nationalism after World War II that forced the Australian government to commit more seriously to regional engagement, and one of those ways was through sponsoring overseas students. The Chifley government's modest scholarship schemes set up the policy framework which was later used for managing Colombo Plan students arriving in Australia. However, Labor's goodwill message conveyed through its scholarship schemes was drowned out by negative publicity surrounding postwar deportations. By contrast, the Menzies government was more discreet in its continued support for a White Australia, and by rapidly expanding the sponsored overseas student program in the 1950s and 1960s, it gained positive publicity both at home and abroad.

APPENDIX: AUSTRALIA'S GREATEST PRIME MINISTER?

Keynote speech delivered to the Robert Menzies Institute Second Annual Conference 2022

The Hon George Brandis KC

LET ME BEGIN by acknowledging the work of the Robert Menzies Institute, and in particular its director, Georgina Downer, in perpetuating the legacy of the statesman it describes as 'Australia's greatest prime minister'.

Was Menzies our greatest prime minister? Of course, the greatness of historical figures is a subjective judgement, and when the figure is a political leader, inevitably a largely partisan one as well: few Labor voters would call Menzies our greatest prime minister, just as few Liberals would award that accolade to such Labor heroes as, say, Gough Whitlam or Paul Keating.

There are *some* objective metrics, the most obvious being longevity. On that score, as we all know, Menzies wins hands down: eighteen years, 163 days, across two terms as prime minister: the first brief and unsuccessful, the second—slightly more than sixteen years—by far the longest of any holder of the office. To put that length of service into historical perspective, by the time he retired on Australia Day 1966, Menzies had been prime minister for slightly more than a quarter of the entire history to date of the Australian Commonwealth. He was one of only five prime ministers—the others being Cook (very briefly), Fisher, Hughes, and Chifley—to have led the nation during both peace and world war. By the time he left office, he was the senior statesman of the Commonwealth—in an era when the Commonwealth meant much more than it does today.

Of course, longevity is not the test of greatness. However, it does tell us at least two important things. First, no political leader in a democratic system remains in office for such a long time without winning a lot of elections, and on the measure of electoral victories alone, Menzies was certainly Australia's most successful politician.[1] His score—one loss (1946), seven wins (at every election between 1949 and 1963)—would be the envy of any sporting team, let alone any political leader. As a result of his stupendous electoral success, his time in government exceeded that of all but one other political leader[2] in a comparable parliamentary democracy in the twentieth century. And in non-Westminster democracies as well: he was in office longer than any American president, French president, German chancellor, Indian prime minister, or Japanese prime minister of the last century. Only dictators who do not have to seek a periodic electoral mandate—and only a small number of them—led their nations for longer.

Secondly, the perspective which longevity gives enables us to get a better *sense* of a political leader, for the simple reason that the longer their time in office, the greater opportunity they have to shape the direction of the nation. On the other side of the coin, since politics is a uniquely hazardous occupation, the longer a leader serves, the better we are able to judge how they handle themselves during times when the political waters become choppy.

In the case of the long post-war Menzies government, its longevity coincided with a period of stability and economic prosperity unmatched in Australia's history. Perhaps 'coincided' is the wrong word, because there was unquestionably a causal relationship between policy and prosperity.

Before I turn to the actual achievements of the Menzies governments, let me say something about the man himself. Because, in his prime, he seemed the very embodiment of the Australian 'establishment', it is often forgotten how humble Menzies's origins were: the classic scholarship boy, who came to Melbourne from the tiny rural town of Jeparit. In fact, it is arguable that his background was more modest than that of any other Liberal prime minister, and of some Labor ones as well—Whitlam's father, for instance, was the Commonwealth crown solicitor.

Menzies enjoyed a brilliant career as a law student—he studied in the very room, then the Law Faculty library, where we meet today—which culminated in the Supreme Court Prize for 1918, which was (and still is) awarded to the most outstanding law graduate of the year. His exceptional intellectual ability produced early success at his chosen calling, the Bar. Famously, in 1920, at the age of just twenty-five, without a senior counsel to lead him and facing the cream of Australia's most senior barristers, he won the *Engineers' Case*[3]—by far the most important constitutional decision of the High Court in the first half of the twentieth century. (This was the case that decided that, in interpreting the Constitution, the Commonwealth heads of legislative power in s. 51 should be given their full meaning, free of implied limitations on their scope upon which earlier High Courts, with more sensitivity to the rights of the states, had insisted. It led to a significant rebalancing of the Federation towards the central government.)

After his victory in *Engineers,* Menzies's career at the Bar was made, and in the 1920s and early 1930s he appeared in many of the most important cases in the Supreme Court of Victoria, the High Court, and the Privy Council. The leader of the Victorian Bar in those years, Owen Dixon KC, chose him as his preferred junior and made him his protégé. Dixon is said to have despaired at Menzies's decision to abandon the Bar for politics (although, as his diaries reveal, that did not stop him feasting on the juicy political gossip which the young Menzies would share with him in his chambers). When, in 1952, Menzies appointed Dixon as Chief Justice of the High Court, it was not lost on any intelligent observer that this was an office which Menzies, had he not chosen the political path, may well himself have filled.

No other Australian prime minister enjoyed such an illustrious career before they entered Parliament, and no other prime minister—or political leader—comes close to Menzies intellectually. The claim is sometimes made that HV Evatt was his equal or better, though those who make that claim are not in a position to judge. When I was young, I was befriended by Sir John Kerr, who knew both men very well—was, indeed, at one time Evatt's protégé—and I remember asking him about the two. He told me, quite emphatically, that there was no doubt that Menzies was the better lawyer and had the better mind.[4]

So it is surely an aspect of Menzies's claim to greatness that he was—I would submit, by a very wide margin—the most *talented* Australian ever to have occupied the position of prime minister. His talents were not just as one of the most—arguably *the* most—brilliant barristers of his generation. His erudition beyond the law, the massive range of his reading and scholarship, particularly in literature and history—which the thousands of volumes of Menzies's personal library, of which this Institute is the custodian, bespeak—is evidence of that (although it is possible that his intellectual breadth in fields beyond the law was matched by Alfred Deakin).

One little-known fact about Menzies—as is evident from his library—was his devotion to poetry. He was actually himself given to the occasional composition of verse, but it must be said that it seldom rose above the level of witty doggerel, often delivered in after-dinner speeches to his beloved Savage Club. And we have it from Heather Henderson's memoir of her father that, the evening before he was to give a major speech, it was his habit to read not government briefing papers, but poetry—to get the rhythms running through his mind, the better to find the right cadence on the morrow.

All of that being said, neither precocious professional accomplishment as a barrister, nor a mind deeply steeped in history and well furnished with the best literature, are enough of themselves to make a great prime minister—or even a good one. For that, the ultimate and really the only test is what is achieved in the furnace of politics. And on that score alone, Menzies's claim to greatness is, in my view, secure.

As we know, he single-handedly fashioned the Liberal Party from the wreckage of non-Labor politics in the early 1940s, and led it for twenty-one years, all but the first five of them in government. In doing so, he created Australia's most successful political party: an 'election winning machine', as my former colleague Christopher Pyne once described it, with nineteen victories out of thirty elections, including seven of the last ten. No other Australian political leader has ever done what Menzies did: built, effectively from the ground up, the structure of one side of politics.

Great though the creation of the Liberal Party was as a purely political achievement, it was essentially a mechanistic one. It is to what he achieved in government—the legacy he left—that one ultimately must look in appraising Menzies' political career. Although the focus of this conference is on the period between 1943 and 1954, for the purposes of this keynote I want to take a longer view, of the whole period of the Menzies governments, but concentrate in particular on the importance of the election of 1949.

There are many signal achievements, the exploration of some of which are the subject of detailed discussion in the papers we will enjoy over the coming days. Let me mention just a few of the big ones: the ANZUS Treaty of 1951, one of the world's longest-enduring alliances and the bedrock of Australian security for more than seventy years; the development of Canberra as a great capital city, a project in which he took particular pride, most of which took place during his tenure and with his guidance; the Colombo Plan, one of the most important diplomatic achievements of the 1950s and beyond, which was foundational to our engagement with our Asian neighbours in the post-colonial world; and the significant expansion of Australian universities, following the Murray Report of 1957. Menzies's passion for expanding educational opportunity is evident as well in the Commonwealth Scholarship scheme, which for the first time opened the doors of our universities, on a meritocratic and competitive basis, to working-class and many more middle-class kids (like Menzies himself); and—again in the field of education—the extension, from 1964, of Commonwealth funding (in the language of the time, 'state aid') to non-government schools, the vast majority of which were relatively poor Catholic schools. This latter was more than merely a significant advance in education policy: at a time when Australia was still significantly divided on religious and sectarian lines—and as someone who attended one such Catholic school in the 1960s, I remember it—it was a massive statement, coming from a political party at that time dominated by Protestants, of what we would today call 'inclusion'.

Every prime minster (well, almost every prime minister) can point to a list of achievements. Menzies's achievements were on a scale and of a significance more lasting, more impressive, than most. But there is something deeper, which I think is the real key to Menzies' claim to greatness. It is the *kind* of society he created in the years after World War II. Some, though by no means all, subsequent governments made important changes—Whitlam's extension of social democratic policies, Hawke and Keating's internationalisation of the economy, Howard's reforms to the tax system—but they were adjustments of, and improvements to, the society Menzies created: a property-owning democracy, undergirded by a social safety net, structured with ladders of opportunity, both aspirational and egalitarian.

There are some—particularly historians of the Left—who mock those years of peace and prosperity as a kind of lotus land of quiescence and unadventurous mediocrity. Commentators like that no doubt prefer the excitement and drama of the Whitlam years. But millions of everyday Australians thought otherwise; for them, the ability to buy a home, raise a family, enjoy a secure job, living in a peaceful community and a stable society, were far to be preferred to the political *sturm und drang* that excites the commentariat.

That predictable, prosperous society is what the post-war Menzies governments delivered, and it remains the bedrock of Australia today. It is captured in the modest but civilised vision which he had rhapsodised in his 'Forgotten People' broadcasts in the early 1940s, when he spoke of homes material, homes human, and homes spiritual:

> [T]he real life of this nation is to be found … in the homes of people who are nameless and unadvertised, and who, whatever their individual religious conviction or dogma, see in their children their greatest contribution. … The home is the foundation of sanity and sobriety; it is the indispensable condition of continuity; its health determines the health of society as a whole.
>
> …
>
> [O]ne of the best instincts in us induces us to have one little piece of earth with a house and a garden which is ours …
>
> …
>
> My home is where my wife and children are. The instinct to be with them is the great instinct of civilized man; the instinct to give them a chance in life—to make them not leaners but lifters—is a noble instinct.[5]

There have been echoes of that speech down the years on the Liberal side of politics: in John Howard's 'white picket fence' view of Australia in the 1980s; in Joe Hockey's 2014 budget speech; in Scott Morrison's 'quiet Australians'. And although the sentiments Menzies expresses are modest, indeed homely, they capture in a very practical way the essence of the liberal view of the relationship between the citizen and the state: that the role of government is a limited one, as an enabler for individual and families. For, as Menzies goes on to say:

> Human nature is at its greatest when it combines dependence upon God with independence of man. We offer no affront—on the contrary, we have the warmest human compassion—toward those whom fate has compelled to live upon the bounty of the State, when we say that the greatest element in a strong people is a fierce independence of spirit. That is the only *real* freedom. ... The moment a man seeks moral and intellectual refuge in the emotions of a crowd, he ceases to be a human being and becomes a cipher.[6]

It is not the *vision* which is modest, but its view of the modest role of the state, and the proper limitations upon its power. The corollary of a modest view of the state is a *bold* vision of an empowered, fiercely independent, self-reliant citizenry.

We have become so used to the idea of Australia as a prosperous, property-owning democracy, with comparatively high standards of living and an enviable quality of life, that it seems almost banal to recite it. *Yet it didn't happen by accident.* It happened because of the policy choices which post-war governments made during the long years of prosperity and stability over which Menzies presided.

There was nothing inevitable about those choices. In fact, if we consider the world as it would have looked at the time of the 1949 election, the most striking thing is that the values and policies on which Menzies based his campaign—the values of the 'Forgotten People' speeches and the political platform of the Liberal Party— were so *against* the tide of the times.

The command economy of wartime was still fresh in people's minds. In the United Kingdom—which most Australians in those days still thought of as 'the mother country', and whose political example they tended to follow—the Attlee government was busily giving effect to the Beveridge Report and building a New Jerusalem of expanded government and nationalised industries. Its outlook was captured in the phrase popularised in those years: 'the man in Whitehall knows best'.[7] Social democratic or socialist governments had recently been elected in France and elsewhere in western Europe, just as communism gripped eastern Europe and threatened Greece and Italy. Even in the avowedly capitalist United States, the trend was towards bigger government, as the Truman administration inherited and adopted the legacy of Roosevelt's New Deal. Almost uniquely in the democratic world, in Australia a government was elected which explicitly advocated free enterprise as the way of the future, opposed the nationalisation (or further nationalisation) of industries, and encouraged middle-class security primarily through property ownership rather than the welfare state.

This was not an embrace of laissez-faire capitalism. It would not be until the 1980s that Liberal Party leaders, notably John Howard, attracted by the examples of Margaret Thatcher and Ronald Reagan, moved somewhat in the direction of significantly shrinking the role of the state and embracing 'small government' as a rhetorical trope. In the concluding sentences of the 'Forgotten People' broadcast, Menzies was quite explicit about this issue:

> Individual enterprise must drive us forward. That does not mean that we are to return to the old and selfish notions of *laissez-faire*. The functions of the State will be much more than merely keeping the ring within which the competitors will fight. Our social and industrial obligations will be increased.[8]

Nevertheless, at the 1949 election, Menzies and his Liberal Party committed themselves to, and his governments subsequently pursued, a liberal capitalist model, rather than a social democratic, welfarist model. That was both profoundly at odds with the direction of most of the democracies at the time and, I would argue, the foundation of modern Australia's prosperity.

Was Menzies Australia's greatest prime minister? I certainly think so, but, as I said at the beginning, that is inevitably a subjective and partisan judgement. What I think can be said with somewhat less subjectivity and partisanship is that in those post-war years, he set the direction of Australia more powerfully than any other prime minister has done. In doing so, he was the architect of modern Australia.

BIBLIOGRAPHY

Archives

Legal cases

Adelaide Company of Jehovah's Witnesses Inc v The Commonwealth (1943) 67 CLR 116.

Australian Communist Party v The Commonwealth [1951] HCA 5; (1951) 83 CLR 1.

Barak, A. HCJ 5100/94, *The Public Committee against Torture v The State of Israel* 53(4) PD 817, 845.

National Archives of Australia

Aid to Indonesia under the Post-UNRRA & UNESCO Schemes—Post-UNRRA Scholarships (General), A4357/3 352/1.

Aid to Indonesia under the Post-UNRRA & UNESCO Schemes. The Macmahon Ball Mission, A4357 352 PART 1.

Australia: Scholarship for Overseas Students at Australian Universities, A981/4 AUS 88.

Chinese Merchants and Students. Arrangements Governing Entry into Australia, A2998/1 1951/2129.

Chinese Merchants and Students. Conditions Governing Entry into Australia, A2998/1 1951/2130.

Chinese Students and Merchants—Conditions under which they will be Admitted to the Commonwealth, D596 1913/268.

Correspondence between R.G. Casey (Minister for External Affairs) and Alfred Brookes.

Cultural Relations. Educational Facilities in Australia for Overseas Students, A1068 PI47/13/2.

Dedman Papers.

Economic & Technical Assistance—Australian Government Overseas Scholarships Outside the Colombo Plan, A1838/294 2047/1.

Education. Nauru. Education and Training of Nauruans outside Territory [5cm], A518/1 C818/1/2 PART 5.

Immigration—Overseas Offices (miscellaneous correspondence), CP815/1/1 021.175.

Liberal Party of Australia Records.

Private Students—policy review—part 6, A446/216 1970/95146.

Scholarships for Asiatic Students, A1068 P147/13/2/4.

W Macmahon Ball's [W Macmahon BALL] S.E. Asian Educational and Relief Mission, A1838/278 381/1/3/1.

National Archives United Kingdom

'Policy and Special Procedure for the Handling of Top Secret Information in Connection with the Leakage of Cabinet Information and Investigations of Soviet Espionage Activity in Australia' (The National Archives (UK), 1950 1948), KV 4/450, KV 4/451, KV 4/452.

National Library of Australia

Papers of the Casey Family, MS 6150.

Papers of Sir Robert Menzies, MS 4936.

Papers of William Macmahon Ball.

Records of the Institute of Public Affairs (NSW), MS 6590 and MS Acc06.084.

Newspapers

The Advertiser (Adelaide)
The Age
The Australian
The Argus
Brisbane Telegraph
The Bulletin
The Canberra Times
Catholic Worker

Courier-Mail
Daily Mercury (Mackay)
Daily News (Perth)
The Daily Telegraph
Education News
Freedom
Gosford Times and Wyong District Advocate
The Mercury (Hobart)
The News (Adelaide)
News Weekly
Pacific Islands Monthly
Queensland Times (Ipswich)
The Sydney Morning Herald
The Sunday Mail (Brisbane)
The Times (London)
Warwick Daily News

Parliamentary papers

Commonwealth Parliamentary Debates (CPD), House of Representatives.
Commonwealth Parliamentary Debates (CPD), Senate.

Interviews

Brookes, Alfred. interviewed by Peter Edwards, 2004, National Library of Australia, https://nla.gov.au/nla.obj-208689401/listen.
Dean, Roger L. interviewed by Pat Shaw and Michael Saward in the Parliament's bicentenary oral history project, Transcript, 1984, p. 112.
Howard, John. *Transcript of the Prime Minister the Hon John Howard MP Press Conference (St Regis Hotel, Beijing, China),* 22 May 2002.
Weeden, WJ & Peter Biskup. William Weeden Interviewed by Peter Biskup [sound recording], ORAL TRC 2670, National Library of Australia digitised item.

Books and theses

Alexander, Fred. *From Curtin to Menzies and After*, Thomas Nelson, Melbourne, 1973.

Badcock, Blair & Andrew Beer. *Home Truths: Property Ownership and Housing Wealth in Australia*, Melbourne University Press, Melbourne, 2000.

Bagehot, Walter. *The English Constitution*, Fontana, Glasgow, 1867.

Barwick, Garfield. *A Radical Tory: Reflections and Recollections*, The Federation Press, Sydney, 1995.

Beale, Howard. *This Inch of Time: Memoirs of Politics and Diplomacy*, Melbourne University Press, Melbourne, 1977.

Behm, Alan. *No, Minister: So You Want to Be a Chief of Staff?*, Melbourne University Press, Melbourne, 2015.

Belloc, Hillaire. *The Servile State*, Foulis, London, 1912.

Bittman, Michael & Jocelyn Pixley. *The Double Life of the Family*, Allen & Unwin, Sydney, 1997.

Blackshield, Tony, Michael Coper & George Williams (eds). *The Oxford Companion to the High Court of Australia*, Oxford University Press, Melbourne, 2007.

Blainey, Geoffrey. *Gold and Paper*, Georgian House, Melbourne, 1958.

Booth, Douglas. *Australian Beach Cultures: The History of Sun, Sand and Surf*, Cass, London, 2001.

Bramston, Troy. *Robert Menzies: The Art of Politics*, Scribe Publications, Melbourne, 2019.

Brawley, Sean. *The White Peril: Foreign Relations and Asian Immigration to Australasia and North America 1919–1978*, UNSW Press, Sydney, 1995.

Brett, Judith. *Robert Menzies' Forgotten People*, Macmillan, Sydney, 1992.

——*Australian Liberals and the Moral Middle Class*, Cambridge University Press, Cambridge, 2003.

Broinowski, Alison. *About Face: Asian Accounts of Australia*, Scribe Publications, Melbourne, 2003.

Brown, Nicholas. *Governing Prosperity: Social Change and Social Analysis in Australia in the 1950s*, Cambridge University Press, Melbourne, 1995.

Brown, Wallace. *Ten Prime Ministers: Life Among the Politicians*, Longueville Books, Double Bay, 2002.

Bunting, John. *R.G. Menzies: A Portrait*, Allen & Unwin, Sydney, 1988.

Burnley, Ian & Peter Murphy. *Sea Change: Movement from Metropolitan to Arcadian Australia*, UNSW Press, Sydney, 2004.

Chavura, Stephen & Greg Melleuish. *The Forgotten Menzies: The World Picture of Australia's Longest-Serving Prime Minister*, Melbourne University Press, Melbourne, 2021.

Chipp, Donn & John Larkin. *Don Chipp: The Third Man*, Rigby, Adelaide, 1978.

Chrimes, SB [Stanley Bertram]. *English Constitutional History*, Oxford University Press, Oxford, 1948.

Colley, Linda. *Britons: Forging the Nation 1707–1837*, 6th edn, Yale University Press, London, 2014.

Coombs, HC. *Trial Balance*, Macmillan, 1981.

Cramer, John. *Pioneers, Politics and People: A Political Memoir*, Allen & Unwin, Sydney, 1989.

Crawford, JG (ed.). *Australian Trade Policy 1942–1966: A Documentary History*, ANU Press, Canberra, 1968.

Crisp, LF. *Ben Chifley*, Longmans, Melbourne, 1963.

Davison, Graeme. *Car Wars: How the Car Won our Hearts and Conquered our Cities,* Allen & Unwin, Sydney, 2004.

Day, David. *Chifley*, HarperCollins, Sydney, 2001.

Deakin, Alfred. *Federated Australia: Selections from Letters to the Morning Post 1900–1910*, ed. JA Lanauze, Melbourne University Press, Melbourne, 1968.

Deane, RP. *The Establishment of the Department of Trade: A Case Study in Administrative Reorganization*, ANU Press, Canberra, 1963.

Dicey, AV. *Introduction to the Study of the Law of the Constitution,* 8th edn, Liberty Classics, Indianapolis, 1915.

Downer, Alexander. *Six Prime Ministers*, Hill of Content, Melbourne, 1982.

Dutton, Geoffrey. *Sun, Sea, Surf and Sand—The Myth of the Beach,* Oxford University Press, Melbourne, 1985.

Evatt, Herbert V, *The King and His Dominion Governors: A Study of the Reserve Powers of the Crown in Great Britain and the Dominions*, Oxford University Press, Oxford, 1936.

——*William Holman: Australian Labour Leader* (1940), abridged edition, Angus & Robertson, Sydney, 1979.

Fahey, John. *Australia's First Spies: The Remarkable Story of Australia's Intelligence Operations, 1901–1945*, Allen & Unwin, Sydney, 2018.

Fadden, Arthur. *They Called Me Artie: The Memoirs of Sir Arthur Fadden*, The Jacaranda Press, Milton, 1969.

Fitzherbert, Margaret. *So Many Firsts: Liberal Women from Enid Lyons to the Turnbull Era*, The Federation Press, Sydney, 2009.

Frame, Tom. *Harold Holt and the Liberal Imagination*, Australian Biographical Monographs 2, Connor Court Publishing, Redland Bay, 2018.

——*A Very Proper Man: The Life of Tony Eggleton*, Connor Court Publishing, Brisbane, 2022.

Fraser, Malcom & Margaret Simons. *Malcolm Fraser: The Political Memoirs*, Melbourne University Publishing (The Miegunyah Press), Carlton, 2010.

Freestone, Robert. *Urban Nation: Australia's Planning Heritage*, CSIRO Publishing, Collingwood, 2010.

Furphy. S (ed.). *The Seven Dwarfs and the Age of the Mandarins: Australian Government Administration in the Post-War Reconstruction Era*, ANU Press, Canberra, 2015.

Gorman, Zachary. *Joseph Cook*, Australian Biographical Monographs 19, Connor Court, Brisbane, 2023.

Hagland, Trent A. *Think Tanks in Australia: Policy Contributions and Influence*, dissertation, University of Sydney, November 2021.

Hancock, Ian. *National and Permanent? The Federal Organisation of the Liberal Party of Australia 1944–1965*, Melbourne University Press, Melbourne, 2000.

Hancock, WK. *Australia*, Ernest Benn Limited, London, 1930.

——*Discovering Monaro: A Study of Man's Impact on his Environment*, Cambridge University Press, London and New York, 1972.

Hasluck, Paul. *The Office of Governor-General*, Melbourne University Press, Melbourne, 1979.

——*The Chance of Politics*, Text Publishing, Melbourne, 1997.

——*Sir Robert Menzies*, Melbourne University Press, Carlton, 1980.

Hazlehurst, Cameron. *Menzies Observed*, George Allen & Unwin, Sydney, 1979.

Hogben, Paul & Judith O'Callaghan (eds). *Leisure Space: The Transformation of Sydney 1945–1970*, UNSW Press, Sydney, 2014.

Hoskins, Ian. *Coast: A History of the New South Wales Edge*, UNSW Press, Sydney, 2014.

Howard, Colin, *Australia's Constitution*, Penguin Books, Melbourne, 1978.

——*The Constitution, Power and Politics*, Fontana, Melbourne, 1980.

Howard, John. *The Menzies Era: The Years that Shaped Modern Australia*, HarperCollins, Sydney, 2014.

Henderson, Anne. *Joseph Lyons: The People's Prime Minister*, NewSouth Publishing, Sydney, 2011.

——*Menzies at War*, NewSouth Publishing, Sydney, 2014.

Henderson, Gerard. *Menzies' Child: The Liberal Party of Australia: 1944–1994*, Allen & Unwin, Sydney, 1994.

Hyde, John. *Dry: In Defence of Economic Freedom*, Institute of Public Affairs, Melbourne, 2002.

Joske, Percy. *Sir Robert Menzies, 1894–1978: A New, Informal Memoir*, Angus & Robertson, Sydney, 1978.

Karskens, Grace. *People of the River: Lost Worlds of Early Australia*, Allen & Unwin, Sydney, 2020

Keir, David L. *The Constitutional History of Modern Britain*, Adam & Charles Black, London, 1938.

Kelly, Andrew. *ANZUS and the Early Cold War: Strategy and Diplomacy between Australia, New Zealand and the United States, 1945–1956*, Open Book Publishers, Cambridge, 2018.

Kelly, Paul. *The End of Certainty: The Story of the 1980s*, Allen & Unwin, Sydney, 1992.

——*100 Years: The Australian Story*, Allen & Unwin, Sydney, 2001.

Kemeny, Jim. *The Great Australian Nightmare: A Critique of the Home-Ownership Ideology,* Georgian House, Melbourne, 1983.

Kemp, David. *A Liberal State: How Australians Chose Liberalism over Socialism 1926–1966*, Miegunyah Press, Melbourne, 2021.

Kiernan, Colin. *Calwell: A Personal and Political Biography*, Thomas Nelson (Australia) Limited, Melbourne, 1978.

Killen, James. *Killen: Inside Australian Politics*, Methuen Haynes, North Ryde, 1985.

Lee, HP & Georgie Winterton. *Australian Constitutional Landmarks,* Cambridge University Press, Melbourne, 2003.

Lee, David. *The Second Rush: Mining and the Transformation of Australia*, Connor Court, Redland Bay, 2016.

Lowe, David & Daniel Oakman. *Australia and the Colombo Plan 1949–1957,* Australian Department of Foreign Affairs and Trade, Canberra, 2004.

Lowe, David. *Menzies and the 'Great World Struggle': Australia's Cold War 1948–1954*, UNSW Press, Sydney, 1999.

Lyons, Enid. *Among the Carrion Crows*, Rigby, Adelaide, 1972.

Macintyre, Stuart. *Australia's Boldest Experiment: War and Reconstruction in the 1940s*, NewSouth Publishing, Sydney, 2015.

——*A Concise History of Australia*, 5th edn, Cambridge University Press, Melbourne, 2021.

Martin, AW. *Henry Parkes: A Biography*, Melbourne University Press, Melbourne, 1980.

——*Robert Menzies: A Life, Volume 1, 1894–1943*, Melbourne University Press, Melbourne, 1993.

——*Robert Menzies: A Life, Volume 2, 1944–1978*, Melbourne University Press, Melbourne, 1999.

Mathews, Race. *Of Law and Liberty: Distributism in Victoria 1891–1966*, University of Notre Dame Press, Notre Dame, Indiana, 2018.

May, LA. *The Battle For the Banks*, Sydney University Press, Sydney, 1968.

McCalman, Janet. *Journeyings: The Biography of a Middle Class Generation 1920–1990*, Melbourne University Press, Melbourne, 1993.

McDaniel, Carl N & John Gowdy. *Paradise for Sale: A Parable of Nature*, University of California Press, Berkeley, 2000.

McEwen, John. *His Story*, privately published, Canberra, 1983.

McKinley, Brian, *Australian Labor History in Documents, Vol. 2: The Labor Party*, Collins Dove, Melbourne, 1990.

McMullin, Ross. *The Light on the Hill: The Australian Labor Party 1891–1991*, Oxford University Press, Oxford, 1991.

Meaney, NK. *Australia and the World: A Documentary History from the 1870s to the 1970s*, Longman Cheshire, Melbourne, 1985.

Menzies, Robert. *The Forgotten People and Other Studies in Democracy*, Angus & Robertson, Sydney, 1943.

——*Speech Is of Time: Selected Speeches and Writings by the Right Honourable Robert Gordon Menzies*, Cassell & Company Ltd, London, 1958.

——*Afternoon Light: Some Memories of Men and Events*, Cassell Australia, Melbourne, 1967.

——*Central Power in the Australian Commonwealth*, Cassell, London, 1967.

——*The Measure of the Years*, Cassell Australia, Melbourne, 1970.

——*Dark and Hurrying Days: Menzies' 1941 Diary*, eds Allan Martin & Patsy Hardy, Goanna Press, Canberra, 1993.

——*Letters to My Daughter: Robert Menzies, Letters, 1955–1975*, ed. Heather Henderson, Murdoch Books, Sydney, 2011.

——*Menzies: The Forgotten Speeches*, ed. David Furse-Roberts, Jeparit Press, Redland Bay, Qld, 2017.

Métin, Albert. *Socialism without Doctrine*, trans. Russell Ward, Alternative Pub. Co-operative, Chippendale, 1977.

Morgan, Patrick. *Melbourne before Mannix: Catholics in Public Life 1880–1920*, Connor Court, Ballan, 2012.

Murphy, John. *Imagining the Fifties: Private Sentiment and Political Culture in Menzies' Australia*, UNSW Press, Sydney, 2000.

Murray, Robert. *The Split: Australian Labor in the Fifties*, Cheshire, Melbourne, 1970.

——*Labor and Santamaria,* Australian Scholarly Publishing, Melbourne, 2016.

Oakman, Daniel. *Facing Asia: A History of the Colombo Plan*, ANU Press, Canberra, 2010.

Odgers, JR. *Australian Senate Practice* (1953), 5th edn, Australian Government Publishing Service, Canberra, 1976.

O'Neill, Robert. *Australia in the Korean War 1950–53*, Australian War Memorial, Canberra, 1981.

Page, Earle. *Truant Surgeon: The Inside Story of Forty Years of Australian Political Life*, Angus & Robertson, Sydney, 1963.

Parnaby, Owen. *Queen's College University of Melbourne: A Centenary History*, Melbourne University Press, Melbourne, 1990.

Peel, Mark & Christina Twomey. *A History of Australia*, Palgrave Macmillan, New York, 2011.

Perkins, Kevin. *Menzies: The Last of the Queen's Men*, Rigby, Adelaide, 1968.

Pinkstone, Brian. *Global Connections: A History of Exports and the Australian Economy*, Australian Government Publishing Service, Canberra, 1992.

Rich, Andrew. *Think Tanks, Public Policy, and the Politics of Expertise*, Cambridge University Press, Cambridge, 2004.

Robin, Eleanor. *The Quest for Eden-Monaro: A Core Sample of Australian Democracy*, Australian Scholarly Publishing, North Melbourne, 2022.

Rolls, Eric. *A Million Wild Acres: 200 Years of Man and an Australian Forest*, Nelson, Melbourne, 1981.

Rowse, Tim. *Nugget Coombs: A Reforming Life*, Cambridge University Press, Melbourne, 1992.

Salt, Bernard. *The Big Shift*, Hardie Grant, South Yarra, 2001.

Sandercock, Leonie. *Cities for Sale*, Melbourne University Press, Melbourne, 1975.

——*Sand in Our Souls: The Beach in Australian History*, Melbourne University Press, Melbourne, 2001.

Santamaria, BA. *Against the Tide,* Oxford University Press, Melbourne, 1981.

Schedvin, CB. *Australia and the Great Depression*, Sydney University Press, Sydney, 1988.

——*In Reserve: Central Banking in Australia, 1945–75*, Allen & Unwin, Sydney, 1992.

Seth, Ronald. *R.G. Menzies*, Cassell, London, 1960.

Shenk, Catherine. *Britain and the Sterling Area: From Devaluation to Convertibility in the 1950s*, Routledge, London, 1994.

Snedden, Billy & Bernie Schedvin. *Billy Snedden: An Unlikely Liberal*, Macmillan, South Melbourne, 1990.

Souter, Gavin. *Acts of Parliament: A Narrative History of the Senate and House of Representatives*, Commonwealth of Australia, Melbourne University Press, Melbourne, 1988.

Spearritt, Peter. *Sydney's Century*, UNSW Press, 2000.

Spender, Percy. *Exercises in Diplomacy: The ANZUS Treaty and the Colombo Plan*, Sydney University Press, Sydney, 1969.

——*Politics and a Man*, Collins, Sydney, 1972.

Tavan, Gwenda. *The Long, Slow Death of White Australia*, Scribe Publications, Carlton North, 2005.

Tilley, Paul. *Changing Fortunes: A History of the Australian Treasury*, Melbourne University Press, Melbourne, 2019.

Tiver, P. *The Liberal Party Principles and Performance*, The Jacaranda Press, Milton, 1978.

Toohey, Brian & William Pinwill. *Oyster: The Story of the Australian Secret Intelligence Service*, William Heinemann Australia, Melbourne, 1989.

Tweedie, Sandra. *Trading Partners: Australia & Asia 1790–1993*, UNSW Press, Sydney, 1994.

Twomey, Anne. *The Veiled Sceptre: Reserve Powers of Heads of State in Westminster Systems*, Cambridge University Press, Cambridge, 2018.

van der Ende, Lorraine. Strengthening Australia's Counter-Terrorist Capabilities: Balancing National Security Concerns with the Protection of Civil Liberties, Honours thesis, UWA Law School, 2002.

Viviani, Nancy. *Nauru: Phosphate and Political Progress*, ANU Press, Canberra, 1970.

Wallace, Chris. *Political Lives: Australian Prime Ministers and Their Biographers*, UNSW Press, Sydney, 2023.

Watt, Alan. *The Evolution of Australian Foreign Policy 1938–1965*, Cambridge University Press, London, 1967.

Webb L. *Communism and Democracy in Australia: A Survey of the 1951 Referendum,* Cheshire, Melbourne, 1954.

Weller, Patrick, Joanne Scott & Bronwyn Stevens. *From Postbox to Powerhouse: A Centenary History of the Department of the Prime Minister and Cabinet*, Allen & Unwin, Sydney, 2011.

West, K. *Power in the Liberal Party*, FW Cheshire, Melbourne, 1965.

Wevill, Richard. *Britain and America after World War II: Bilateral Relations and the Beginnings of the Cold War*, Bloomsbury, London, 2020.

Whitington, Don. *The House Will Divide: A Review of Australian Federal Politics*, revised edn, Landsdowne Press, Melbourne, 1969.

Whitwell, Greg. *The Treasury Line*, Allen & Unwin, Sydney, 1986.

Journal articles and chapters in edited collections

Andrew, Christopher. 'The Evolution of Australian Intelligence', *Studies in Intelligence*, Fall (1988), pp. 67–97.

Barker, Joanne & Anna Kent. 'International Education Recovery through Scholarships: A Case for a New Approach', *Australian Universities Review*, Vol. 64, No. 1, 2022, pp. 39–44.

Brett, Judith. 'Robert Menzies's Debt to Deakinite Liberalism', in Z. Gorman (ed.), *The Young Menzies: Success, Failure, Resilience (1894–1942)*, Melbourne University Press, Melbourne, 2022, pp. 63–76.

Broomhill, R. 'Australian Economic Booms in Historical Perspective', *Journal of Australian Political Economy*, No. 61.

Boyd, Jodie & Nicola Charwat. 'Ideology and the Economy: Capital Issues Controls, Inflation and the Menzies Government 1950–51', *Australian Journal of Politics and History*, Vol. 60, 2014, pp. 503–17.

British Medical Association. 'National Health In Australia', *The British Medical Journal*, Vol. 1, No. 4455, 25 May 1946, p. 153.

Byrne, Caitlin. 'Australia's New Colombo Plan: Enhancing Regional Soft Power through Student Mobility', *International Journal*, Vol. 71, No. 1, 2016, pp. 107–28.

Carment, David. 'Roger Levinge Dean (1913–1998)', *Australian Dictionary of Biography*, 2022.

Carr, Andrew & Benjamin T Jones. 'Civic Republicanism and Sir Robert Menzies: The Non-liberal Side of the Liberal Leader', *Journal of Australian Studies*, Vol. 37, No. 4, 2013, pp. 485–502.

Chamedes, Giuliana. 'The Vatican, Nazi-Fascism, and the Making of Transnational Anti-communism in the 1930s', *Journal of Contemporary History*, Vol. 51, No. 2, April 2016, pp. 261–90.

Charlesworth, Max. 'Australian Catholic Intellectuals: The Catholic Worker and the Movement', in Brian Head and James Walter (eds), *Intellectual Movements and Australian Society*, Oxford University Press, Melbourne, 1988, pp. 274–9.

Clohesy, Lachlan. 'A House Committee on Un-Australian Activities? An Alternative to the Dissolution Act', *Australian Historical Studies,* Vol. 44, 2013, pp. 23–36.

Collins, Hugh. 'Political Ideology in Australia: The Distinctiveness of a Benthamite Society', *Daedalus*, Vol. 114, No. 1, 1985, pp. 147–69.

Conley Tyler, M, R Matthews & E Brockhurst. 'Think Tank Diplomacy', *Brill Research Perspectives in Diplomacy and Foreign Policy*, Vol. 2, No. 3, 2017, pp. 1–96.

Cook, Malcolm. 'The Vernon Report: An Anatomy of an Assassination', *Journal of Economic and Social Policy*, Vol. 1, No. 1, 1995, pp. 39–43.

Cornish, Selwyn. 'The Keynesian Revolution in Australia: Fact or Fiction?', *Australian Economic History Review*, Vol. 33, 1993, pp. 42–68.

——'HC Coombs: Governor of Australia's Central Bank 1949–1968', *Reserve Bank of Australia Bulletin*, December 2022.

Cowper, N. 'Action Against Communism', *Australian Quarterly,* Vol. 22, No. 1, 1950, pp. 5–12.

Cunneen, C. 'Sir Ernest Keith White (1892–1983)', *Australian Dictionary of Biography*, Vol. 18, 2012.

Darian-Smith, Kate & James Waghorne. 'Australian–Asian Sociability, Student Activism, and the University Challenge to White Australia in the 1950s', *Australian Journal of Politics and History*, Vol. 62, No. 2, 2016, pp. 203–18.

Edelman, James & Angela Kittikhoun. 'Menzies and the Law', in Zachary Gorman (ed.), *The Young Menzies: Success, Failure, Resilience 1894– 1942*, Melbourne University Press, Melbourne, 2022.

Edwards, PG. 'Menzies and the Imperial Connection', in Cameron Hazlehurst (ed.), *Australian Conservatism: Essays in Twentieth Century Political History*, ANU Press, Canberra, 1979, pp. 194–212.

Fitzherbert, Margaret. 'Deakin and the Australian Women's National League', in JR Nethercote (ed.), *Liberalism and the Australian Federation*, The Federation Press, Sydney, 2001, pp. 98–112.

——'Menzies and the Representation of Women', in JR Nethercote (ed.), *Menzies: The Shaping of Modern Australia*, Connor Court Publishing, Cleveland, Qld, 2016, pp. 77–91.

Gorman, Zachary. 'George Reid's Anti-socialist Campaign in the Evolution of Australian Liberalism', in Greg Melleuish (ed.), *Liberalism and Conservatism*, Connor Court Publishing, Ballarat, Vic., 2015, pp. 17–38.

——'How Communist Fears Changed Australia', *Agora*, Vol. 57, No. 2, 2022, pp. 11, 12.

——'Sampson, Sydney (1863–1948)', *People Australia*, National Centre of Biography, 2023.

Gyngell, Alan. 'The Rumble of Think Tanks: National Security and Public Contestability in Australia', in Dan Marsten and T Leahy (eds), *War, Strategy and History: Essays in Honour of Professor Robert O'Neill*, ANU Press, Canberra, 2016, pp. 265–84.

Hancock, Ian. 'Sir Thomas Malcolm Ritchie (1894–1971)', *Australian Dictionary of Biography*, Vol. 16, 2002.

Henderson, Anne. 'Robert Menzies: War and Peace', in JR Nethercote (ed.), *Liberalism and the Australian Federation*, The Federation Press, Sydney, 2001, pp. 27–42.

Henderson, Gerard. 'Democratic Labor's Last Hurrah', *The Australian Quarterly*, Vol 47, No. 1, March 1975, pp. 77–89.

Horne, Julia. 'International Students in Australia since the Early 1900s', in Julia Horne & Matthew Thomas (eds), *Australian Universities: A Conversation about Public Good*, Sydney University Press, Sydney, 2022, pp. 103–17.

Kemp, David. 'Liberalism and Conservatism in Australia since 1944', in Brian Head & James Walter (eds), *Intellectual Movements and Australian Society*, Oxford University Press, Melbourne, 1988, pp. 322–62.

——'Menzies' Forgotten People and Howard's Battlers', in Tom Frame (ed.), *The Ascent to Power, 1996: The Howard Government, Volume 1*, UNSW Press, 2017, pp. 20–36.

——'Robert Menzies: The Long Assessment', in Zachary Gorman (ed.), *The Young Menzies: Success, Failure, Resilience (1894–1942)*, Melbourne University Press, 2022, pp. 1–15.

Lee, David. The National Security Planning and Defence Preparations of the Menzies Government, 1950–1953', *War & Society*, Vol. 10, 1992, pp. 119–38.

——'The 1949 Election: A Reinterpretation', *Australian Journal of Political Science*, Vol. 29, 1994, pp. 501–19.

——'Cabinet', in Scott Prasser, JR Nethercote & John Warhurst (eds), *The Menzies Era: A Reappraisal of Government, Politics and Policy*, Hale & Iremonger, Sydney, 1995, pp. 123–36.

Lloyd, C. 'The Rise and Fall of the United Australia Party', in JR Nethercote (ed.), *Liberalism and the Australian Federation*, The Federation Press, Sydney, pp. 134–62.

Lowe, David. 'Canberra's Colombo Plan: Public Images of Australia's Relations with South and Southeast Asia in the 1950s', *South Asia: Journal of South Asian Studies*, Vol. 25, No. 2, 2002, pp. 183–204.

——'Brave New Liberal: Percy Spender', *Australian Journal of Politics and History*, Vol. 51, No. 3, 2005, pp 389–99.

Lowe, David. 'Percy Spender and the Colombo Plan', *Australian Journal of Politics and History*, Vol. 40, No. 2, 1994, pp 162–76.

——'Spender, Sir Percy Claude (1897–1985)', *Australian Dictionary of Biography*, Vol. 18, 2012.

Markwell, Donald. 'The Office of Governor-General', *Melbourne University Law Review*, Vol. 38, 2015, pp. 1098–117.

Martin, Allan. 'Robert Menzies', in Michelle Grattan (ed.), *Australian Prime Ministers*, New Holland, Chatswood, 2000.

Marsh, Ian & Diane Stone. 'Australian Think Tanks', in Diane Stone & Andrew Denham (eds), *Think Tank Traditions: Policy Analysis Across Nations*, Manchester University Press, Manchester, 2004, pp. 247–63

Mathews, Race. 'Collateral Damage: B.A. Santamaria and the Marginalising of Social Catholicism', *Labour History*, No. 92, May, 2007, pp. 89–111.

McCafferie, Brendan & Chris Aulich. 'For Whom the Bellwether Polls: The Electorate of Eden-Monaro as an Indicator of Australian Electoral Trends', *Australian Journal of Politics and History*, Vol. 62, No. 3, 2016, pp. 452–66.

Meaney, Neville. 'Look Back in Fear: Percy Spender, the Japanese Peace Treaty and the ANZUS Pact', *Japan Forum*, Vol. 15, No. 3, 2003, pp. 399–410.

Megarrity, Lyndon. 'Indigenous Education in Colonial Papua New Guinea: Australian Government Policy (1945–1975)', *History of Education Review*, Vol. 34, No. 2, 2005, pp. 41–58.

Melleuish, Gregory. 'A Short History of Australian Liberalism', Centre for Independent Studies, *Occasional Paper 74*, 2001.

——'Menzies: Democracy, Spirit and Education', in Zachary Gorman, ed., *The Young Menzies: Success, Failure, Resilience (1894–1942)*, Melbourne University Press, Melbourne, 2022, pp. 47–61.

Milner, Ian. 'Referendum Retrospect', *The Australian Quarterly*, Vol. 16, No. 4, December 1944, pp. 38–29.

Murray, R. 'Sir William Hewson Anderson (1897–1968)', *Australian Dictionary of Biography*, Vol. 13, 1993.

Nethercote, John. 'Canberra Knights: The Rise and Fall of the Public Service Mandarins, 1936–86', in Henry Ergas & Jonathan Pincus (eds), *Power, Politics & Parliament: Essays in Honour of John R. Nethercote*, Connor Court, Redland Bay, Qld, 2022, pp. 281–308.

Nethercote, John R. 'Menzies and the Institutions of Government and Parliament', in his (ed.) *Menzies: The Shaping of Modern Australia*, Connor Court, Redland Bay, Qld, 2016, pp. 323–60.

Nicholas, HS. 'Fifty Years of the Constitution', *The Australian Quarterly*, Vol. 23, No. 2, June 1951, pp. 29–34.

Oakman, Daniel. '"Young Asians in Our Homes": Colombo Plan Students and White Australia', *Journal of Australian Studies*, No. 72, 2002, pp. 89–98.

Richardson, Charles. 'A CIA Scheme? A Royal Plot? Whitlam Conspiracy Theories Poppycock', *Crikey*, 12 November 2015.

——'On Saving the Governor-General, Part I', *The World is Not Enough*, 25 August 2022.

Roskam, J. 'Charles Denton Kemp (1911–1993)', *Australian Dictionary of Biography*, Vol. 19, 2021.

Schwartz, Adam. 'Confronting the "Totalitarian Antichrist": Christopher Dawson and Totalitarianism', *The Catholic Historical Review*, Vol. 89, No. 3, July 2003, pp. 464–88.

Scotton, R. 'The Vernon Report and Australian Government', *Australian Journal of Public Administration*, Vol. 25, No. 2, June 1966, pp. 133–45.

Siracusa, Joseph M, & Glen St John Barclay. 'Australia, the United States and the Cold War, 1945–51: From V-J Day to ANZUS', *Diplomatic History*, Vol. 5, No. 1, 1981, pp. 39–52.

Smart, J. 'Dame Elizabeth May Couchman (1876–1982)', *Australian Dictionary of Biography*, Vol. 17, 2007.

Stapledon, Nigel. 'The Inexorable Rise in House Prices in Australia since 1970: Unique or Not?', *The Australian Economic Review*, Vol. 49, No. 3, 2016, pp. 317–27.

Starr, Graeme. 'Menzies and Post War Prosperity', in JR Nethercote (ed.), *Liberalism and the Australian Federation*, The Federation Press, Sydney, 2001, pp. 177–95.

Stone, Diane. 'Introduction', in Diane Stone & Andrew Denham (eds), *Think Tank Traditions: Policy Analysis Across Nations*, Manchester University Press, Manchester, 2004, pp. 1–16.

Tregenza, Ian. 'The "Servile State" Down Under: Hilaire Belloc and Australian Political Thought, 1912–53', *Journal of the History of Ideas*, Vol. 82, No. 2, 2021, pp. 305–27.

Tsokhas, Kosmas. 'Dedominionization: The Anglo-Australian Experience, 1939–1945', *The Historical Journal*, Vol. 37, 1994, pp. 861–83.

Walter, J. 'Ministers, Minders and Public Servants: Changing Parameters of Responsibility in Australia', *Australian Journal of Public Administration*, Vol. 65, No. 3, September 2006, pp. 22–7.

Waters, Christopher. 'The Great Debates: H.V. Evatt and the Department of External Affairs, 1941–49', in Joan Beaumont, Christopher Waters & David Lowe with Garry Woodward, *Ministers, Mandarins and Diplomats: Australian Foreign Policy Making 1941–1969*, Melbourne University Press, Melbourne, 2003, pp. 45–61.

Whitwell, Greg. 'Economic Policy', in Scott Prasser, JR Nethercote & John Warhurst (eds), *The Menzies Era: A Reappraisal of Government, Politics and Policy*, Hale & Iremonger, Sydney, 1995, pp. 166–84.

Williams, George. 'Australian Values and the War Against Terrorism', *UNSW Law Journal*, Vol. 26, No. 1, 2003, pp. 191, 192.

Winterton, George. 'The Significance of the *Communist Party* Case', *Melbourne University Law Review*, Vol. 18, No. 3, 1992, pp. 630–58.

Speeches and broadcasts

Chief Justice Higgins. *Address to Isaacs Law Society Ball*, 7 October 2005, p. 7.

Menzies, Robert. '1946 Election Speech', Camberwell, 20 August 1946.

Menzies, Robert. '1949 Election Policy Speech', Melbourne, 10 November 1949.

NOTES

Introduction

1 The infamous line 'the Commonwealth Government is not concerned with making the workers into little capitalists', referring to private homeownership, was said by Minister for Postwar Reconstruction John Dedman, 'Commonwealth and State Housing Agreement Bill 1945', CPD, House of Representatives, 2 October 1943, p. 6265.

2 'Ministry's Policy', *The Sydney Morning Herald*, 27 April 1939, p. 9.

3 Collins, pp. 147–69.

4 Métin.

5 Hancock, *Australia*, p. 72.

6 Wallace, p. 75.

7 Menzies said in January 1949, 'Australia with its seven and a half million people could not live for 10 years without great and powerful friends in the world—it would be blotted out of existence', and he would repeat the phrase numerous times once in office, 'Big Crowd Hear Mr. Menzies', *The Advertiser* (Adelaide), 28 January 1949, p. 1. The phrase had previously been used in the singular to describe America during World War II, so Menzies was partly making the point that Britain still mattered, which fits in with Stoltz's chapter.

Chapter 1   Menzies's Miracle?

1 Nicolle Flint was the federal member for Boothby from 2016 to 2022 and now acts as a public commentator.

2 It is worth noting that Joseph Cook argued that the original Labor Party died with the introduction of the caucus pledge, hence that he had never been a member of the version of the Labor Party that he would subsequently oppose in federal politics. See Gorman, *Joseph Cook*.

3 Hancock, *National and Permanent?*, p. 4.

4 ibid.

5   ibid.

6   Starr, p. 178.

7   ibid.

8   Henderson, *Menzies' Child*, p. 80.

9   Henderson, 'Robert Menzies: War and Peace', p. 40.

10 ibid.

11 Gorman, *Joseph Cook*.

12 Gorman, 'George Reid's Anti-socialist Campaign in the Evolution of Australian Liberalism', pp. 17–38.

13 Fitzherbert, 'Deakin and the Australian Women's National League', pp. 102–3.

14 Fitzherbert, pp. 110–11; Henderson, 'Robert Menzies War and Peace', pp. 34–9.

15 Tiver, pp. 23–4.

16 Tiver, p. 24; NAA, 'Stanley Bruce: Elections'.

17 Parliament of Australia, Parliamentary Library, 'Detailed Results: House of Representatives 1922–1940'. See also NAA.

18 Lloyd, p. 137.

19 ibid., pp. 142–8.

20 Lloyd, pp. 143–5; Kemp, *A Liberal State*, p. 111.

21 Lloyd, pp. 146–9; Kemp, *A Liberal State*, pp. 124–8.

22 Lloyd, pp. 154–5.

23 ibid., p. 156.

24 ibid., p. 157.

25 ibid., pp. 157–9.

26 ibid., pp 157–8.

27 Hancock, *National and Permanent?*, pp. 13, 23–5; Cunneen.

28 Henderson, *Menzies' Child*, pp. 62–5.

29 Fitzherbert, So Many Firsts, pp. 19–23; Fitzherbert, 'Menzies and the Representation of Women', pp. 77–91. Henderson, *Menzies' Child*, pp. 70–71; Hancock, *National and Permanent?*, p. 15; Smart.

30 Hancock, *National and Permanent?*, pp. 13–14, 26, 34; Murray, 'Sir William Hewson Anderson'; Henderson, *Menzies' Child*, p. 70; Kemp, *A Liberal State*, pp. 275–6.

31 Hancock, *National and Permanent?*, pp. 26–7.

32 Henderson, *Menzies' Child*, pp. 62–5; Hancock, *National and Permanent?*, pp. 17–27; Kemp, *A Liberal State*, pp. 287–94.

33 Letter from R Menzies to A Mair, Leader of the Opposition, 5 November 1943, Papers of RG Menzies, Series 14. Liberal Party, 1939–1978, Original Consignment, National Library of Australia (Images 28–29).

34 Hancock, *National and Permanent?*, pp. 23–6; Henderson, *Menzies' Child*, pp. 63–5.

35 Hancock, *National and Permanent?*, pp. 26–7; Kemp, *A Liberal State*, pp. 288–94.

36 Henderson, *Menzies' Child*, p. 67.

37 Henderson, *Menzies' Child*; see also Hancock, *National and Permanent?*, pp. 28–9.

38 Letter from R Menzies to F Davis, President, Young Nationalists Organisation of Victoria, Papers of RG Menzies, Formation of the Liberal Party 1943–1944, Class Consignment received 1993, National Library of Australia, (Image 51).

39 Letter from R Menzies to F Davis, President, Young Nationalists Organisation of Victoria, Papers of RG Menzies, Formation of the Liberal Party 1943–1944, Class Consignment received 1993, National Library of Australia, (Images 47–48).

40 Letter from R McDonald, Legislative Assembly of Western Australia, to Hon R Menzies MP, 3 October 1944, Papers of RG Menzies, Formation of the Liberal Party 1943–1944, Class Consignment received 1993, National Library of Australia, (Images 0–5).

41 Letter from E White, President, Liberal Democratic Party of Australia, New South Wales, to R Menzies, 3 October 1944, Papers of RG Menzies, Formation of the Liberal Party 1943–1944, Class Consignment received 1993, National Library of Australia, (Images 39–45).

42 Letter from A Mair, Deputy Leader of the Opposition, Legislative Assembly of New South Wales, to Hon R Menzies MP, 27 September 1944, Papers of RG Menzies, Formation of the Liberal Party 1943–1944, Class Consignment received 1993, National Library of Australia, (Images 28–29).

43 Letter from G Stewart, Hon. Secretary, Queensland Women's Electoral League, to R Menzies, 5 October 1944, Papers of RG Menzies, Formation of the Liberal Party 1943–1944, Class Consignment received 1993, National Library of Australia, (Image 55).

44 Letter from H Warby to Sir Sydney Snow, 1 September 1943, Papers of RG Menzies, Formation of the Liberal Party 1943–1944, Class

Consignment received 1993, National Library of Australia, (Images 30–38).

45 Kemp, *A Liberal State*, p. 296, pp. 296–8.

46 ibid., pp. 296–8.

47 List of delegates & observers—Canberra Conference, 13–16 October 1944, Papers of RG Menzies, Formation of the Liberal Party 1943–1944, Class Consignment received 1993, National Library of Australia, (Images 56–60).

48 Henderson, 'Robert Menzies War and Peace', pp. 183–4; Kemp, *A Liberal State*, pp. 294–5.

49 Hancock, *National and Permanent?*, p. 21.

50 Bramston, chapter 4, 'Barrister at Law'.

51 For an excellent summary, see Kemp, *A Liberal State*, pp. 10–11.

52 Menzies, 'Australia's Place in the Empire', *International Affairs*, vol. XIV, No. 4, July–August 1935, Papers of RG Menzies, Articles and Statements 1917–1935, Original Consignment, National Library of Australia, (Images 73–82).

53 Menzies, 'Australia's Place in the Empire' (Images 75–76).

54 Menzies, 'Marketing of Primary Products Bill', Parliamentary Debates, State of Victoria, 13 August 1930, Papers of RG Menzies, Articles and Statements 1917–1935, Original Consignment, National Library of Australia, (Images 185–196). See also Menzies, 'Address by RG Menzies, President of the United Australia Organisation at the First Annual Conference 21 September 1932', Papers of RG Menzies, Articles and Statements 1917–1935, Original Consignment, National Library of Australia, (Images 96–98).

55 Menzies, 'Industrial Peace. A New Conciliation System: Overhauling the Machine', *The Argus*, July–August 1929, Papers of RG Menzies, Articles and Statements 1917–1935, Original Consignment, National Library of Australia, (Images 102–103).

56 Brett, 'Robert Menzies's Debt to Deakinite Liberalism', pp. 63–4.

57 Bramston, Appendix.

58 Menzies, Untitled, 16 June 1944, Papers of RG Menzies, Letters, Class Consignment received 1993, National Library of Australia, (Image 58).

59 Bramston, chapter 5, 'Spring Street'.

60 West, p. 214; Bramston, chapter 5, 'Spring Street'.

61 'The Selected Anti-Socialist Candidates', *The Argus*, 7 December 1906, p. 5.

62 Bramston, chapter 4, 'Barrister at Law'.

63 ibid.

64 West, p. 215; Fitzherbert, 'Menzies and the Representation of Women', p. 80; Kemp, *A Liberal State*, pp. 97–8.

65 West, p. 215; Lloyd, p. 140.

66 Lloyd, p. 140; Kemp, *A Liberal State*, pp. 103–7.

67 Menzies, 'Address by RG Menzies, President of the United Australia Organisation at the First Annual Conference 21 September 1932'.

68 Bramston, chapter 7, 'Wartime Prime Minister'; Henderson, A, chapter 6, 'War at a Distance', chapter 7, 'Menzies' Dark and Hurrying Day'.

69 Henderson, *Menzies' Child*, p. 48.

70 ibid., p. 51.

71 Brett, *Robert Menzies' Forgotten People*, pp. 226–30.

72 Kemp, *A Liberal State*, p. 307.

73 Bramston, chapter 9, 'The Liberal Party of Australia'.

74 Hancock, *National and Permanent?*, p. 4.

75 Hancock, *National and Permanent?*, pp. 35–6.

76 Menzies, 'Opening Speech by the Rt. Hon. RG Menzies KC MP (Leader of the Opposition), Canberra, Conference, 13 October 1944', Speeches etc., Original Consignment, National Library of Australia, (Images 0–11).

77 Henderson, *Menzies' Child*, pp. 82–9; Roskam.

78 Fitzherbert, So Many Firsts, pp. 21–2; Kemp, *A Liberal State*, pp. 308–9.

79 Kemp, *A Liberal State*, pp. 306–08.

80 Cunneen.

81 Hancock, *National and Permanent?*, pp. 55–9; Hancock, 'Sir Thomas Malcolm Ritchie'.

Chapter 2 Menzies and the Movement

1 Lucas McLennan is a Melbourne-based senior history teacher, who has completed a Masters thesis on nineteenth-century Australian education policy at the University of Melbourne.

2 Charlesworth, p. 277.

3 Murray, *Labor and Santamaria*, pp. 40–2.

4 Henderson, 'Democratic Labor's Last Hurrah', p. 78.

5 ibid., p. 88.

6 Chavura and Melleuish, p. 14.

7 ibid.

8 ibid., pp. 18–19.

9 Brett, *Robert Menzies' Forgotten People*, p. 59.

10 Carr & Jones, pp. 485–502.

11 Menzies, Election Speech, 20 August 1946.

12 Morgan, pp. 149–67.

13 Charlesworth, p. 275.

14 Santamaria, pp. 16–17.

15 Tregenza, p. 307.

16 ibid.

17 Belloc, p. 16.

18 Santamaria, p. 16.

19 *Catholic Worker*, 5 February 1938.

20 Charlesworth, p. 277.

21 ibid.

22 *Freedom*, 5 January 1944.

23 *Freedom*, August 1943.

24 *Freedom*, 24 January 1945.

25 *Freedom*, 1 November 1944.

26 *Freedom*, 19 December 1945.

27 *News Weekly*, 20 August 1946.

28 *Freedom*, 12 February 1945.

29 Chifley on China, quoted in McKinley, p. 133.

30 ibid.

31 *News Weekly*, 7 February 1950.

32 *News Weekly*, 7 February 1950.

33 *News Weekly*, 12 September 1951.

34 Milner, p. 38.

35 ibid.

36 *Freedom*, 30 October 1943.

37 *Freedom*, 30 October 1943.

38 *Freedom*, 30 October 1943.

39 *Freedom*, 28 June 1944.

40 *Freedom*, 28 June 1944.

41 *Freedom*, 28 June 1944. Industrial conscription meant being legally compelled to take up a civil occupation in the same way one might be legally compelled to join the military. It was an issue that had been raised by the circumstances of the war, but which was also associated with the implementation of a fully socialist state.

42 In 1944, Menzies supported the efforts of the Australian Constitutional League to oppose the fourteen powers. The league used hyperbole to persuade the public. One advertisement compared Australia to 1933 Germany, where Hitler had used a fraudulent referendum to grant full powers to the general German government (and he as Führer). Another factor in the referendum's defeat was the silence (until 21 July) to support the 'Yes' vote.

43 *Freedom*, 2 August 1944.

44 *Freedom*, 30 August 1944.

45 *News Weekly*, 2 June 1948.

46 *News Weekly*, 2 June 1948.

47 *News Weekly*, 2 June 1948.

48 *British Medical Journal*, 26 May 1946.

49 Robert Menzies, leader of the Opposition (3 April 1946). 'Constitution Alteration (Social Services) Bill 1946: Second Reading' (PDF); CPD, House of Representatives, p. 900.

50 *British Medical Journal*, 26 May 1946.

51 *News Weekly*, 12 July 1944.

Chapter 3   Menzies and the Banks

1   Anne Henderson AM is the deputy director of the Sydney Institute and a prolific author on Australian history.

2   Menzies, The Measure of the Years, p. 109.

3   Crisp, p. 326 and p. 329.

4   Schedvin, pp. 94–5.

5   Crisp, p. 167.

6   ibid., p. 170.

7   Blainey, p. 361.

8   May, p. 8.

9   Menzies, *Afternoon Light*, p. 129.

10 Martin, *Robert Menzies: A Life, Volume 2*, p. 66.

11 *The Sydney Morning Herald*, 17 September 1947, p. 1.

12 Blainey, chapter 22, 'The Fight', pp. 356–72.

13 May, pp. 26–9.

14 Blainey, p. 367.

15 *The Sydney Morning Herald*, Wednesday 17 September 1947, p. 1.

16 Australia, House of Representative Debates, 17 September 1947.

17 Australia, House of Representatives, Debates, 18 September 1947.

18 Martin, *Robert Menzies: A Life, Volume 2*, p. 77.
19 *The Argus*, 28 October 1947, p. 1.
20 Martin, *Robert Menzies: A Life, Volume 2*, p. 77.
21 Australia, House of Representatives Debates, 23 October 1947.
22 *The Sydney Morning Herald*, 13 November 1947, p. 1.
23 Blackshield, Coper & Williams, p. 53.
24 Blainey, pp. 370–1.
25 Day, p. 468.
26 Menzies, *The Measure of the Years*, pp. 110–15.
27 Menzies, *Afternoon Light*, p. 130.

Chapter 4   Liberalism Applied?

1 Tom Switzer is executive director of the Centre for Independent Studies in Sydney and a presenter at the ABC's Radio National. He is a former editor of the *Spectator Australia*, opinion editor at *The Australian*, editorial writer at the *Australian Financial Review* and assistant editor of the Washington-based American Enterprise Institute.
2 See Macintyre, *Australia's Boldest Experiment*.
3 Melleuish, 'A Short History of Australian Liberalism', p. 26.
4 Martin, 'Robert Menzies', in Grattan, p. 189.
5 Martin, *Robert Menzies: A Life, Volume 2*, p. 62.
6 'Mr. Menzies Critical', *The Age*, 18 August 1947, p. 1.
7 Museum of Australian Democracy, Election Speeches, 1949, Robert Menzies on behalf of the Liberal/Country Party Coalition, Melbourne, 10 November 1949.
8 See Gorman, 'George Reid's Anti-socialist Campaign in the Evolution of Australian Liberalism', pp. 17–38.
9 'Fadden to Get Dollars for Industries', *The Daily Telegraph*, 18 November 1949, p. 7.
10 Mike Steketee, 'Liberal Lessons in Appeal', *The Australian*, 5 December 2009; Brett, *Australian Liberals and the Moral Middle Class*.
11 Kemp, *A Liberal State*, p. 364.
12 NAA, 'John Gorton: Elections'. Australian Electoral Commission, 'House of Representatives: Two Party Preferred Results 1949–Present'.
13 Paul Kelly, 'How Chifley Dimmed the Light', *The Australian*, 13 March 2001.
14 'The Age of Menzies', *The Bulletin*, 29 January 1966.

15 Paul Kelly, 'A Nation Comes of Age—WW II 60th Anniversary Series: Part 7 Australia's War', *The Australian*, 13 August 2005.

16 Howard, *The Menzies Years*, p. 576.

17 Paul Kelly, 'Time to Reconsider the Many Faces of Menzies', *The Australian*, 17 November 1999.

18 Norman Abjorensen, *Canberra Times*, 3 December 2019.

19 Menzies's copy survives in the Menzies Collection, housed in the Baillieu Library at the University of Melbourne, and shows signs of intensive use.

20 Norman Abjorensen, *Canberra Times*, 3 December 2019; Martin, 'Robert Menzies', in Grattan, pp. 194–5.

21 Martin, 'Robert Menzies', in Grattan, p. 194.

22 ibid., pp. 125–6.

23 Bunting, p. 125.

24 Coombs, p. 133.

25 Martin, *Robert Menzies: A Life, Volume 2*, p. 153; Kemp, *A Liberal State*, p. 375.

26 Martin, *Robert Menzies: A Life, Volume 2*, p. 136, Kemp, *A Liberal State*, p. 375; Paul Kelly, 'A Nation Comes of Age—WW II 60th Anniversary Series: Part 7 Australia's War', *The Australian*, 13 August 2005.

27 Howard, *The Menzies Years*, p. 595.

28 Australian Government, Department of the Prime Minister and Cabinet, PM Transcripts—Transcripts from the Prime Minister of Australia.

29 Howard, *The Menzies Years*, p. 596.

30 Kelly, 100 Years; ABC documentary, *100 Years: The Australian Story*, Episode Three, 'Land of the Fair Go', 14 March 2001.

31 Kemp, *A Liberal State*, p. 376.

32 Kemp, *A Liberal State*, p. 376.

33 Martin, 'Robert Menzies', in Grattan, p. 196.

34 Martin, *Robert Menzies: A Life, Volume 2*, p. 203.

35 ibid., p. 210.

36 Kemp, *A Liberal State*, p. 377.

37 ibid, p. 378.

38 Howard, *The Menzies Years,* p. 605.

39 Melleuish, 'A Short History of Australian Liberalism', p. 26.

40 This was to be a contributory scheme, much like modern superannuation, an approach which allowed the centre-right to maintain that it had

a distinctive policy that was more financially sound than Labor's, even if it was seeking to achieve similar goals.

41 George Brandis, 'The Howard Paradox', *The Australian*, 23 October 2008.

42 Gorman, 'Sampson, Sydney'.

43 Howard, *The Menzies Years*, pp. 586–7.

44 Australian Government, Department of the Prime Minister and Cabinet PM Transcripts—Transcripts from the Prime Minister of Australia.

45 Mike Steketee, 'Liberal Lessons in Appeal', *The Australian*, 5 December 2009.

46 Howard, *The Menzies Years*, p. 631.

47 Menzies, *The Forgotten People*.

48 Mike Steketee, 'Liberal Lessons in Appeal', *The Australian*, 5 December 2009.

49 Menzies, *The Forgotten People*.

50 Macintyre, *Australia's Boldest Experiment,* p. 476.

Chapter 5   Early Think Tanks and their Influence on the Menzies Government

1 Andrew Blyth, formerly group manager for the Public Leadership Research Group–John Howard Prime Ministerial Library at UNSW Canberra, is doing a PhD thesis on think tanks.

2 Kemp, 'Robert Menzies: The Long Assessment', p. 3.

3 National Film and Sound Archive, 'Australian History Timeline 3'.

4 Treasury, 'Australia's Century since Federation at a Glance'.

5 David Kemp, 'Power Struggle on the Edge of an Abyss', *The Australian*, 1 January 2007, p. 12.

6 Broomhill.

7 For a fuller account, see Behm, pp. 120–45.

8 Scotton, p. 140; see also Nicholas.

9 Walter, p. 22.

10 Ian Marsh, 'Canberra Turns Increasingly to the Think-tank', *Australian Financial Review*, 24 July 1992, p. 5, claims by 1970 there were fifteen think tanks in Australia, and seventy-five by 1992, 'spread nearly equally among federal government departments, universities and the private sector—and the number was still growing'.

11 Marsh and Stone, in Stone & Denham, pp. 247–63. British and American think tanks with a focus on international affairs have been

popping up for the past hundred years or so and have strong global reputations. In the United States, the RAND Corporation was formed in 1946. Committed exclusively to national security research and funded primarily by the United States Air Force, RAND was formed during the presidency of Harry S Truman (April 1945–January 1953).

12 Hagland, p. 93.

13 Abelson, DE, 'A World of Their Own: Think Tanks and Global Politics', presentation to Blanquerna Communication School of Universitat Ramon Lull, April 2014.

14 Gyngell, quoted in Noel Turnbull & Clare Shanier, 'Think Tanks and Their Influence', in Mark J Sheehan (ed.), *Advocates and Persuaders*, Australian Scholarly Publishing, North Melbourne, pp. 72–94.

15 The Australian Institute of Political Science was established in 1932, the Australian Institute of International Affairs (AIIA) in 1933; and the Institute of Public Affairs (IPA) opened officially in 1943. The Committee for Economic Development of Australia (CEDA) was formed in 1960 and the Strategic and Defence Studies Centre (SDSC), located at the Australian National University, was formed in 1966, after Menzies had left office.

16 Interview with the author, 17 January 2020.

17 Stone, in Stone & Denham, p. 2.

18 Rich, p. 11.

19 Suzuki, T, *Think Tanks and Policy Formation in Japan*.

20 McGann, '2018 Global Go to Think Tank Index Report', 2019, *TTCSP Global Go To Think Tank Index Reports*, p. 12.

21 ibid., p. 13.

22 See Conley Tyler, Matthews & Brockhurst.

23 Roskam.

24 Hyde, p. 111.

25 Records of the Institute of Public Affairs (NSW), MS 6590 and MS Acc06.084.

26 Institute of Public Affairs, *Looking Forward—A Post War Policy For Australian Industry*, ANU Archives.

27 Hyde, p. 111.

28 For a counter-argument to this claim, see Henderson, *Menzies' Child*, pp. 89–96.

29 See Kemp, 'Menzies' Forgotten People and Howard's Battlers'.

30 NAA, 'Robert Menzies: During Office: The Menzies Era'.

31 Adapted from Kemp's 'Menzies' Forgotten People and Howard's Battlers', p. 29.

32 Address given by Mr RG Menzies at Dinner, The Athenaeum Club, 10 April 1954, provided to the author by Dr David Kemp, 22 March 2022.

33 See Frame, *A Very Proper Man*, suggesting, 'Menzies' reluctance to meet with people outside of his immediate political circle, also extended to members of the press gallery', p. 48.

34 Commonwealth of Australia, *Report of the Committee on Australian Universities*, September 1957, Extract, Appendix A, p. 127.

35 Melleuish, 'Menzies: Democracy, Spirit and Education'.

36 See Frame, *Harold Holt and the Liberal Imagination*, p. 61.

37 See Cook.

38 JR Nethercote, 'What Did the Vernon Report Say?', *The Sydney Morning Herald*, 5 October 2015.

39 Scotton.

40 A model replicated by his protégé John Howard some thirty years later when establishing two statutory 'think tank' authorities: the Productivity Commission (1998) and the Australian Strategic Policy Institute (2001).

41 CPD, House of Representatives, 21 September 1965, pp. 1078–85 (Robert Menzies, Prime Minister).

42 Scotton, p. 139.

43 ibid., p. 145.

44 John Hyde in *Dry: In Defence of Economic Freedom* claims McEwen had built a bureaucratic base in the Department of Trade, with Trade and Treasury pitted against the other in formulating policy, p. 48.

45 Howard, J, *The Menzies Era*, p. 242.

46 Bramston, p. 167.

47 Bramston, p. 150, records that in 1950, the Cabinet met 158 times, considered 237 submissions, and made 456 decisions; by 1965, the Cabinet met 159 times, considered 618 papers, and made 785 decisions.

Chapter 6   What Liberty for the Enemies of Liberty?

1 Lorraine Finlay is Australia's Human Rights Commissioner. This paper is based upon a presentation given at the Second Annual Conference of the Robert Menzies Institute, *Coming to Power, Learning to Govern and Gathering Momentum 1943–1954* on 17–18 November 2022.

2 Specifically the constitutional validity of the Security Legislation Amendment (Terrorism) Bill 2002 (No. 2) and the Australian Security Intelligence Organisation Legislation Amendment (Terrorism) Bill 2002.

3 Parliamentary Joint Committee on ASIO, ASIS, and DSD, An advisory report on the Australian Security Intelligence Organisation Legislation Amendment (Terrorism) Bill 2022, p. vii.

4 Williams, D (The Hon.) (Attorney-General), Australian Security Intelligence Organisation Legislation Amendment (Terrorism) Bill 2002: Second Reading Speech, p. 1607.

5 van der Ende, p. 59.

6 Barak, p. 845.

7 Second reading speech on the Communist Party Dissolution Bill: CPD, House of Representatives, 27 April 1950, p. 1995.

8 Menzies, 13 February 1946, quoted in Webb, p. 22; Fadden, p. 97.

9 Menzies: CPD, House of Representatives, 15 May 1947, p. 2460.

10 *National Security (Subversive Associations) Regulations 1940* (Cth), reg. 3; Commonwealth Gazette, No. 110, 15 June 1940.

11 Evatt: CPD, House of Representatives, 28 January 1943, p. 111. See also 'End of Ban on Communists', *The Sydney Morning Herald*, 19 December 1942, p. 8, quoted in Webb, p. 9.

12 *Adelaide Company of Jehovah's Witnesses Inc v Commonwealth* (1943) 67 CLR 116.

13 Clohesy, p. 24.

14 Winterton, p. 634.

15 George Williams, 'Menzies Turned Referendum Loss to Long-term Advantage', *The Australian*, 2 October 2021.

16 Williams, p. 192.

17 'Liberal Party Declares for Ban on Communist Party', *The Canberra Times*, 12 March 1948, p. 4, quoted in Clohesy, p. 26.

18 See, for example, Clohesy, p. 26.

19 'Liberal Plan to Ban Communists', *The Sydney Morning Herald*, 19 January 1949, p. 3, quoted in Winterton, p. 635.

20 'Drastic Action on Communists', *The Sydney Morning Herald*, 11 November 1949, p. 5, quoted in Winterton, p. 635.

21 Gorman, 'How Communist Fears Changed Australia', p. 12.

22 Williams, p. 193.

23 CPD, House of Representatives, 27 April 1950, p. 1997 (Robert Menzies, Prime Minister).

24 CPD, House of Representatives, 9 May 1950, p. 2242.

25 CPD, House of Representatives, 27 April 1950, p. 1996.

26 ibid., p. 1994.

27 ibid., p. 1994.

28 'War on Communism' (editorial), *The Mercury* (Hobart), 28 April 1950, p. 3, quoted in Winterton, p. 642.

29 'Drastic Remedy for Cancer', *The Canberra Times*, 28 April 1950, p. 4, quoted in Winterton, p. 643.

30 'Defence of Liberty' (editorial), *The Courier-Mail* (Brisbane), 2 May 1950, p. 2, quoted in Winterton, p. 643.

31 'Dealing with the Communists' (editorial), *The Age*, 28 April 1950, p. 2, quoted in Winterton, p. 643.

32 See Winterton, p. 643.

33 'Anti-Communist Bill in Australia: Many Misgivings About Methods', *The Times* (London), 29 April 1950, p. 5, quoted in Winterton, p. 643.

34 Letter from ten professors and twenty-two readers and lecturers, *The Sydney Morning Herald*, 19 May 1950, p. 2, quoted in Winterton, p. 644.

35 Letter, *The Age*, 24 May 1950, p. 2, quoted in Winterton, p. 644.

36 Cowper, p. 7.

37 Winterton, p. 645.

38 George Williams, 'Menzies Turned Referendum Loss to Long-term Advantage', *The Australian*, 2 October 2021.

39 ibid.

40 *Australian Communist Party v The Commonwealth* [1951] HCA 5; (1951) 83 CLR 1.

41 Edelman & Kittikhoun, p. 43.

42 Lee & Winterton, p. 108.

43 *Australian Communist Party v The Commonwealth* [1951] HCA 5; (1951) 83 CLR 1, p. 263.

44 *Australian Communist Party v The Commonwealth* [1951] HCA 5; (1951) 83 CLR 1, p. 258.

45 See Edelman & Kittikhoun, p. 44.

46 Winterton, p. 653.

47 'The Battle for Barton', *The Sun* (Sydney), 15 April 1951, p. 16.

48 George Williams, 'Menzies Turned Referendum Loss to Long-term Advantage', *The Australian*, 2 October 2021.

49 ibid.

50 ibid.

51 John Howard (Prime Minister), Transcript of the Prime Minister the Hon John Howard MP Press Conference (St Regis Hotel, Beijing, China), 22 May 2002.

52 Parliamentary Library (Department of Parliamentary Services), Online Parliamentary Handbook.

53 Chief Justice Higgins.

Chapter 7 The Art of Power

1 Troy Bramston is a senior writer and columnist with *The Australian* newspaper, and the author of best-selling biographies of multiple Australian prime ministers.

2 This chapter draws on my biography, *Robert Menzies: The Art of Politics*.

3 Interview with William Heseltine, 22 June 2017, Sydney.

4 Interview with Tony Eggleton, 14 October 2013, Canberra.

5 Robert Menzies, 'Cabinet List', Robert Menzies Papers, MS 4936, Series (2000 Addition), Box 6, Folder 43, National Library of Australia, Canberra.

6 See Bramston, p. 92.

7 Frances McNicoll interview with Robert Menzies, 14 May 1972, Papers of Frances McNicoll, MS 9246, Series 6, Box 15, Files 1–3, National Library of Australia, Canberra.

8 Interview with Heather Henderson, 13 October 2017, Canberra.

9 Interview with Lenox Hewitt, 10 October 2018, via email.

10 *Robert Menzies, Mr Prime Minister*, Episode 7: 'Robert Gordon Menzies', ABC TV, 1966.

11 Lyons, pp. 90–91.

12 Barry York interview with Frank Jennings, Oral History Program, Old Parliament House, 29 October 2007.

13 Interview with Doug Anthony, 20 April 2017, via phone.

14 Interview with Ian Sinclair, 7 April 2017, Taree.

15 Interview with Jim Forbes, 14 December 2018, Adelaide.

16 Bramston, p. 154.

17 McNicoll interviews with Menzies, 13 May 1972 and 17 May 1972.

18 Robert Menzies, 'Note of conversation between the Prime Minister and the Minister for Labour and National Service, 23 September 1959', Papers of Robert Menzies, Correspondence with William McMahon, M2576/2, NAA.

19 Interview with Malcolm Fraser, 6 September 2002, Melbourne.

20 Spender, *Politics and a Man*, pp. 152–4.

21 Menzies, *Afternoon Light*, p. 57.

22 Interview with John Carrick, 9 March 2017, Sydney.

23 McNicoll interview with Menzies, 18 May 1972.

24 Bramston, pp. 120, 122.

25 R Maley, 'Menzies Nips Revolt in the Bud', *The Argus*, 3 March 1951, p. 3.

26 Downer, pp. 2–3.

27 Brown, p. 22.

28 Interview with Ian Sinclair, 7 April 2017, Taree.

29 Souter, p. 340.

Chapter 8   Menzies, Evatt, and Constitutional Government

1 Charles Richardson earned his PhD from Rutgers University, specialising in ethical theory and political philosophy. He is currently an independent scholar based in Melbourne.

2 Chrimes, p. 2. For a more critical account, see Howard, *The Constitution, Power and Politics*, pp. 88–93.

3 See Markwell, pp. 1106–08, who distinguishes between a de jure and de facto head of state.

4 See particularly *R (Miller) v The Prime Minister and Cherry v Advocate General for Scotland*, [2019] UKSC 41, which supersedes many earlier authorities.

5 Keir, p. 538.

6 Dicey, p. 393.

7 Edwards, p. 207.

8 Balfour Declaration, section II.

9 Keir, p. 542.

10 Alexander, p. 127.

11 Nethercote, 'Menzies and the Institutions of Government and Parliament', p. 325. Much of this paper is a rather one-sided dialogue with John Nethercote, who passed away a few months before it was presented; I would particularly like to record my appreciation for his support over the years, and I regret that my argument could not benefit from his no doubt valuable criticism.

12 Nethercote, 'Menzies and the Institutions of Government and Parliament', p. 323 (opening words).

13 Martin, *Robert Menzies: A Life, Volume 1*, p. 150.

14 Menzies, *Afternoon Light*, p. 250.

15 See Twomey, pp. 38–41.

16 Evatt, *The King and His Dominion Governors*, chapter XIV, esp. p. 130. His *William Holman*, pp. 319–21, is also relevant. Compare Twomey, pp. 202–03.

17 Hasluck, *The Chance of Politics*, p. 80.

18 Murray, *The Split*, pp. 10–11. Compare McMullin, p. 205: 'In sheer intellect he had no peer, but in political astuteness he had much to learn'.

19 CPD, House of Representatives, 25 August 1937, p. 83.

20 CPD, House of Representatives, 7 October 1942, p. 1434; Menzies, *The Forgotten People*, chapter XXIX, 'The Statute of Westminster' (delivered 9 October 1942).

21 Keir, p. 546.

22 Twomey, p. 745. Compare Nethercote, 'Menzies and the Institutions of Government and Parliament', p. 329, on the appointment of Lord Gowrie in 1938: his reference to the Statute of Westminster is anachronistic since it had not been adopted in Australia at that time, but the procedure was within the scope of the Balfour Declaration.

23 CPD, House of Representatives, 20 February 1947, p. 17; compare Menzies, *Afternoon Light*, p. 254.

24 Evatt, *The King and His Dominion Governors*, pp. 197–8.

25 CPD, House of Representatives, 20 February 1947, p. 19.

26 Martin, *Robert Menzies: A Life, Volume 2*, p. 64.

27 Howard, *Australia's Constitution*, p. 94.

28 Nethercote, 'Menzies and the Institutions of Government and Parliament', p. 354; compare Odgers, p. 33.

29 Parliament of the Commonwealth, Documents Relating to the Simultaneous Dissolution. Menzies's post-retirement account, in his *The Measure of the Years*, pp. 37–43, follows this closely.

30 Evatt, *The King and His Dominion Governors*, p. 45.

31 Howard, *The Menzies Era*, p. 117. Compare Richardson, 'On Saving The Governor-General'.

32 Martin, *Robert Menzies: A Life, Volume 2*, p. 240.

33 Menzies, *Afternoon Light*, pp. 255–8.

34 Howard continues, 'It would not have occurred to any PM since then to advise the Queen to appoint anyone other than an Australian to the vice-regal post' (*The Menzies Era*, pp. 85–6).

35 Nethercote, 'Menzies and the Institutions of Government and Parliament', p. 331; compare Menzies's letter to John McEwen of 10 June 1959, printed in Henderson, p. 29: 'I have a working arrangement with [the Queen] to the effect that, from my point of view, it is not a matter of just nominating someone and saying "Take it or leave it." We should by a process of discussion come to a complete agreement on somebody who pleases her and pleases us'.

36 Letter to Heather Henderson, 21 February 1969, in Menzies, *Letters to My Daughter*, p. 206.

37 Discussed in Nethercote, 'Menzies and the Institutions of Government and Parliament', pp. 327–8.

38 CPD, House of Representatives, 2 December 1953, pp. 783 and 820.

39 Hasluck, *The Office of Governor-General*, p. 16; Howard, *The Constitution, Power and Politics*, p. 124. Compare Twomey, pp. 380–2.

40 CPD, House of Representatives, 26 October 1955, p. 1895.

41 Richardson, 'A CIA Scheme?'.

Chapter 9   The Forgotten People by the Sea?

1 Dr Christopher Beer has conducted research which has spanned many aspects of urban development. He has previously completed his doctoral studies at the Australian National University and held adjunct positions at the University of Canberra and Macquarie University.

2 McCalman, p. 3.

3 Rolls; Hancock, *Discovering Monaro*; Karskens.

4 Robin; McCafferie & Aulich, pp. 452–66.

5 National Population Inquiry, *Population and Australia: A Demographic Analysis and Projection—Volume One*, Commonwealth of Australia, Canberra, 1975, p. 151.

6 See, for example, Burnley & Murphy; Salt.

7 Freestone; Spearritt.

8 Brown, pp. 87–125.

9 See, for example, Davison; Hogben & O'Callaghan.

10 Menzies, *The Measure of the Years*, p. 129.

11 Menzies, 'The Forgotten People', speech reproduced in Brett, *Robert Menzies' Forgotten People*, p. 23.

12 ibid., p. 28.

13 ibid., p. 27.

14 ibid., p. 23.

15 The term has a broad history of use to encapsulate certain trends in Western polities post-World War II. In the Australian context, see, for example, Sandercock.

16 Stapledon, p. 324; see also Badcock & Beer; Kemeny.

17 Kemeny, p. 15.

18 Murphy, p. 107.

19 Bittman & Pixley.

20 Hoskins, pp. 341–2.

21 'Getting Away From All of What', *The Bulletin*, 23 January 1971, p. 33.

22 Calculation based on a 1950s male average income of between approximately £500 at the start of the decade and £1000 at the decade's end, derived from Australian Bureau of Statistics, Average Weekly Earnings Australia 1941–1990, 1992, p. 5.

23 Commonwealth Bureau of Census and Statistics, Census of the Commonwealth of Australia 30 June 1954—Volume I Part III: New South Wales, pp. 100 and 107.

24 This observation is based on the proportion of dwellings unoccupied at the time of the Census, i.e. a mid-winter Wednesday. See Commonwealth Bureau of Census and Statistics. Census of the Commonwealth of Australia 30 June 1954—Volume I: New South Wales, pp. 6–7.

25 Commonwealth Bureau of Census and Statistics, Census of the Commonwealth of Australia 30 June 1954—Volume I—Part I: New South Wales, pp. 15–16 and 37.

26 Wardlaw, H, 'Plan for the Shire of Gosford', Report commissioned by the Shire of Gosford Council, 1958, p. 21.

27 T Stephens, 'Drainage a Down to Earth Issue in Godzone', *The Sydney Morning Herald*, 27 February 1990, p. 6.

28 Assuming the Sydney CBD as a primary destination/origin. See Wardlaw, H, 'Plan for the Shire of Gosford', p. 12.

29 Wardlaw, 'Plan for the Shire of Gosford', p. 23.

30 'Roger Dean Criticises "Pommy" Attitude to New Australians', *Gosford Times and Wyong District Advocate*, 9 February 1951, p. 1.

31 'Flora Society Praised by Town Planner', *Gosford Times and Wyong District Advocate*, 22 January 1954, p. 1.

32 Chief Electoral Office for the Commonwealth, State of New South Wales—Statistical Returns—The General Elections for the House of Representatives 1949, p. 10.

33 Chief Electoral Office for the Commonwealth, State of New South Wales—Statistical Returns—The General Elections for the House of Representatives 1951, p. 11.

34 Chief Electoral Office for the Commonwealth, State of New South Wales—Statistical Returns—The General Elections for the House of Representatives 1954, p. 5.

35 'How Australia Voted at the Referendum', *The Sydney Morning Herald*, 23 September 1951, p. 5.

36 At the state level, much of the region was covered by the Gosford electorate from 1950 onwards, which was also held by the Liberal Party during this period.

37 'Roger L Dean, interviewed by Pat Shaw and Michael Saward in the Parliament's bicentenary oral history project', Transcript, 1984, p. 112.

38 Carment.

39 'Roger L Dean interviewed by Pat Shaw and Michael Saward', p. 111.

40 ibid., p. 33.

41 'Surprising Lessons from the Backbenchers', *The Sydney Morning Herald*, 20 May 1959, p. 2.

42 'Roger Dean CBE—Obituary', *The Sydney Morning Herald*, 13 January 1998, p. 33.

43 ibid., p. 33.

44 'Menzies Warns Commercial Radio Stations', *The Daily Telegraph*, 26 September 1949, p. 6; 'Menzies on Socialism', *Townsville Daily Bulletin*, 27 September 1949, p. 3; 'Fed. Poll Crucial, Warns Menzies', *The Sun*, 23 September 1949, p. 7.

45 'Mr Menzies Fights a Hard Federal Campaign', *The Age*, 18 May 1954, p. 2.

46 'PM Warns Aust', *The Sydney Morning Herald*, 20 April 1958, p. 7.

47 'Roger L. Dean interviewed by Pat Shaw and Michael Saward', p. 39.

48 ibid., p. 35.

49 ibid., p. 181.

50 ibid., p. 140.

51 'Mr Dean Lashes Out at Socialistic Program', *Gosford Times and Wyong District Advocate*, 7 May 1954, p. 7.

52 'Afraid to Speak Freely', *The Sydney Morning Herald*, 3 December 1949, p. 3.

53 'Council Rebuffs Red League', *The Sydney Morning Herald*, 24 March 1955, p. 4.

54 Riley, M, 'MacMasters Beach', Manuscript, 2004, p. 39.

55 'Roger L Dean interviewed by Pat Shaw and Michael Saward', p. 105.

56 ibid., p. 162.

57 ibid., p. 149.

58 'Egg Export Market Worry', *The Age,* 20 January 1955, p. 4.

59 Dean, R (Letter), 'Restrictions on Shopkeepers', *The Sydney Morning Herald*, 15 November 1951, p. 2.

60 'Water Scarce in Gosford Tourist Area', *The Sydney Morning Herald*, 24 December 1957, p. 4.

61 'Roger Dean CBE', *The Sydney Morning Herald*, 13 January 1998, p. 32.

62 Sandercock, *Sand in Our Souls*, Booth; Dutton.

63 Bongiorno, 'Foreword', in Robin, p. xiii.

Chapter 10   Menzies and Economic Management, 1950–54

1 David Lee is associate professor in the School of Humanities and Social Sciences at the University of New South Wales, Canberra.

2 May.

3 Wevill.

4 Tsokhas, pp. 861–3.

5 Shenk.

6 Deane, pp. 8–9.

7 Speech by Robert Menzies for the Liberal/Country Party Coalition, Melbourne, 10 November 1949.

8 ibid.

9 Lee, 'The 1949 Federal Election', p. 515.

10 ibid.

11 Martin, *Robert Menzies: A Life, Volume 1*, chapter 16.

12 Whitington, p. 149.

13 Martin, *Robert Menzies: A Life. Volume 2*, chapter 6.

14 Lee, 'Cabinet', p. 127.

15 Weller et al., p. 47.

16 Lee, 'Cabinet', p. 127.

17 ibid.

18 Nethercote, 'Canberra Knights', pp. 281–308.

19 Rowse.

20 Martin, *Menzies: A Life, Volume 2*, p. 160.

21 Pinkstone, pp. 150–6.

22 Tweedie.

23 Lowe, *Menzies and the 'Great World Struggle'*.

24 Lee, 'The National Security Planning and Defence Preparations of the Menzies Government', pp. 119–38.

25 Boyd & Charwat, pp. 503–17.

26 O'Neill.

27 Submission by RG Casey, Minister for External Affairs, to Cabinet, 'The Economic and Financial Future', 24 June 1952, NAA: A571, 1952/1161 Part 2.

28 Cornish, 'Keynesian Revolution', pp. 42–68 and 'HC Coombs: Governor of Australia's Central Bank 1949–1968'.

29 FH Wheeler, First Assistant Secretary, 'Budget 1950/51 Summary of Effect of Cabinet Decisions of 3/10/50 and of Items Still Requiring Decision', 5 October 1950, NAA; A571, 1950/1677.

30 Arthur Fadden, Submission to Cabinet, 'Economic Policy—June 1952', 12 June 1952, NAA: A571, 1952/1161 Part 2.

31 '10 p.c. Tax Slug Forecast in Budget', *The Sun* (Sydney), 26 September 1951; 'Severe Taxes to Curb Inflation', *The Age*, 27 September 1951.

32 Whitwell, p. 105.

33 Sir Douglas Copland, 'Some Comments on the Budget', ABC News Commentary, 27 September 1951, NAA: A571, 1951/2248.

34 'Budget Press Comment', Treasury paper, 3 October 1951, NAA: A571, 1951/2248.

35 ibid.

36 'Drastic Budget Revision is Imperative', *The Sydney Morning Herald*, 3 October 1951.

37 Tilley, p. 63.

38 Grindle, NL, 'Recent International Discussions on Wool', in United States of America, State Department Bulletin, Vol. XXV, July–Dec 1951, p. 116.

39 ibid.

40 'US Delegation in Wool Talks', *The Canberra Times*, 11 November 1950.

41 'No Interference with Wool Auction System', *The Age*, 29 November 1950.

42 'Statement by Australian Representative on United States Proposal for Allocations with Ceiling Prices', July 1951, NAA: A621, S794 Part 5.

43 Letter from Crawford to Moroney, 31 July 1951, NAA: A621, S794 Part 4.

44 Press statement by Menzies, 22 August 1951, in Crawford, p. 399.

45 Deane, p. 18.
46 Cabinet Minute, Decision no. 328, 'Submission no. 214—Australia's Balance of Payments and International Reserves', 6 March 1952, Crawford Papers, NLA4514, Box 4 'file S'.
47 ibid.
48 Furphy.
49 Lee, *The Second Rush*.
50 NLA, Remarks by John Stone interviewed by Bernie Schedvin, 15 May 1991 – 8 July 1994, P.7:6 to 7:9.

Chapter 11   A Prudent and Urgent Measure

1 Dr William A Stoltz conducted this research as a visiting fellow at the Robert Menzies Institute. Dr Stoltz was policy director at the National Security College until February 2023.
2 Fahey.
3 Deakin.
4 Casey, RG, 'Subseries 4.3. Lord Casey's Diaries (Originals)', in Papers of the Casey Family (National Library of Australia, 1820).
5 Casey.
6 Andrew, pp. 67–97.
7 ibid.
8 Brookes, A, Alfred Deakin Brookes interviewed by Peter Edwards, 2004, National Library of Australia.
9 Andrew.
10 ibid.
11 'A Brief Historical Note on a Security Organisation' (Dedman Papers, 7 February 1949), NAA.
12 Andrew.
13 MI5 is Britain's counter-intelligence agency aimed at protecting Britain from acts of espionage and covert action, as opposed to MI6, which engages in such acts against foreign nations.
14 'Policy and Special Procedure for the Handling of Top Secret Information in Connection with the Leakage of Cabinet Information and Investigations of Soviet Espionage Activity in Australia', The National Archives (UK), 1950 1948, KV 4/450, KV 4/451, KV 4/452.
15 'Policy and Special Procedure for the Handling of Top Secret Information in Connection with the Leakage of Cabinet Information and Investigations of Soviet Espionage Activity in Australia'.

16 Similar to the relationship between MI5 and MI6, ASIO is Australia's counter-intelligence agency aimed at protecting Australia from acts of espionage and covert action, as opposed to ASIS, which engages in such acts against foreign nations.

17 Casey, 'Subseries 4.3. Lord Casey's Diaries (Originals)'.

18 Liberal Party of Australia, 'Liberal Party of Australia—Federal Secretarial—Policy Research Committee', NAA, 1950 1946, p. 5 Part 4.

19 Liberal Party of Australia, 'Liberal Party of Australia—Federal Secretarial—Policy Research Committee', NAA, n.d., p. 5 Part 4.

20 Brookes, A, Alfred Deakin Brookes interviewed by Peter Edwards.

21 Casey, RG, 'Subseries 4.3. Lord Casey's Diaries (Originals)'.

22 ibid.

23 ibid.

24 ibid.

25 Brookes, A, Alfred Deakin Brookes interviewed by Peter Edwards.

26 Toohey & Pinwill, pp. 20–30.

27 ibid., p. 15.

28 Hope, R, 'Royal Commission on Intelligence and Security Fifth Report [Re Australian Secret Intelligence Service]—Volume I', Canberra, 1976, p. 26.

29 Casey, RG, 'Subseries 4.3. Lord Casey's Diaries (Originals)'.

30 Report on the Australian Secret Intelligence Service, Public edn, Australian Government Publishing Service, Canberra, 1995.

31 Toohey & Pinwill, see Appendix A.

32 ibid.

33 ibid.

34 Casey, RG, 'Subseries 4.3. Lord Casey's Diaries (Originals)'.

35 Toohey & Pinwill.

36 ibid.

37 ibid.

38 ibid.

39 Casey, R & Brookes, A, 'Correspondence between R.G. Casey (Minister for External Affairs) and Alfred Brookes', NAA, n.d., A7133.

40 ibid.

41 ibid.

42 ibid.

43 Brookes, A, Alfred Deakin Brookes interviewed by Peter Edwards.

44 ibid.

45 ibid.

46 ibid.

47 Andrew.

Chapter 12   An Innovative Realist

1   David Furse-Roberts is a research fellow at the Menzies Research Centre who has published widely on Menzies and the Menzies era.

2   Menzies, R, 'Policy Speech', Melbourne, 10 November 1949. Papers of Sir Robert Menzies, NLA, MS 4936, Box 254, Folder 22.

3   Lowe, 'Spender, Sir Percy Claude'.

4   ibid.

5   'Middle Class Legion of the Lost', *The West Australian*, 5 April 1943, p. 2.

6   Lowe, 'Brave New Liberal', p. 395.

7   ibid., p. 393.

8   Spender, *Exercises in Diplomacy*, p. 195.

9   Oakman, *Facing Asia*, p. 16.

10 Lowe, 'Percy Spender and the Colombo Plan', p. 163.

11 Oakman, *Facing Asia*, p. 16.

12 Macmahon Ball, cited in Oakman, *Facing Asia*, p. 17.

13 Oakman, *Facing Asia*, p. 14.

14 ibid., pp. 14–15.

15 ibid., p. 15.

16 Spender, *Exercises in Diplomacy*, p. 196.

17 Lowe, 'Percy Spender and the Colombo Plan', p. 164.

18 Spender, *Exercises in Diplomacy*, p. 200.

19 ibid., p. 276.

20 Lowe, 'Percy Spender and the Colombo Plan', p. 166.

21 Spender, *Exercises in Diplomacy*, p. 267.

22 ibid., p. 267.

23 Oakman, *Facing Asia*, p. 44.

24 Lowe, 'Percy Spender and the Colombo Plan', p. 166.

25 Oakman, *Facing Asia*, p. 60.

26 Spender, P, *Current Notes on International Affairs*, Vol. 21, No. 8 (August 1950), p. 582, cited by Siracusa & Barclay, p. 49.

27 Oakman, *Facing Asia*, p. 12.

28 Kelly, *ANZUS and the Early Cold War*, p. 85.

29 ibid., pp. 85–6.

30 Siracusa & St John Barclay, p. 50.

31 ibid.

32 Spender, *Exercises in Diplomacy*, pp. 174–6.

33 Kelly, *ANZUS and the Early Cold War*, p. 90.

34 Spender, *Politics and a Man*, p. 304.

35 Menzies, *The Measure of the Years*, p. 54.

36 Spender, *Exercises in Diplomacy*, p. 50.

37 ibid., p. 52.

38 Meaney, 'Look Back in Fear', pp. 405–6.

39 Spender, *Exercises in Diplomacy*, p. 52.

40 ibid., p. 54.

41 Kelly, *ANZUS and the Early Cold War*, p. 78.

42 Spender, *Exercises in Diplomacy*, p. 54.

43 ibid., p. 59.

44 Meaney, 'Look Back in Fear', p. 408.

45 ibid.

46 Spender, *Politics and a Man*, p. 265.

47 ibid., p. 266.

48 ibid., p. 322.

49 Oakman, *Facing Asia*, p. 11.

50 Spender, 'Statement of Foreign Affairs', CPD, House of Representatives, Vol. 206, 9 March 1950, cited in Spender, *Politics and a Man*, p. 326.

51 Spender, *Politics and a Man*, p. 326.

Chapter 13   Overseas Students in Australia

1   Lyndon Megarrity is an adjunct lecturer at James Cook University, with a PhD from the University of New England.

2   'For more than seventy years, the Australian government has supported the education of emerging leaders from developing countries, through the Colombo Plan in the 1950s to today's Australia Awards.' Department of Foreign Affairs (DFAT), 'Australia Awards'. See also Luke Slattery, 'A Broad Lesson Plan', *The Australian*, 8 July 2009, p. 32.

3   Peel & Twomey, pp. 142–5.

4   'It has been customary for members of the Tongan ruling family to attend Newington College in Sydney'. 'From Nauru', *The Warwick Daily News*, 16 May 1933, p. 6. See also 'Education of Nauru Boys Here Defended', *The Herald* (Melbourne), 8 November 1940, p. 3.

5 'Asiatic Merchants and Travellers', *The Queensland Times* (Ipswich), 7 December 1905, p. 14.

6 In a list of 'Chinese Admitted on Passports' from 1913 and 1914, it is noted that Harry Gee Fat Wong entered Brisbane on 23 January 1914, but was 'previously admitted for educational purposes in 1904'. See 'Chinese Admitted on Passports [enclosure in Departmental memo for Minister for External Affairs, 17 November 1914]', Chinese Merchants and Students. Conditions Governing Entry into Australia, A2998/1 1951/2130, NAA.

7 'Chinese Students: Questions of Admission', *The Herald* (Melbourne), 10 June 1912, p. 8.

8 Chinese Students and Merchants—Conditions under which they will be Admitted to the Commonwealth, D596 1913/268, NAA.

9 Prime Minister (Billy Hughes) to Governor-General (Sir Ronald C Munro Ferguson), 10 September 1920, Chinese Merchants and Students. Conditions Governing Entry into Australia, A2998/1 1951/2130, NAA.

10 GF Pearce to VC Thompson, 3 June 1924, in Chinese Merchants and Students. Conditions Governing Entry into Australia, A2998/1 1951/2130, NAA.

11 See, for example, LRO Bevan, *The Age*, 8 February 1909, p. 6; William Yinson Lee, Letter to the Editor, 'Chinese Students at Australian Universities', *The Daily Telegraph* (Sydney), 24 March 1910, p. 12; 'Japanese Students', *The Advertiser* (Adelaide), 31 March 1904, p. 7.

12 'China: Opportunities for Australia', *The Canberra Times*, 23 January 1937, p. 1.

13 ibid., p. 1.

14 By 1924, the Home and Territories Minister was stating that 'In future no Chinese under the age of 14 years would be admitted [as a student]'. 'Chinese Influx: Students under 14 excluded', *The Herald* (Melbourne), 19 May 1924, p. 5. By at least 1933, 'The Commonwealth arrangement regarding Chinese students permits them to come here between the ages of 10 and 19 years, and to remain here, as a rule, up to the age of 24 years.' Statement by JA Perkins (Minister for the Interior), in 'Chinese: Treatment Fair in Australia', *The Canberra Times*, 14 February 1933, p. 2.

15 A total of 225 Chinese students were admitted to the Commonwealth between 1921 and the first quarter of 1924. It is likely that greater

Commonwealth restrictions on Chinese student migration after this point prevented the numbers from moving upwards during the rest of the inter-war period. See Statement Regarding Chinese Children Admitted Temporarily to Australia for Educational Purposes (Home and Territories Department Memo dated 4 April 1924), in Chinese Merchants and Students. Conditions Governing Entry into Australia, A2998/1 1951/2130, NAA.

16 'Chinese Students: Ex-Missionary and Her School', *Evening Sun*, 17 May 1924, in Chinese Merchants and Students. Conditions Governing Entry into Australia, A2998/1 1951/2130, NAA.

17 'Indian Student to Study Here', *Daily News* (Perth), 21 February 1939, p. 3.

18 From 1919 Nauru was a League of Nations mandated territory ostensibly run by Britain, Australia, and New Zealand, each of which had a share in the island's phosphate deposits through the British Phosphate Commission. After World War II, Nauru became a United Nations Trust Territory run by Australia until Nauruan independence in 1968. Viviani, pp. 40–5; McDaniel & Gowdy, p. 44. The Australian administration's practice of sending Nauruans to study in Australia ultimately led to several former students gaining government employment. See, for example, Administrator, 'Report to the Council of the League of Nations on the Administration of Nauru during the year 1926, *Commonwealth Parliamentary Papers*, Vol. II, 1926–27–28, p. 1399; Administrator, 'Report to the Council of the League of Nations on the Administration of Nauru during the year 1937', *Commonwealth Parliamentary Papers*, Vol. III, Session 1937–38–39–40, pp. 272, 279.

19 'Education of Nauru Boys Here Defended', *The Herald* (Melbourne), 8 November 1940, p. 3. See also HE Hurst to Secretary, London Missionary Society (Sydney branch), 25 May 1945, in Education. Nauru. Education and Training of Nauruans outside Territory [5cm], A518/1 C818/1/2 Part 5, NAA.

20 M Ridgway to Hurst, 22 August 1944, in Education. Nauru. Education and Training of Nauruans outside Territory [5cm], A518/1 C818/1/2 Part 5, NAA. In the same file, see also M Ridgway to External Territories Assistant Secretary (JR Halligan), 21 April 1944; Hurst to Ridgway, 20 August 1944; Hurst to Halligan, 9 January 1945; Secretary, External Affairs to Director of Research, Department of the Army, 31 July 1945.

21 'From Nauru: First University Student', *The Warwick Daily News*, 16 May 1933, p. 6; Administrator, 'Report to the Council of the League of Nations on the Administration of Nauru during 1932', Commonwealth of Australia, Canberra, 1933, p. 19.

22 For more details on Bernicke, see Student card for Austin Bernicke, University of Melbourne Archives; Viviani, p. 105; 'These Men Will Run Nauru', *Pacific Islands Monthly*, 1 February 1968, p. 22; 'Austin Bernicke Dead', *Pacific Islands Monthly*, 1 March 1977, p. 17; Parnaby, p. 171.

23 Darian-Smith & Waghorne, p. 205; Secretary of Immigration (THE Heyes) to Secretary (External Affairs), 2 June 1947, in Cultural Relations. Educational Facilities in Australia for Overseas Students, A1068 PI47/13/2, NAA.

24 At least four students sponsored by the Chinese government arrived in Australia to study various subjects such as geography, mainly at Sydney University. See correspondence in Chinese Merchants and Students. Arrangements Governing Entry into Australia, A2998/1 1951/2129, NAA especially Australian Legation (Chungking) to External Affairs, cable dated 25 February 1946 and Rex Stumbles (Clerk, Immigration) to Tasman Heyes (Secretary, Immigration), 7 October 1947. Australian-sponsored scholarship programs for South Pacific students from Nauru, PNG and elsewhere were initiated during the post-war years, but they were modest compared with those which were offered to Asian students. For Nauru scholarships, see, for example, Commonwealth Office of Education, *Annual Report 1960*, Commonwealth of Australia, Sydney, 1961, p. 13; Commonwealth Office of Education, *Annual Report for 1966*, Commonwealth of Australia, Canberra, 1968, p. 13. For PNG scholarships, see, for example, Megarrity, pp. 41–58.

25 As early as 1941, the British Council had proposed an exchange of students between Netherlands East Indies and Australasian universities. The circumstances of World War II prevented the scheme from going ahead. See R Harry (External Affairs) to HA Peterson (Australian Government Commissioner, Batavia), 23 September 1941, in Australia: Scholarship for Overseas Students at Australian Universities, A981/4 AUS 88, NAA.

26 'Unesco Fellowships and Scholarships', *Education News*, Vol. 2, No. 5, October 1949, p. 11.

27 There were three categories of scholarships: Senior Fellowships (living allowance of £600 per annum), Junior Fellowships (£400 per annum)

and Scholarships (£200 per annum). For details, see the following correspondence items in Aid to Indonesia under the Post-UNRRA & UNESCO Schemes- Post-UNRRA Scholarships (General), A4357/3 352/1, NAA: WB Pritchett, Acting Australian Consul-General, Jakarta to Dr Ali Sastroamidjojo, Minister for the State of Education of the Government of Indonesia, Jakarta, 27 May 1949; Secretary of External Affairs (John Burton), Memorandum, 14 June 1949; Australian Consulate General, memo dated 8 July 1949. See also *The Sydney Morning Herald*, 27 May 1948, clipping in W Macmahon Ball's [W Macmahon BALL] S.E. Asian Educational and Relief Mission, A1838/278 381/1/3/1, NAA.

28 David Dexter (Acting Head of the Economic and Technical Assistance Branch, External Affairs) to JK Waller (Assistant Secretary, External Affairs), 25 May 1956, in Economic & Technical Assistance– Australian Government Overseas Scholarships Outside the Colombo Plan, A1838/294 2047/1, NAA.

29 Prime Minister's statement, 12 January 1948, in Aid to Indonesia under the Post-UNRRA & UNESCO Schemes. The Macmahon Ball Mission, A4357 352 Part 1, NAA.

30 'UNESCO Fellowships and Scholarships', *Education News*, Vol. 2, No. 5, October 1949, pp. 12–14.

31 'Summer School for South-East Asian Students', *Education News*, Vol. 2, No. 8, April 1950, pp. 3–5. The article notes (p. 3) that 'Fellows and scholars … had expressed a need for reliable information about the Australian environment'. For Colombo Plan administration, see, for example, 'The Training of Asian Students in Australia Under the Colombo Plan', *Education News*, Vol. 6, No. 11, October 1958, pp. 4–6.

32 *Melbourne Sun*, cited in '"Bar Immigration Talk": Evatt: Cable sent to Macmahon Ball', *The Straits Times*, 9 June 1948, in William Macmahon Ball Papers, Series 12, Folder 7, MS 7851, National Library of Australia.

33 Waters, p. 57. See also 'White Australia and Coloured Asian' by Kularb Saipradit, translation from *Nakorn Sarn*, 10 May 1949, in Immigration— Overseas Offices (miscellaneous correspondence), CP815/1/1 021.175, NAA.

34 'Alien's Case to Menzies', *Brisbane Telegraph*, 6 August 1949, p. 3; 'Chinese Potato Grower Ordered to Leave Australia', News (Adelaide), 28 November 1949, p. 2.

35 Arthur Fadden (leader of the Australian Country Party), CPD, House of Representatives, 15 April 1948, p. 913.

36 Macintyre, *A Concise History of Australia*, p. 207.

37 Weeden, WJ & P Biskup, William Weeden interviewed by Peter Biskup [sound recording], ORAL TRC 2670, National Library of Australia digitised item.

38 Secretary, Department of External Affairs to Secretary, Prime Minister's Department, 17 April 1947, in Scholarships for Asiatic Students, A1068 P147/13/2/4, NAA.

39 'Brief for Cabinet for Commonwealth Conference, Colombo', December 1949, A1838 532/7 Part 1, NAA, in Lowe & Oakman, p. 22.

40 ibid., p. 29.

41 Lowe, pp.183–6.

42 The Liberal government allowed the Filipino Lorenzo Gamboa to return to Australia to rejoin his Australian family after Labor had had him deported. Moreover, the new regime did not continue with Labor's War-Time Removal Bill (1949), which attempted to remove the loophole whereby non-European immigrants could remain permanently in Australia if they were married to Australian citizens. This had been Calwell's response to the Australian High Court's decision to prevent the deportation of Mrs Annie O'Keefe and her seven children. The High Court ruled that as an Indonesian married to an Australian, she was a British subject and entitled to stay. Kiernan, pp. 146–9; Brawley, pp. 252–3; 'Exemptions Granted Wartime Migrants', *Daily Mercury* (Mackay), 17 February 1950, p. 1.

43 Watt, p. 116. Britain (6256 students) and the US (15709) accepted more Colombo Plan scholars during the same period. See Oakman, *Facing Asia*, p. 82.

44 Tavan, p. 84.

45 See Broinowski, p. 129; Barker & Kent, p. 41.

46 Crocker, W, 'Notes on Colombo Plan Aid in India', 25 April 1953, quoted in Casey to Shaw, 29 December 1954, CRS A10299/1 C15, NAA, cited in Oakman, '"Young Asians in Our Homes"', p. 91.

47 In 1951, private overseas student numbers in Australia were listed as 1543. By 1962, the number had grown to 10903. Private Students—policy review—part 6, A446/216 1970/95146, NAA.

48 'Students from Asia are Finding us Hard to Understand', *The Sydney Morning Herald*, 19 January 1954, p. 2; '"Young Asians Made Victims of Color Bar"', *The Argus* (Melbourne), 11 October 1954, p. 9.

49 MG Swinburne, Letter to the Editor, *The Age*, 29 May 1954, p. 2.

50 See the comments of Oakman, *Facing Asia*, pp. 212–13.

51 'Govt. Delay in Defence of White Australia Attacked by Liberals', *The Age*, 8 July 1954, p. 4.

52 H Cox, 'Asian Students Taught us a Real Lesson!', *Sunday Mail* (Brisbane), 11 July 1954, p. 17.

53 By the late 1970s, references to the Colombo Plan student program in official reports were becoming less detailed, and it is virtually impossible to verify the total number of Colombo Plan students who studied in Australia. See, for example, Australian Development Assistance Bureau, *Annual Review 1980–81*, AGPS, Canberra, 1982, p. 8. However, in August 1980, the statistics section of the Australian Development Assistance Bureau produced a table which indicated that the total number of Colombo Plan students studying in Australia between 1951 and 31 December 1979 was 18 592. The total number of students and trainees financed by Australia between 1945/46 and 1979 (including those under the Colombo Plan) was 28 203. Australian Development Assistance Bureau, Central Statistical Service, *Bulletin: Technical Co-operation: Sponsored Overseas Students and Trainees in Australia 1979*, Statistics Section, ADAB, Department of Foreign Affairs, August 1980, copy in possession of author.

54 See Meaney, *Australia and the World*, pp. 16–17.

55 DFAT, 'New Colombo Plan'. See also Byrne, pp. 107–28.

56 DFAT, 'Australia Awards'.

57 See Horne, pp. 113–15.

Appendix: Australia's Greatest Prime Minister?

1 At the national level. A small number of state premiers were in office for longer, including Sir Thomas Playford in South Australia and Sir Johannes Bjelke-Petersen in Queensland.

2 Canada's William Mackenzie King, who served more than twenty-one years.

3 *Amalgamated Society of Engineers v Adelaide Steamship Co* (1920) 28 CLR 129.

4 Private conversation in the mid-1980s. Interestingly, Evatt was one of the barristers who Menzies beat in the *Engineers' Case*.
5 Menzies, *The Forgotten People*, chapter 1.
6 ibid.
7 First used by the Attlee Cabinet Minister Douglas Jay in his 1937 book *The Socialist Case*. What Jay actually wrote was: 'In the case of nutrition and health, just as in the case of education, the gentleman in Whitehall really does know better what is good for people than the people know themselves.' In the past couple of years, we have only to substitute 'Spring Street' for 'Whitehall' to capture the illiberal spirit of the times, although it would be inappropriate in more ways than one to describe Melbourne's pandemic era policymakers as 'gentlemen'.
8 Menzies, *The Forgotten People*, chapter. 1.

INDEX

Abelson, Donald E 64
Acheson, Dean 175
activism *see* pressure groups
ACTU (Australian Council of Trade
    Unions) 52
*Adelaide Company of Jehovah's Witnesses
    Inc v Commonwealth* 79–80
Afternoon Light (Menzies) 58
agriculture xvii, 138, 139–40, 141,
    143–5
airline policy 53
All for Australia Leagues 6
Allied Intelligence Bureau (AIB) 151
ALP *see* Australian Labor Party (ALP)
Amalgamated Society of Engineers
    Engineers' Case 10, 199
Anderson, William 3, 7, 15
Anglo-Protestant establishment xiii, 22
    Catholic suspicion of 22, 25–6
    see also Protestantism
Anthony, Doug 96
Anthony, Larry 136
anti-communism 17–33, 79–88,
    128, 154, 155, 168; *see also*
    Communist Party of Australia
    (CPA); Korean War
Anti-Socialists (formerly Liberal Free-
    Traders) 4
ANZAC Pact ('Canberra Pact') 174
ANZUS Treaty xviii, 69, 97, 144,
    166, 174–82, 201
arbitration 22, 52

Asian students in Australia 184–6,
    187–95
Asia-Pacific region
    ALP policies 27, 171
    intelligence operations in 150, 151,
        156–7
    regional forum for the Pacific 171
    Spender insight 166, 168–70,
        180–1
    turmoil x–xi
    see also ANZUS Treaty; Colombo
        Plan; Indonesian Republic; Japan;
        Japanese Peace Treaty (1951);
        Korean War; Malayan Emergency
ASIO *see* Australian Security
    Intelligence Organisation (ASIO)
ASIS *see* Australian Secret Intelligence
    Service (ASIS)
Australia
    ANZUS Treaty xviii, 69, 97, 144,
        166, 174–82, 201
    cities and regions 117–20; *see also*
        Central Coast of New South
        Wales
    Federation 46, 104
    Japanese Peace Treaty (1951) xviii,
        155, 166, 177–80
    society *see* Australian society
    system of government *see*
        parliamentary government in
        Australia
Australia Party 5

Australia–Japan Commerce Agreement (1957) *see* Japan—trade agreement with

Australian Bankers Export Re-finance Corporation 43

Australian Constitutional League 31

Australian Council of Trade Unions (ACTU) 52

Australian economy 59–60, 62, 72–4, 133–48
  1951 budget 142
  Chifley government management of 134–6
  inflation control 140–3
  international reserves 134, 135, 136, 145, 146–7
  Menzies government management of 136–48
  Vernon Report (1965) 73–4
  see also Australian society; economic policy

Australian Labor Party (ALP)
  bank nationalisation attempt *see* bank nationalisation
  and CPA ban 85, 86
  economic policy (1950s) 55
  Lyons's defection 6, 12
  the Movement and 18–19, 29–33
  post-war agenda *see* post-war reconstruction
  on recognition of PRC 27
  split (1955) 18, 114
  see also Chifley government; Curtin government; Hawke government; Keating government; Whitlam government

Australian National Federation *see* Nationalist Party

Australian Parliament
  double dissolutions xvi, 5, 43, 50, 87, 110–12
  Senate voting system reform 110
  see also elections (federal)

Australian political system *see* parliamentary government

in Australia; political career (Menzies); political parties

Australian Secret Intelligence Service (ASIS) 149–64
  abolition proposal 162–3
  advocates for 151–2, 154–5
  establishment xvii–xviii, 155, 156–9, 163
  legislation 159
  operations 159–60
  purpose and functions xvii, 150, 157–9, 161–2
  structure and budget 158, 160–1

Australian Security Intelligence Organisation (ASIO) 153, 162–3

Australian society xiii, 62–3, 202–6
  Central Coast of NSW 117–31
  cities and regions 117–20; *see also* Central Coast of New South Wales
  middle-class people *see* middle-class
  prosperity v, xvi–xvii, 62, 198–9, 202–5
  see also Australian economy

Australian Women's National League 3, 5, 7, 15

'Australia's greatest prime minister' question xviii, 197–206

Ball, William Macmahon 170

bank nationalisation xiii–xiv, 35–44, 57, 58
  community protest 38–41, 43
  High Court and Privy Council challenges 42
  legislation 42
  Menzies's opposition to 39–44, 46, 47–8

banking system 36–7, 43, 53
  Banking Act of 1945 36–7
  Banking Act of 1947 42, 43

Barton, Edmund 4

Barwick, Garfield 98

Beale, Howard 136

Belloc, Hilaire 21, 22–3, 25

Berendsen, Carl 176
Bernicke, Austin 187
Bevin, Ernest 173
Blainey, Geoffrey 37, 39
Bland, Henry 52
Boyd, Jodie 140
Bradman, Don 99
Bramston, Troy xvi, 13–14, 75
Brandis, George, on Menzies 56, 197–206
Brett, Judith 11, 19, 48
Bretton Woods Agreement 38, 145–6
Britain see United Kingdom
British Commonwealth of Nations 105, 127, 157–8, 166, 175, 180–1, 190, 191, 194; see also Colombo Plan
British Council 187–8
British intelligence services see MI5; MI6
British liberal tradition 17, 19–21, 24
British Medical Association in Australia 32–3
broadcasts see radio broadcasts
Brookes, Alfred Deakin 151–2, 154–5, 156–7, 159–63, 164
Brookes, Herbert 5
Brookes, Ivy 5
Brookings Institution 64
Brown, Allen 51, 92, 101, 137
Bruce, Stanley Melbourne 5, 6, 16
Bunting, John 51, 101, 137
bureaucracy see public service
Burke, Edmund 11
Burton, John 169–70, 171, 190
Bury, Les 97

Cabinet and ministry (Menzies) 94–8, 100, 102, 136–9, 155
Cabinet secretariat 137, 147
Cain government (Victoria) 41
Calwell, Arthur 42, 91, 189, 191
Canberra (city) 53, 96, 117, 201–2
'Canberra Pact' (ANZAC Pact) 174

capitalism
civilised 49, 59
'little capitalists' x
see also economic policy
Carr, Andrew 20
Carrick, John 99
Casey, Richard 6, 94, 95, 99, 113, 136, 192
and ASIS xvii, 151, 153–7, 158, 160, 161–2
Catholic schools state aid 72, 202
Catholic social thought xiii, 22–4, 25; see also the Movement (Catholic Social Studies Movement)
Catholic Worker 21–2, 23
Central Coast of New South Wales xvi–xvii
commuters 122–3
demography 118–19, 122–3, 131
development 121–3, 129–30
electoral history 119, 123, 124–9, 130–1
environment 118, 123, 131
Central Intelligence Agency (CIA, USA) 152–3, 156, 160, 162–3
centralisation 28–32
Charwat, Nicola 140
Chatham House 64
Chavura, Stephen 19
Chesterton, GK 21, 22, 25
Chifley, Ben x, 25, 91, 92, 198
bank nationalisation attempt see bank nationalisation
and CPA ban 85
and intelligence services 152–3, 155
Menzies on 44
on recognition of PRC 27
Chifley government x, 28–9, 45
achievements 45–6, 49, 57–8
bank nationalisation attempt see bank nationalisation
defeat 46, 48
economic management 134–6
economic policy 45–6, 50, 58, 59
education initiatives 98

enduring policy agenda 49, 50–3, 58
foreign policy 171
overseas students policy 187–9, 190, 195
referendums 10, 13, 20, 29–32
Senate voting system reform 110
senior public servants 50–2, 92, 101
child endowment 135–6
China (People's Republic of China, PRC) 26–7, 140, 175
Chinese Civil War x
Chinese students in Australia 184–6
Chipp, Don 97
Christian social principles 23–4, 31; see also Catholic social thought; Protestantism
CIA see Central Intelligence Agency (CIA, USA)
cities and regions 117–20; see also Central Coast of New South Wales
Citizens League 6
Coalition governments 15–16, 18, 36, 46, 48, 60, 95, 100–1; see also Menzies government (1949–66)
Cold War x–xi, 17, 27, 163, 177
Colley, Linda 19
Colombo Plan xviii, 97, 127, 166, 169–74, 183, 188, 190–5, 202
Committee of Economic Inquiry (Vernon Inquiry) 73–4
Commonwealth Bank 36–7, 40, 51, 53, 133, 135, 138, 141, 143
Commonwealth Banking Corporation 43
Commonwealth funding to non-government schools 72, 202
Commonwealth government expenditure 53
Commonwealth government role xiii–xiv, 53–7, 60, 63, 204, 205; see also state intervention
Commonwealth Office of Education 188–9, 190

Commonwealth Oil Refineries 55
Commonwealth parliament see Australian Parliament; parliamentary government in Australia
Commonwealth Party 7
Commonwealth powers 53–4
Communist Party Case 86–7
defence powers 140
Engineers' Case 10, 199
petrol distribution 135
referendums concerning 10, 13, 20, 29–31
Commonwealth Scholarship scheme 202
Commonwealth Trading Bank 43
communism x–xi, 80–1
in trade unions 25–6, 38, 81, 83
see also anti-communism; socialism
Communist Party Dissolution Act 1950 (Cth) and Bill 82–5
High Court challenge 86–7
Communist Party of Australia (CPA)
High Court challenge to ban 86–7
Menzies's attempts to ban xv, 28, 33, 79–88, 154, 155
Menzies's resistance to proposed ban xv, 78–9, 80–2, 84
and radical union actions 38
referendum on xv, 28, 87–8, 125
support for bank nationalisation 42
support for central powers referendum 30–1
see also anti-communism
constitutional law
bank nationalisation case 42
Communist Party Case 86–7
counter-terrorism legislation validity 77–8
Engineers' Case 10, 199
see also Commonwealth powers; parliamentary government in Australia
Cook, Joseph 4, 5, 16, 50, 198

Coombs, HC ('Nugget') 50–1, 138, 141
Copland, Douglas 142
the Corner 4
Cornish, Selwyn 141
Costello, Peter 60
Couchman, Elizabeth 3, 7, 14–15
counter-intelligence agencies *see* Australian Security Intelligence Organisation (ASIO); MI5
counter-terrorism legislation 77–8
Country Party ix, xii, 5, 51, 80, 94, 95
coalition relations with Liberal Party 95, 100–1, 102; *see also* Menzies government (1949–66)
ministers 94, 95, 101, 136
covert action xvii, 150, 151, 156–60
Cowper, Norman 84
CPA *see* Communist Party of Australia (CPA)
Crawford, John 52, 138, 144–5, 147
Crocker, Walter 192
Cromwell, Oliver 106
cultural puritanism 19
Curtin, John ix–x
Curtin government 2, 28–9, 45, 57, 79–80, 101, 171, 174

Davis, Frank 8
Dawson, Christopher 21, 25
Day, David 43
De L'Isle, Viscount 113
Deakin, Alfred 4, 5, 16, 55, 56, 150, 200
Deakinite liberalism 55–9
foreign policy 181
Deakin, Ivy *see* Brookes, Ivy
Dean, Roger xvi, 123–9
defence expenditure 53–4, 140
democratic freedoms
individual rights versus national security 77–89
see also liberalism
Democratic Labour Party (DLP) xiii, 18, 27, 33; *see also* the Movement

(Catholic Social Studies Movement)
Department of Commerce and Agriculture 138, 147
Department of Defence 152, 158, 159, 160–2; *see also* Shedden, Frederick
Department of Education 72
Department of External Affairs 152, 158, 160–2, 169–70, 171, 176, 187, 190–1; *see also* Evatt, HV (Bert); Spender, Percy
Department of Foreign Affairs and Trade 194
Department of Post-War Reconstruction 138
Economic Division 137
Department of Trade 147
Department of Trade and Customs 138, 147
Dicey, AV 105
Dixon, Owen 47, 199–200
DLP *see* Democratic Labour Party (DLP)
Donovan, Bill 156
double dissolutions of Australian Parliament xvi, 5, 43, 50, 87, 110–12
Downer, Alexander (Alick) 99
Downing, RI 73
Dulles, Allen 162
Dulles, John Foster 162, 175–6, 177–80
Dunrossil, Lord 113

Easton, James 163
economic management 133–48
Chifley government 134–6
Menzies government 136–48
wartime controls 133–6
economic policy
changes in (1980s) 59–60
Chifley government 45–6, 50, 58, 59
Deakinite Liberalism 55–7, 58

external advice on 72–4; *see also* think tanks
Keynesian economics x, xvii, 45, 52, 56–7, 62–3, 133, 139–43, 147
Menzies government (1949–66) xvii, 46, 49, 50, 53–5, 58–9, 62–3, 72–4
education
Murray Report (1957) 71–2
overseas students in Australia 183–95; *see also* Colombo Plan
state aid to non-government schools 72, 202
universities xiv, 53, 71–2, 98, 194, 202
Eggleton, Tony 93–4
elections (federal)
1910 4
1913 5
1930s 6
1943 ix–x, xii, 6–7, 11
1946 15, 37, 47
1949 36, 43, 48–9, 80, 82, 92, 99, 135–6
1951 43, 87–8
1954 and 1955 114
1961 and 1969 18
Central Coast of NSW electoral history 119, 123, 124–9, 130–1, 135–6
Coalition victories 18, 36
Menzies's success 15, 36, 48, 198
UAP victories 6
elections (state)
1930, NSW 5
1947, Victoria 41
electoral Division of Robertson (NSW) 124–9
Elizabeth I, Queen 149–50
Elizabeth II, Queen 112–14
Ellis, Dick 152, 157
Engineers' Case 10, 199
espionage 149–63
Evatt, HV (Bert) 35, 91, 152, 166, 200

ANZAC Pact 174
bank nationalisation case 42
career 103, 107, 108
on CPA bans 79–80, 86, 87–8
and intelligence services 152–3, 155
personal characteristics 107
regional forum for the Pacific 171
on vice-regal role and powers 107, 109–10, 112, 114, 115
expert advice *see* think tanks
exports 139–40, 144–5
external affairs *see* Department of External affairs; foreign policy

Fabian Society 64
Fadden, Arthur xii, 48, 94, 95, 101, 136, 137, 141, 142, 189
federal parliament *see* Australian Parliament
federal–state relations *see* Commonwealth government role; Commonwealth powers; constitutional law
Federation 46, 104
Fisher, Andrew 198
Fisher government 184–5
Fitzherbert, Margaret 5
Forbes, Jim 96–7
foreign policy x–xi, xviii, 26, 154, 161, 163
Spender achievements 165–82
tradition 181
see also ANZUS Treaty; Colombo Plan; Japanese Peace Treaty (1951); national security
'forgotten people' theme xii, 11, 19, 48, 58, 69, 120, 203–5
fourteen powers referendum *see* referendums
Fraser, James 32
Fraser, Malcolm 46, 97
'free' market *see* Keynesian economics
free speech 79
free trade 59, 60; *see also* protectionism

Freedom (publication) 23, 24–6, 30–1; *see also News Weekly*
Fullagar, Wilfred 86–7

Gamboa, Lorenzo 191
General Agreement on Tariffs and Trade 146
Gorton, John 46, 72, 95
government role *see* Commonwealth government role
governments (Menzies) *see* Menzies government (1939–41); Menzies government (1949–66)
governor-general role xvi, 105, 107
  Evatt on 107, 109–10, 112, 114, 115
  insecurity of tenure of viceroy 107, 110, 115–16
  McKell appointment opposed 109–10, 113
  Menzies's appointments 112–13
  monarch's exercise of powers 113–14
Great Britain *see* United Kingdom
Greenwood, Ivor 88
Gullett, Jo 97

Hancock, Ian 3–4, 10, 14
Hancock, WK xiv, 118
Harrison, Eric 94, 95, 136, 178
Harry, Ralph 176
Hasluck, Paul 95, 97, 107, 113, 114
Hawke government 60, 202
Hayek, Friedrich 50, 67
head of state 104; *see also* governor-general role
health schemes *see* national health schemes
Henderson, Anne 3
Henderson, Gerard 3
Henderson, Heather 95, 200–1
Heseltine, William 93
Hewitt, Lenox 95
High Court of Australia 80
  bank nationalisation case 42

Chief Justice appointment 200
  Communist Party Case 86–7
  Engineers' Case 10, 199
  historiography xii, xv, xvi, 117–18, 121
Hockey, Joe 203
Holt, Harold 46, 52, 72, 94, 95, 97, 136, 137, 147, 177, 193
home building and ownership 119–22, 129
Howard, Colin 111, 114
Howard, John 49, 52, 53, 57, 60, 88, 112, 113, 203, 205
Howard government 63, 202
  counter-terrorism legislation 77–8
Hughes, William Morris (Billy) 5, 16, 97, 198
Hyde, John 67

ideology *see* political philosophy
immigration policy 52, 55–6, 127
  deportations 184, 189, 191, 195
  White Australia Policy xviii, 98, 184, 186, 189, 193, 195
  see also overseas students in Australia
import licensing 54, 133, 134–5, 145–8
independent schools state aid 72, 202
Indian students in Australia 184, 187
individual enterprise 20, 48, 59, 68, 69, 128, 204, 205
individual rights versus national security 77–89
Indonesian Republic x, 152
industrial disputes 25–6, 38, 81, 128, 136
  Engineers' Case 10, 199
industrial relations policy 22, 52
industry protection *see* protectionism
Institute of Public Affairs New South Wales 7, 67, 68
Institute of Public Affairs Victoria (IPA) xiv, 3, 7, 9, 13, 14, 17, 54, 67–71
intelligence agencies *see* Allied Intelligence Bureau (AIB); Australian Secret Intelligence

Service (ASIS); Australian
Security Intelligence Organisation
(ASIO); Central Intelligence
Agency (CIA, USA); MI5; MI6
international affairs *see* foreign policy
international aid *see* Colombo Plan
International Bank for Reconstruction
and Development (World Bank)
138–9
International Monetary Fund 38,
145–6
international students *see* overseas
students in Australia
Interstate Committee 6
Isaacs, Isaac 109

Jang, Frank 189, 191
Japan
intelligence operations against 151
suspicion of 155
trade agreement with 59, 97, 148,
180
trade potential 156
Japanese Peace Treaty (1951) xviii,
155, 166, 177–80
Japanese students in Australia 184
Jayewardene, JR 173
Jennings, Frank 96
Jones, Benjamin 20

Karskens, Grace 118
Keating, Paul, on Chifley government
achievements 49
Keating government 60, 202
Keir, DL 105–6, 108
Kelly, Andrew 176
Kelly, Bert 97
Kelly, Paul 48–9, 64
Kemp, Charles 3, 14, 67–8, 70
Kemp, David xii, 9, 48, 53, 55, 61
Kerr, John 200
Keynes, John Maynard x, 50–1, 67
Keynesian economics x, xvii, 45, 52,
56–7, 62–3, 133, 139–43, 147
Killen, Jim 97

Korean War xvii, xviii, 69, 138, 139,
140, 143–4, 155, 175

Labor Party (Australia) *see* Australian
Labor Party (ALP)
labour movement
communism in trade unions 25–6,
38, 81, 83
the Movement and 18, 21–4, 28,
29, 30, 31, 32
see also industrial disputes
Latham, John 42
leadership 14–16
of Liberal Party *see* Menzies
government (1949–66); political
career (Menzies)
Leckie, John William (Pattie Menzies's
father) 12
Liberal Democratic Party of Australia,
New South Wales 3, 7, 9, 15
Liberal Free-Traders (later the Anti-
Socialists) 4
Liberal Party (1909–17) 4–5, 6
Liberal Party of Australia
Casey as federal director 154
electoral success 15–16, 36, 48,
198, 201
foundation xii–xiii, 1–16
leadership 15–16, 37–8, 47, 99, 201
the Movement's attitude to 18,
24–6, 31
name 58
opposition to communism 17, 18
opposition to referenda on
Commonwealth powers 20
parliamentary party 98–100
policy platform 9, 10–11, 45,
52–5, 58–9, 68–9, 81
seen as representative of business
class 24–5, 26, 31, 69
structure 8–9, 12
see also Menzies government
(1949–66); political career
(Menzies)
Liberal Party of Victoria 15

Liberal Protectionists 4
liberalism 46, 54–5, 57, 60, 205
    British liberalism 17, 19–21, 24
    Deakinite liberalism 55–9
    see also political philosophy
'little capitalists' x
Looker, Cecil 102
Looking Forward (IPA, 1944) 14, 68
Lowe, David 166
Lyons, Enid 13, 94, 96
Lyons, Joseph 2, 6, 12, 13, 16
Lyons government 108, 167

McBride, Philip 94, 95, 136, 156
McCalman, Janet 118
McConnan, Leslie J 37, 39, 43
McEwen, John 46, 74, 94, 95, 96, 97,
    101, 136, 137, 138, 139, 147
Macintyre, Stuart 59
McKell, William 92, 109–10, 111–12
McLeay, George 95, 136
McMahon, William (Billy) 46, 97
McTiernan, Edward 42
Mair, A (NSW Leader/Deputy Leader
    of the Opposition) 7, 9
Malayan Emergency 155, 156–7
Mannix, Daniel 21, 26
Marsh, Ian 63
Martin, AW (Allan) 46–7, 52, 110
May, AL 39
The Measure of the Years (Menzies)
    119–20
medical and health schemes see
    national health schemes
Meere, Frank 52, 138, 146
Melleuish, Gregory 19, 46, 58
Menzies, Heather see Henderson,
    Heather
Menzies, James (father) 11
Menzies, Pattie 12, 96
Menzies, Robert Gordon 26
    anti-communism xiii, xv, 17, 18,
        19–21, 25–6, 33, 79–88
    career at the Bar 10, 86–7,
        199–200

career in politics see political career
    (Menzies)
on Chifley 44
as civic republican 20–1
Deakinite Liberalism 55–9
early life 199
education 199
historiography xii, xv, xvi
and Keynesianism 56–7, 58,
    139–43
legacy 49, 50–1, 74–5
the Movement's attitude to 18,
    24–6, 31
opposition to socialism xiv, 47, 56,
    59
personal characteristics 2, 13–14,
    37, 93–4, 106
personal library 61, 200
political career see political career
    (Menzies)
pragmatism xiv
Protestantism xiii, 20
publications see publications by
    Menzies
respect for public service xiv, 50–2,
    58, 71, 73, 101–2, 147
respect for tradition 19, 21, 51, 58
work practices, office and staff
    92–4
Menzies, Stewart 158
Menzies government (1939–41) 2, 46
    CPA ban 79–80
    Menzies's resignation as prime
        minister 2, 102
    Spender as minister 167
Menzies government (1949–66) 17,
    49–60
    achievements xviii, 59, 75, 127,
        147–8, 166, 177, 200–6
    anti-communism 17, 18, 26–8, 33
    bipartisanship 45–6, 49, 52–3,
        59–60
    Cabinet and ministry 94–8, 100,
        102, 136–9
    Cabinet secretariat 137, 147

CPA dissolution attempts xv, 28, 33, 79–88
double dissolution (1951) xvi, 43, 50, 87, 110–12
economic management 136–48
economic policy xvii, 46, 49, 50, 53–9, 62–3, 69, 72–4
foreign policy 26–7, 33, 69, 89, 140, 165–82
governor-general appointments 112–13
immigration policy 193, 195; see also White Australia Policy
leadership style and party management xv–xvi, 91–102
legacy 49, 50–1, 74–5
longevity 197–9
Murray Report (1957) 71–2; see also universities
overseas students policy see Colombo Plan
parliamentary party 98–100
policy advice see public service; think tanks
policy agenda see liberalism; political philosophy
prime minister's office 92–4
protectionist 52–3, 55, 59
relations with Country Party (coalition management) 95, 100–1, 102
relations with Liberal Party organisation 100
senior public servants xi, 50–2, 62, 92, 101, 147, 169, 170; see also public service
Vernon Report (1965) 73–4
Menzies in Opposition see Opposition leader (Menzies); political career (Menzies)
Métin, Albert xiii
MI5 152, 153
MI6 (Secret Intelligence Service, SIS) 149, 151, 152–3, 157, 158, 159–60, 162–3

middle class 39, 48, 49, 120, 205
education 72, 202
'forgotten people' xii, 11, 19, 48, 58, 69, 120, 203–5
Middle Class Party 7
mineral exports 139
ministry see Cabinet and ministry (Menzies's)
Monk, Albert 52
Morrison, Herbert 175
Morrison's 'quiet Australians' 203
the Movement (Catholic Social Studies Movement) 17–19, 21–33
alignment with Menzies's ideas 24, 28, 29, 32, 33
anti-communism 22, 24, 25–8, 31, 33
attitude to Menzies and Liberal Party 18, 24–6, 31
attitude to national health scheme 33
and labour movement 18, 21–4, 28, 29, 30, 31, 32
Muhammad, Ghulam 173
Murray, Keith xiv, 71
Murray, Robert 107
Murray Report (1957) 71–2, 202; see also universities

National Bank of Australasia (NBA) 37, 39, 43
national health schemes
Labor plans 29, 32–3
Menzies government 97
pre-World War II 23, 56
National Party see Country Party
National Secretariat for Catholic Action 21
national security 88–9, 154, 155–64
versus individual rights 77–89
intelligence agencies see Allied Intelligence Bureau (AIB); Australian Secret Intelligence Service (ASIS); Australian

Security Intelligence Organisation
(ASIO); MI5; MI6
*National Security (Subversive
Associations) Regulations 1940*
(Cth) 79–80
National Security Resources Board
(NSRB) 53, 140
National Service 140
nationalisation
of banks *see* bank nationalisation
of healthcare *see* national health
schemes
Nationalist Party 5, 15
infrastructure 6
Young Nationalists 8, 12
Nauru students in Australia 186–7
NBA *see* National Bank of Australasia
(NBA)
Nethercote, John xvi, 106
New Colombo Plan 194
New Hebrides 150
New South Wales
Central Coast *see* Central Coast of
New South Wales
Leader/Deputy Leader of the
Opposition (Mair) 7, 9
non-Labor forces 3, 7
New South Wales Institute of Public
Affairs *see* Institute of Public
Affairs New South Wales
New Zealand *see* ANZUS Treaty
News Weekly 18, 23, 24, 25, 26, 27,
29, 31–2, 33; *see also Freedom*
(publication)
Nixon, Richard 97
non-government advisory
organisations *see* think tanks
non-Labor groups 1–2, 3, 4–7
in-fighting in state groups 6–7
see also Country Party; Liberal Party
(1909–17); Liberal Party of
Australia; United Australia Party
(UAP)
NSRB *see* National Security Resources
Board (NSRB)

Oakman, Daniel 171
One Parliament for All Australia 7
Opposition leader (Menzies) xii, 4,
13, 20, 24–32, 37, 40
O'Sullivan, Neil 136–7
overseas students in Australia 183–95;
see also Colombo Plan

Pacific Islander students in Australia
184, 186–7, 194
Pacific region *see* Asia-Pacific region
Page, Earle 13, 94, 97, 136
Parkhill, Archdale 5, 167
parliamentary government in Australia
103–16
balance of power 103–4
governor-general role xvi, 105,
107, 109–12, 115–16
head of state 104
imperial relationship 104–6, 108–9
see also Australian Parliament;
Commonwealth government
role; Commonwealth powers;
Westminster system of
government
Pearce, George 185
People's Party (Queensland) 15
People's Republic of China (PRC)
26–7, 140, 175
petrol distribution and rationing 135,
139
Playford, Thomas 99
policy advice *see* public service; think
tanks
political career (Menzies) 115, 200–6
election campaigning 41, 91,
135–6, 153–4
electoral defeat 15, 37, 47
electoral success 15, 36, 48, 198,
201
historiography xii, xv, xvi
international experience 12–13
leadership 14–16, 37–8, 46–7,
91–102
longevity 197–9

national network 10
Opposition leader xii, 4, 13, 20,
    24–32, 37, 40
opposition to bank nationalisation
    39–44, 46, 47–8
opposition to McKell appointment
    109–10
political party practical experience
    11–12
political philosophy 10–11, 19–21,
    46, 55–60, 75, 106, 203–5
position on Chifley government
    referendums 31–2
prime ministership see Menzies
    government (1939–41); Menzies
    government (1949–66)
revival of xii, 37–8, 46
role in foundation of Liberal Party
    1–16
state politics 10
Statute of Westminster debates
    108–9
wartime loss of power 46
see also Menzies government
    (1949–66)
political parties
Menzies's practical experience
    11–12
non-Labor groups 1–2, 3, 4–7
see also Australian Labor Party
    (ALP); Communist Party of
    Australia (CPA); Country Party;
    Liberal Party (1909–17); Liberal
    Party of Australia; Nationalist
    Party; United Australia Party
    (UAP)
political philosophy xiii–xiv
Menzies 10–11, 19–21, 46, 55–60,
    75, 106, 203–5
Spender 168
see also liberalism
post-war reconstruction ix–x, 24,
    28–9
Chifley government achievements
    45–6, 49

enduring post-war legacy 49, 50–1
Menzies's opposition to Labor
    agenda 21, 33
the Movement's approach 23–4,
    33
Presbyterian Women's Mission Union
    186
pressure groups 6; see also think tanks
prices and rents control referendum
    (1948) 31–2
Prime Minister's Department 101–2,
    137–8, 147
Economic Policy Division 137–8
prime minister's office (Menzies's)
    92–4
prime ministership
'Australia's greatest prime minister'
    question xviii, 197–206
Menzies's leadership style 91–102
Menzies's views on prime ministerial
    power 95
in parliamentary government 104
see also Menzies government
    (1939–41); Menzies government
    (1949–66); political career
    (Menzies)
principles see liberalism; political
    philosophy
private banks 36–40; see also bank
    nationalisation
privatisation 55, 60
Privy Council
bank nationalisation case 42
prosperity v, xvi–xvii, 62, 198–9,
    202–5
protectionism 4, 12, 46, 52–3, 55,
    58, 59, 62
US and European 139–40
Protectionists' party see Liberal
    Protectionists
Protestantism xiii, 17, 19–20, 22,
    25, 26; see also Anglo-Protestant
    establishment
public policy think tanks see think
    tanks

public service
  Cabinet secretariat 137, 147
  contestability of advice 70–1, 73,
    75
  economic advice 137–8, 141
  expansion of 50, 62–3
  Menzies's respect for xiv, 50–2, 58,
    71, 73, 101–2, 147
  senior public servants xi, 50–2, 62,
    92, 101, 147, 169, 170
  and Vernon Report
    recommendations 74
publications about Menzies
  (historiography) xii, xv, xvi
publications by Menzies
  Afternoon Light 58
  'forgotten people' broadcasts xii,
    11, 19, 48, 58, 69, 120, 203–5
  The Measure of the Years 119–20
Pyne, Christopher 201

Queensland Labor Party 18
Queensland People's Party 15
Queensland Women's Electoral League
  9
'quiet Australians' 203

radio broadcasts
  'forgotten people' broadcasts xii,
    11, 19, 48, 58, 69, 120, 203–5
record-keeping 137
referendums 20, 26, 28, 29–32
  on Communist Party xv, 28, 87–8,
    125
  Powers Referendum (1944) 10, 13,
    20, 29–31
  on social services x, 29, 31, 32
regions and cities 117–20; *see also*
  Central Coast of New South
  Wales
Reid, Alan 49
Reid, George 4–5, 16, 47, 56
rents and prices control referendum
  (1948) 31–2
republicanism 20–1

Reserve Bank of Australia 43
Ritchie, Thomas 3, 15
Robert Menzies Institute xi
Robertson (electoral division) 124–9
role of the state *see* Commonwealth
  government role; Commonwealth
  powers; state intervention
Rolls, Eric 118
Rourke, Brigadier 51
Royal Commission into Monetary and
  Banking Systems (1935–37) 36
Royal Commission into Soviet
  Espionage (1954–55) 89
Royal United Services Institute 64
Rusk, Dean 175
Russell Sage Foundation 64

Sampson, Sydney 4, 11–12, 56
Santamaria, BA xiii, 18, 21–4; *see also*
  the Movement (Catholic Social
  Studies Movement)
Scullin, James 109
Scullin government 35, 36
Secret Intelligence Service (Australia)
  see Australian Secret Intelligence
  Service (ASIS)
Secret Intelligence Service (SIS, UK)
  149, 151, 152–3, 157, 158,
  159–60, 162–3
Services and Citizens' Party 3, 7, 15
servility 22–3
Shedden, Frederick 160, 162, 176–7
Sinclair, Ian 96, 101
Slim, William 113, 114
Snow, Sydney 9
social services referendum (1946) x,
  29, 31, 32–3
social welfare 22–4, 45, 53, 55, 56
socialism 47–8
  Menzies's opposition to xiv, 47,
    56, 59
  'socialisme sans doctrines' xiii
  state socialism 20, 21, 22–3
  see also bank nationalisation;
    communism

society *see* Australian society
South Australia
　bank nationalisation challenge 42
　vote on CPA ban 88
South Pacific Commission 171
South-East Asian Fellowship Scheme
　188, 189
Soviet espionage 152–3, 163
Soviet Union 27–8, 80; *see also*
　communism
Spender, Percy 165–82
　ANZUS Treaty xviii, 97, 166,
　　174–82
　ASIS 155, 156, 158, 159, 163
　bio 166–7
　Colombo Plan 97, 166, 169–74,
　　190, 191
　foreign policy outlook xviii, 166,
　　168–70, 180–2
　Japanese Peace Treaty xviii, 166,
　　177–80
　political career 95, 99, 136, 167–70
　political philosophy 168
spies *see* Australian Secret Intelligence
　Service (ASIS); Secret Intelligence
　Service (SIS, UK)
Spry, Charles 163
Starr, Graeme 3
state aid to non-government schools
　72, 202
state intervention xiii, 45–6, 49,
　54–7, 62, 135, 146–7, 167–8; *see
　also* Commonwealth government
　role
states' reserved powers *see*
　Commonwealth powers
Statute of Westminster (1931) 105–6,
　108–9
Stone, Diane 63
Stone, John 148
strikes *see* industrial disputes
suburbanisation *see* Central Coast
　of New South Wales; cities and
　regions
Swan, Trevor 51

Tange, Arthur 160, 161
tariffs *see* protectionism
think tanks xiv, 61–75
　definition and description 65–7
　IPA xiv, 3, 7, 9, 13, 14, 17, 54,
　　67–71
　origins 63–4
Thomas, Josiah 184–5
Tilley, Paul 142–3
trade unions *see* labour movement
trading banks *see* bank nationalisation;
　private banks
Treasury 133, 138, 141–3
Treaty of San Francisco *see* Japanese
　Peace Treaty (1951)
Truman, Harry S 152, 175, 177

UNESCO 187–9, 190
United Australia Movement 6
United Australia Organisation 7, 12
United Australia Party (UAP) 15
　1943 election loss ix–x, xii, 6–7, 11
　election wins 6
　formation 6, 12
　fragmentation ix, xii, 2
　Spender expulsion 167
　see also Lyons government; Menzies
　　government (1939–41)
United Kingdom
　attitude to ANZUS Treaty 174–5
　Beveridge report and public policy
　　204–5
　British liberal tradition 17, 19–21,
　　24
　dominions 104–6, 108–9
　post-war economic situation 134–5
　Secret Intelligence Service (SIS)
　　149, 151, 152–3, 157, 158,
　　159–60, 162–3
　Statute of Westminster 105–6,
　　108–9
　think tanks 64
　Westminster system xvi, 13, 51,
　　106
United Nations 152, 176, 181

United Nations Educational, Scientific, and Cultural Organization (UNESCO) 187–9, 190
United States
    ANZUS Treaty xviii, 69, 97, 144, 166, 174–82, 201
    Central Intelligence Agency (CIA) 152–3, 156, 160, 162–3
    Colombo Plan participation 173–4
    Navy visit to Australia 181
    think tanks 64
    see also Korean War
universities xiv, 53, 71–2, 98, 194, 202; see also Colombo Plan; education
University of Melbourne, Robert Menzies Institute xi

Vernon Report (1965) 73–4
vice-regal powers see governor-general role
Victoria
    1947 election 41
    bank nationalisation challenge 42
    non-Labor forces 3, 7
    vote on CPA ban 88
Victorian Institute of Public Affairs see Institute of Public Affairs Victoria (IPA)
Victorian Parliament 10, 11–12
Victorian Young Nationalists Organisation see Young Nationalists Organisation of Victoria

Wake, Nancy 87
Wallace, Chris xv
Walsingham, Francis 149–50
war see Korean War; Malayan Emergency; World War I; World War II

war debts 38, 134–5; see also post-war reconstruction
Warby, H 9
Watson government 184
Watt, Alan 160, 161, 162
Watt, GPN 138, 141
Weeden, William John 190
Wentworth, William (Bill) 97
Western Australian input to Liberal Party of Australia formation 9
Westminster system of government xvi, 13, 51, 106; see also parliamentary government in Australia
White, Ernest 3, 7, 15
White, Thomas 94, 136
White Australia Policy xviii, 98, 184, 186, 189, 191, 193, 195; see also overseas students in Australia
Whitlam, Gough 46, 199
Whitlam government 202, 203
Whitwell, Greg 142
Williams, Daryl 78
Williams, George 83
Willoughby, JR (Bob) 93
Wilson, Roland 52, 138, 141
Winterton, George 87
wool boom xvii, 143–5
wool supply, US-proposed system of international control 138, 144–5
wool tax 141
World Bank loan 138–9
World War I 5, 151
World War II 2, 26
    banking regulations 36
    intelligence operations 151
    leadership see Curtin government
    powers referendums see referendums
    war debts 38, 134–5
    see also post-war reconstruction

Young Nationalists Organisation of Victoria 8, 12